Gendering the GOP

Gendering the GOP

Intraparty Politics and Republican Women's Representation in Congress

CATHERINE N. WINEINGER

OXFORD
UNIVERSITY PRESS

OXFORD
UNIVERSITY PRESS

Oxford University Press is a department of the University of Oxford. It furthers the University's objective of excellence in research, scholarship, and education by publishing worldwide. Oxford is a registered trade mark of Oxford University Press in the UK and certain other countries.

Published in the United States of America by Oxford University Press
198 Madison Avenue, New York, NY 10016, United States of America.

Library of Congress Control Number: 2021951489
ISBN 978–0–19–755655–9 (pbk.)
ISBN 978–0–19–755654–2 (hbk.)

DOI: 10.1093/oso/9780197556542.001.0001

1 3 5 7 9 8 6 4 2

Paperback printed by Marquis, Canada
Hardback printed by Bridgeport National Bindery, Inc., United States of America

For Dan, Ellie, Mom, and Dad

Contents

Acknowledgments

It's impossible for me to adequately express in a few short pages the gratitude I have for everyone who has guided me on my path toward the completion of this book. But here's my best shot.

First, thank you to the funders who invested in me and this project. This research was made possible through financial support from the Institute for Citizens and Scholars (formerly the Woodrow Wilson National Fellowship Foundation), the Dirksen Congressional Center, the Carrie Chapman Catt Center for Women and Politics at Iowa State University, the Institute for Humane Studies at George Mason University, and the American Political Science Association. Funding from these institutions gave me both the confidence and the financial means to pursue this project, and for that I am grateful.

My heartfelt thanks to the team at Oxford University Press, especially Angela Chnapko and Alexcee Bechthold, for guiding me through the publication process. Thank you also to my fantastic copy-editor, Suzanne Copenhagen, and to the anonymous reviewers who took the time to read my manuscript. I truly valued every word of critique, praise, and advice, and I am grateful for their input.

This book would not have been possible without the consistent support of my doctoral dissertation committee at Rutgers University, which comprised four brilliant and inspirational women: Susan J. Carroll, Kira Sanbonmatsu, Sophia J. Wallace, and Ronnee Schreiber. To my committee chair, Sue Carroll, I cannot thank you enough for your continued guidance. Sue believed in me and my work, even when I didn't. She is always available for a phone call and has helped shepherd this project from its earliest stages. I always look forward to her no-nonsense feedback and down-to-earth conversations about sports, politics, and tattoos. Thank you, Sue, for somehow challenging me to be better while simultaneously building my self-esteem. I will always be grateful and honored to have had the opportunity to learn from you.

I thank Kira Sanbonmatsu for her mentorship and constant kindness. I am especially thankful for her practical advice in the field (including the important suggestion to wear comfortable shoes when conducting interviews on

Capitol Hill!), her thoughtful feedback on all my work, and her continued support after graduate school. Thank you also to Sophia Wallace for her commitment to both my own professional development and to creating a more inclusive and diverse discipline. Sophia has always been an inspiration to me, and I am eternally grateful for her guidance during my first years of graduate school, for introducing me to the congressional politics literature, and for her continued mentorship. Thank you, finally, to Ronnee Schreiber. I first read Ronnee's book, *Righting Feminism*, prior to entering graduate school. Her scholarship is what inspired me to write a dissertation, and now a book, on conservative women. I thank her for her work and for her thoughtful comments that push me to think through the connections between conservatism, gender, motherhood, and politics.

I am forever grateful to the Center for American Women and Politics (CAWP) at Rutgers University for making available countless resources and opportunities. This book relies heavily on interviews conducted by scholars at CAWP during the 103rd, 104th, and 114th Congresses. I am particularly thankful to the most recent research team—Kelly Dittmar, Kira Sanbonmatsu, Sue Carroll, Debbie Walsh, and Audra Lubiak—for the extraordinary amount of work they put into this project, encouraging me to participate as a graduate research assistant, and giving me the chance to include my own interview questions. I would also like to thank the members of Congress—especially the sixteen Republican women—who took the time to speak with us in the midst of their busy schedules. This book would not exist without them.

In addition to CAWP, I thank the Department of Political Science, the Women and Politics Program, the Department of Women's and Gender Studies, and the Institute for Research on Women. I feel lucky to have been a part of these Rutgers institutions and to have benefitted from an environment that is wholeheartedly committed to supporting women academics and research on women in politics.

My academic journey and the completion of my first book would not have been possible without the education and mentorship I received as an undergraduate at the University of San Diego (USD). Thank you especially to Casey Dominguez, Noelle Norton, and Gary Gray for cultivating my interest in American politics and for advising me throughout my time at USD. To Karen Shelby, who introduced me to feminist theory and helped transform both my life and my scholarship, thank you for your endless support and inspiration on the road to becoming a fire-eating feminist! I am also thankful for the USD McNair Scholars Program, which has been pivotal in helping me navigate institutions of higher education as a first-generation student.

I am fortunate to have made lasting friendships throughout the eight years of researching, writing, and editing this book. To my friends in the Women and Politics Program who read the earliest drafts of my work, helped me think through my theoretical contributions, shared a pitcher of sangria with me, celebrated with me at my wedding, knitted my daughter a women's suffrage-themed blanket, and so much more—I hope you know how truly grateful I am to have you in my life. Thank you especially to Mary Nugent, Juliana Restrepo Sanín, Jessica Nevin, Amanda Roberti, and Grace Howard for their continued friendship and for keeping me grounded since our first day of grad school together. Thank you also to Noa Balf for being a feminist inspiration and for contributing to this book probably more than she knows.

I would be remiss not to mention my pets, whose positive impact on my mental health cannot be overstated. Mittens, my sweet tabby cat, has been with me for the entirety of this journey, from the beginning of grad school through the submission of my final manuscript; he sat patiently on my lap as I read for class, studied for my comprehensive exams, and wrote each chapter. I'm also thankful for Molly, my "Borador," who can always make me smile and who forces me to take some much-needed breaks.

My final words of love and thanks go out to my bicoastal family. I arrived in New Jersey from California not knowing anyone, and I've left with a big, amazing new family. Thank you for making New Jersey feel like home. Thanks especially to my mother-in-law, Robin Gamatko, for her unwavering support and for watching Ellie every week so I could finish the first draft of this book. To my West Coast family—and especially to my tía y tío, Sonia and Tom Lahaie, who treat me like a daughter; and my cousin, Chris Baker, who treats me like a sister—thank you for always checking in on me. And of course, I am grateful for my incredible parents, Sylvia and Jeff Wineinger, who are truly my best friends and biggest fans, and who never once questioned my decision to major in political science. Thank you for listening without judgment as I obsessively talked about my research on the phone, for subsidizing my work with gift cards to coffee shops, for sneaking into my conference presentations, and for always encouraging me to pursue my passion—even when that meant moving thousands of miles away. I love you lots and so much more.

My daughter, Elena Aurora, didn't exist when this project began, but is now the most amazing, creative, and fiercest little girl I know! Thank you to my Beanie for filling each day with more joy than I could have imagined and, importantly, for not caring at all whether or not I finished this book. Better than anyone else, Ellie has taught me the importance of work/life balance, and for that I am thankful.

No one has played a more significant role in helping me achieve this dream than my husband, Dan Beam. I often feel Dan knows me better than I know myself; he has celebrated every small accomplishment and has walked me through every trial and tribulation. He sent me articles that were relevant to my research, gave important insights into my work, and, above all else, has shown me the power of compassion, patience, and love. I finished this book during the COVID-19 pandemic (which meant no child care!), and it was only possible because Dan sacrificed so much more than he should have for our family and my career. Putting into words what he means to me would be a book in itself, so I will say simply: I love you and thank you. For everything.

I want to stress—if it is not already abundantly clear—that this has been far from an individual endeavor. I am the beneficiary of sacrifices made by those mentioned here and by those whom I have never met. To every woman who blazed this trail for me, I offer my sincerest gratitude and a promise to pay it forward.

1

Introduction

Party Politics through a Gender Lens

Narrowly averting a government shutdown, President Barack Obama and Speaker John Boehner reached a federal budget agreement in the late hours of April 8, 2011. Earlier that day, though, partisan tensions had been mounting. At noon Eastern Time, the Democratic women of the United States Senate held a press conference. Together, they blamed House Republicans for stalling budget negotiations over the inclusion of an anti-abortion policy provision that would have eliminated federal funding for Planned Parenthood.[1] A mere four hours later, Republican women in the House of Representatives held their *own* press conference, defending their party's proposed budget and accusing Democratic senators of wasteful spending. Led by Cathy McMorris Rodgers (R-WA), then-vice chair of the House Republican Conference,[2] a line of 15 Republican women made their way to the podium to "share a little perspective" with the American people.[3]

McMorris Rodgers, who had recently become the first member of Congress to give birth twice while serving in office,[4] opened the press conference by talking about her four-month-old daughter and the need to rein in government spending. Emphasizing her daughter's share of the national debt, she argued, "No mom runs a family budget this way and neither should the federal government."[5] Mary Bono of California, during her remarks, looked around at her colleagues on stage and added, "I'd like to say what an honor it is to be up here with these amazing women. I think it's the first time we've all been together like this as a group, and it's pretty powerful and beautiful."[6] It was an acknowledgment not only of the important perspectives women bring into the policymaking arena, but also of the significance of speaking collectively as *Republican* women.

This scene raises questions about the evolving role of women in Congress. While much of the previous literature on women's congressional representation has focused on the legislative impact of women members, it is becoming necessary to more thoroughly understand how changes in the institutional

Gendering the GOP. Catherine N. Wineinger, Oxford University Press. © Oxford University Press 2022. DOI: 10.1093/oso/9780197556542.003.0001

environment affect the experiences and strategies of congresswomen more broadly. The combination of growing polarization and interparty competition in recent years has resulted in fewer policy deviations by women from their party line. And yet, as evidenced by these press conferences, gender continues to shape the representational behavior of women on both sides of the aisle.

Asymmetric polarization—in which the Republican Party has shifted further to the right than the Democratic Party has shifted to the left (Poole 2007; Mann and Ornstein 2012)—has also affected the composition and characteristics of women in the House of Representatives. While the number of Democratic women has increased steadily over the past several decades, the number of Republican women has remained comparatively stagnant, in part due to the ideological hurdles that disproportionately impact Republican women candidates (see Och and Shames 2018; Thomsen 2015; 2017; 2020).[7] Even in what has been deemed the "Year of the Republican Woman," the 2020 election cycle resulted in a total of 31 House Republican women— a modest gain from their previous record of 25, and still dwarfed by the House Democratic Party's record 89 women.[8] Women in both parties, like their male counterparts, are also more ideologically extreme than members in previous decades. But the impact of polarization has been most notable among *Republican* women, who had once been significantly more moderate than men in their party (Frederick 2009). Evidence shows that, as moderate members have been replaced by more conservative members (Thomsen 2015), House Republican women are now in fact "ideologically indistinguishable" from their Republican male colleagues (Frederick 2009; 2013).

This book delves deeper into the gendered effects of polarization by examining how these institutional changes have affected the rhetoric and experiences of Republican women in the House of Representatives. As Republican congresswomen struggle to gain seats, grow further apart ideologically from their Democratic women colleagues, and operate in an increasingly partisan environment, I argue that it is important to develop a more nuanced understanding of "the difference women make" (Swers 2002) in Congress. Thus, rather than focusing on the legislative impact of Republican women, I examine the evolution of gender dynamics within the House GOP and how women navigate those dynamics.

In moving beyond an analysis of legislative behavior, I further unveil the *process* through which women's representation occurs in a polarized congressional environment. As Karen Beckwith (2014) contends, "Asking about representation of women's interests requires that scholars ask about women's role in their own representation, including within legislatures as legislators themselves" (36). Beckwith asks scholars to separate how female legislators act on behalf of women's interests from the way they act on behalf of *themselves* as women in a legislative institution. She writes, "It is reasonable to ask whether and under what conditions women in legislatures seek to advance their interests as women within the state venue in which they are situated, as well as to ask about their willingness to advance women's interests articulated by those outside the state" (Beckwith 2014, 37). It is through an analysis of these dual acts of representation—representing the interests of women outside of Congress as well as their own institutional interests as congresswomen—that I illustrate the evolving role of women in Republican Party politics.

The first half of this book looks at changes in the way Republican congresswomen define women's issues and claim to represent women. Whereas Democratic women senators, at their April 2011 press conference, emphasized funding for Planned Parenthood as a top priority, the Republican women of the House avoided the topic of abortion, choosing instead to speak about the consequences of government spending from a gendered perspective. This rhetoric was in line with GOP leadership's general messaging on the 2011 budget negotiations. "There's only one reason that we do not have an agreement as yet," Speaker Boehner stressed, "and that issue is spending."[9] For Republican women in this partisan era, representing the interests of women is less about moderating the GOP's stances on conventional "women's issues" and more about using their gendered perspectives to advance conservative issues that align with their party's communication tactics. Examining exactly how their rhetoric has changed over time can shine new light on the way Republican congresswomen work on behalf of women.

Building off this analysis of rhetorical shifts, the second half of the book focuses on changes in the way Republican women work together as women legislators. Through extensive interviews and case studies, I highlight the experiences of Republican congresswomen, their attempts to navigate existing gender dynamics, and the connection between rhetoric and institutional advancement. I show how Republican congresswomen have mobilized around their *partisan-gender identity*, identifying and working together as Republican women in an attempt to gain visibility and institutional power within their party. I further uncover the dynamics that give Republican congresswomen opportunities to become high-profile party messengers while simultaneously constraining their ability to achieve more substantive legislative power.

Throughout this book, I make the case that Republican women's descriptive and substantive underrepresentation in Congress is more complex than it appears from the outset. While it is true that Republican women in Congress, like Republican men, have become more ideologically extreme in recent years, they do not function merely as gender-blind partisans. On the contrary, Republican congresswomen are, in many ways, more attuned to their identity as partisan women than they had been in the past. How they work together at the intersection of their gender and partisan identities shines light on the role of women in the GOP, men's continued presence as gatekeepers, and the future of Republican women's representation.

Congressional Representation: The Issue with "Women's Issues"

In her seminal work, Hanna Pitkin (1967) argues that representation consists of four main dimensions: formalistic, symbolic, descriptive, and substantive. That is, as political representatives are given formal authority and reasonable means of accountability through elections, they have the ability to "stand for" and "act for" their constituents. "Standing for" the represented encompasses symbolic and descriptive representation in that representatives can engage in representation merely through the emotions they evoke (symbolic) or the identities they possess (descriptive). Substantive representation goes further and is defined by Pitkin as "acting in the interests of the represented in a manner responsive to them" (Pitkin 1967, 209). Indeed, as elected officials in a representative democracy, members of Congress are tasked with representing the policy interests of their constituents. Whether and how members substantively represent their constituencies has been a primary focus for congressional scholars, who have found that myriad factors—including public opinion, campaign resources, potential challengers, and issue salience—affect the representational behavior of legislators (Fenno 1977; Mayhew 1974).

Expanding our understanding of congressional representation, scholars of politically underrepresented groups have shown that legislators also have the desire and ability to represent people outside of their geographic districts. For instance, functioning as "surrogate" representatives (Mansbridge 2003), women members of Congress have expressed an obligation to represent the interests of women across the country (Carroll 2002; Dittmar, Sanbonmatsu, and Carroll 2018). Understanding this connection between descriptive and substantive representation has been a principal goal of those who study the legislative representation of politically marginalized populations (Dovi 2002; 2007; Mansbridge 1999; Phillips 1995).

In Congress specifically, members must work within committees, parties, and chambers whose formal rules and informal networks favor cisgender white men. Women of color and other legislators who do not fit this mold thus face unique raced-gendered obstacles and must often work harder to have their voices heard (Brown 2014; Hawkesworth 2003). Nevertheless, scholars have typically found descriptive representation to be an important factor for substantive representation. For racial (Hero and Tolbert 1995; Wallace 2014), sexual (Hansen and Treul 2015), and gender minorities (Carroll 2001; Dodson 2006; Evans, 2005; Rosenthal 2002; Swers 1998; 2002; 2013; Thomas 1994; Vega and Firestone 1995), the identity of legislators can have significant effects on legislation.

Notably, when measuring the substantive impact of women legislators, scholars have most often focused on the way members advocate for certain issues, finding that women members are more likely than their male counterparts to introduce, co-sponsor, and vote for bills related to "women's issues" (Bratton and Haynie 1999; Burrell 1994; Dodson and Carroll 1991; Dodson et al. 1995; Dodson 2006; Gelb and Palley 1996; Norton 1999; Swers 1998; 2002; 2013; Thomas 1994). There have been essentially three main conceptualizations of "women's issues" within the gender politics literature. The first encompasses issues that are "explicitly feminist" in nature (Bratton and Haynie 1999, 665), such as expanding abortion access or advocating for equal pay. Second are issues that directly impact the lives of women, which can include both feminist and *anti-feminist* issues like abortion restrictions or the elimination of affirmative action programs for marginalized communities (Swers 2002, 37). A final conceptualization involves issues that deal with "women's traditional areas of interest," including "bills that reflect women's roles as caregivers both in the family and in society and thus address issues in health care, care of the elderly, education, housing and the environment" (Dodson and Carroll 1991, 53).

These issues—what I refer to in this book as "conventional women's issues"—are not mutually exclusive and capture a broad range of ideologies; nevertheless, it should be noted that they are issues which have been primarily identified by *researchers*, rather than by legislators themselves. While early studies of women in Congress have typically operationalized women's substantive representation as the promotion of conventional women's issues, more recent scholarship has challenged the method by which these issues are identified. Reingold and Swers (2011), for instance, advocate for an "endogenous approach" to the study of women's representation: "If we begin with the assumption that women's interests are socially constructed, politically contested, and empirically contingent, then we can further explore how and why the meaning and significance of women's interests vary across time, space, institutions, groups, and individuals" (430). One goal of this book is to expand scholarly understandings of women's interests by empirically examining changes in the way Republican congresswomen discuss the impact of various policies on women's lives.

In the following sections, I show how institutional changes—in particular, increasing party polarization and competition—have forced scholars to begin to reassess the legislative impact of women in Congress. I further argue that these changes require both a broader interpretation of women's issues and a more in-depth analysis of the way congresswomen represent women within the confines of their political parties.

Party Politics through a Gender Lens

This book examines congressional party politics through a gender lens, focusing on the experiences of Republican women. I begin with three main assumptions rooted in previous scholarship. First and foremost is an acknowledgment that Congress and political parties are raced-gendered institutions (Brown 2014; Dittmar 2021; Hawkesworth 2003; Jones 2017; Wineinger 2021). That is, they are spaces in which "race-specific constructions of masculinity and femininity are intertwined in the daily culture of the institution" (Hawkesworth 2003, 537). An analysis of women's experiences in the House Republican conference is therefore not simply about individual gender identity; more than that, it is a way to uncover existing gender (and racial) power dynamics and to examine how women preserve and/or contest those hierarchies. As Nikol Alexander-Floyd (2008) emphasized in her study of Republican Secretary of State Condoleezza Rice, the presence of prominent Black women in politics may challenge the status quo in some ways without necessarily "displac[ing] the dominant power structure" (446).

Second, American political parties have distinct cultures that shape institutional gender and racial dynamics (Freeman 1986; Grossmann and Hopkins 2015; 2016). As I discuss further in Chapter 3, the Democratic and Republican parties comprise coalitions with fundamentally different identities and interests. As a result, the structures and priorities of the two parties are also fundamentally different. In particular, compared to the Democratic Party, the Republican Party tends to have a more hierarchical power structure, is more ideological, and is less invested in what they consider to be "identity politics"—that is, the explicit promotion of group-based identities and interests (Freeman 1986; Grossmann and Hopkins 2015; 2016). This is not to say, of course, that Republicans do not cater to specific identities; white and Christian identity has become strongly associated with Republican partisanship, in part due to racial appeals made by Republican elites (Jardina 2019; Mason and Wronski 2018). As candidates, many Republican women have worked within this party culture by vocally rejecting the notion of "identity politics" while simultaneously aligning themselves "with white, Christian constructions of family, motherhood, and citizenship" (Wineinger 2021, 580; see also: Wineinger and Nugent 2020). Uncovering how Republican women navigate these tensions within the institution of Congress is one goal of this book.

Finally, the decisions made by party leaders must be understood as part of a broader political strategy. With the goal of winning (and maintaining) legislative majorities, party leaders make policy, fundraising, and messaging decisions based on potential electoral outcomes (Koger and Lebo 2017; Lee 2009; 2016; Valdini 2019). The institutional environment and the broader political landscape—including the saliency of gendered issues—are factors to consider when examining why and how women's voices matter in party politics. For example, the presence of an active women's movement and the voting gender gap can influence parties' outreach efforts, legislative agendas, and overall decisions to elevate women to positions of power (Campbell 2016; Carroll 2014; Sanbonmatsu 2004; Weldon 2002; Valdini 2019).

The strategic decisions made by party leaders, then, are neither race- nor gender-neutral. *Whose* interests are prioritized and *whose* voices are amplified is often at the forefront of party leaders' choices, whether intentionally or not. Throughout this book, I argue that we cannot fully understand congressional party politics without attention to social group identity, and we cannot fully understand the impact of group-identity in Congress without attention to party politics. By looking at intraparty dynamics through a gender lens, I unveil new challenges—and new opportunities—for women in the GOP.

The Gendered Effects of Party Polarization and Competition

One of the most widely studied issues among congressional scholars is that of party polarization (Binder 2016; McCarty, Poole, and Rosenthal 2006; Poole and Rosenthal 1997; Sinclair 2006; Theriault 2008). Based on roll call data and developed by Keith T. Poole and Howard Rosenthal, DW-NOMINATE (Dynamic Weighted Nominal Three-step Estimation) scores are commonly used as a measure of members' ideology; ranging from −1 to 1, a higher DW-NOMINATE score signals a more conservative ideology. Figure 1.1 shows the average ideology of both parties in the House of Representatives from the 89th Congress (1965–1967) to the 116th Congress (2019–2021). Since 1965, the gap between the mean DW-NOMINATE scores of Democrats and Republicans has widened from .547 to .873, with the election of increasingly liberal Democrats and—to a greater extent—increasingly conservative Republicans (Poole 2007; Mann and Ornstein 2012).

In more recent years, the use of DW-NOMINATE scores as evidence that party polarization is the result of shifting individual ideological preferences

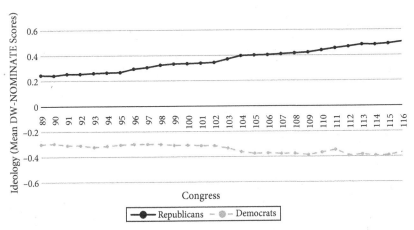

Figure 1.1 Mean Ideology of Congressional Parties, 89th–116th Congresses (1965–2021)

Data source: Lewis, Jeffrey B., Keith Poole, Howard Rosenthal, Adam Boche, Aaron Rudkin, and Luke Sonnet (2020). *Voteview: Congressional Roll-Call Votes Database.* https://voteview.com/

(Poole 2007) has been called into question (Lee 2009). Indeed, while DW-NOMINATE scores measure voting patterns, they do not specifically measure positions taken on issues. That said, with a few exceptions,[10] DW-NOMINATE scores have consistently reflected the ideological scores reported by various interest groups such as Americans for Democratic Action and the US Chamber of Congress (Burden, Caldeira, and Groseclose 2000; McCarty, Poole, and Rosenthal 2006). Thus, I use DW-NOMINATE scores in this book to quantify members' ideology on a liberal-conservative spectrum.

Importantly, however, congressional polarization must be understood both in terms of ideology and partisanship. While it is true that ideological differences between the Democratic and Republican parties have grown significantly since the 1970s due to demographic changes and regional shifts in partisan constituencies (Alphonso 2018; Kabaservice 2012; Karol 2009; Noel 2013), institutional dynamics between party leaders and rank-and-file members also help explain the widening gap between congressional parties. What party polarization shows, after all, is a strengthening of party discipline—that members are more likely to vote together as a party. Within the party politics literature, debates emerged over the extent of party leaders' abilities to control the legislative behavior of rank-and-file members. While some scholars have argued that parties function as cartels with strong leaders (Cox and McCubbins 1993), others have painted a more complex picture, with parties acting more like "teams" (Downs 1957; Lee 2009; 2016) and power dynamics between leaders and members fluctuating depending on electoral interests (Aldrich and Rohde 1997; 2000; 2010; Cox and McCubbins 2005; Koger and Lebo 2017; Pearson 2015).

Indeed, an increasingly competitive electoral environment has shaped congressional party behavior over the past two decades. Prior to 1995, Republicans had been deemed the "permanent minority" in Congress, with Democrats retaining majority party status for four decades (Connelly and Pitney 1994; Mann 1988). The relatively low level of party competition at this time meant there was also a smaller cost to working across the aisle and compromising on certain policies. This dynamic changed following the 1994 "Republican Revolution" during which Republicans campaigned aggressively on conservative policies and won control of the House for the first time in 40 years (Lee 2016; Koger and Lebo 2017). Between 1995 and 2021, control of the House has switched three times. And since 2007 (when Democrats regained control of the House for the first time following the Republican Revolution), Democrats and Republicans have each held a majority in the House four times.[11] As the potential for a shift in party control of government has increased over time, so have the stakes in each congressional election. This intensification of interparty competition has resulted in a growing incentive for members of the minority party to actively oppose and campaign against the policies proposed by the majority (Lee 2016). A focus on messaging and party branding has also become the norm on both sides of the aisle (Heberlig and Larson 2012; Lee 2016).

Several scholars have documented the consequences of party polarization and competition on the policymaking process in Congress, including the implementation of "unorthodox" rules (Sinclair 2016), less deliberation, stronger party leaders, and increasing legislative gridlock (Binder 2003; 2016; Lee 2009; 2016; Pearson 2015). In addition, we have also begun to see the gendered implications of these institutional changes. While female legislators on both sides of the aisle continue to view themselves as surrogate representatives (Dittmar, Sanbonmatsu, and Carroll 2018), they increasingly act for women within the context of their own parties and ideological beliefs. Republican women, for instance, are more likely to adopt anti-feminist policy alternatives (Osborn 2012; Swers 2002) and are less likely than Democratic women to pursue conventional women's issues (Swers 2016). Moreover, despite previous studies showing that women legislators are more likely to collaborate across party lines (Kathlene 1994; Duerst-Lahti 2002; Gelb and Palley 1996), Democratic and Republican women are no longer more bipartisan than their male counterparts (Lawless, Theriault, and Guthrie 2018). One result is that conventional "women's issues" are less likely to make it out of committee and through the legislative process (Volden, Wiseman, and Wittmer 2018).

A main objective of this book is to enhance our current understandings of the gendered impact of party polarization and competition. I argue that these institutional changes have implications beyond legislative behavior; they also shape the way Republican women fight strategically for power within their party. Certainly, I do not claim that polarization is the sole cause of behavioral changes over the past two decades. However, I do show how the combination of ideological cohesion among Republican congresswomen and interparty competition between Republicans and Democrats has enabled Republican women to tactically leverage their gender identity, framing it as an electoral asset to the party.

Republican Women in the House: Trends over Time

The 1992 "Year of the Woman" marked a sharp increase in the election of women to the US Congress. Women gained 22 seats that year, bringing their total number to 54, or 10 percent, of the 535 members.[12] At the time of this writing, a record-breaking 143 women hold seats in the 117th Congress.[13] But these increases in the number of congresswomen have not been consistent on both sides of the aisle. In the House, while Democratic women hold 88 seats, Republican women hold only 31 seats—up from 13 seats in the previous cycle.[14] Figure 1.2 shows the breakdown of the number of women in the House by party; as the number of Democratic women has increased gradually over time, the number of Republican women has remained relatively stagnant since 1993.

Gender politics scholars have sought to understand this "partisan gap" among women in Congress (Elder 2020; 2021; Och and Shames 2018; Thomsen 2015). Research shows that, while all women candidates must learn to navigate a gendered campaign environment (Dittmar 2015), Republican women face specific ideological and cultural barriers. Women candidates of both parties are generally stereotyped as being more liberal than their male counterparts, less competent on issues related to the military and national security, and more capable of handling issues like health care and education (Carroll and Schreiber 1997; Dolan 2010; Huddy and Terkildsen

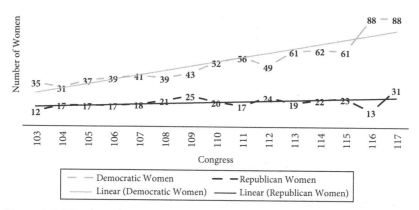

Figure 1.2 Number of Women in the House of Representatives by Party, 103rd–117th Congresses (1993–2023)

Data source: Center for American Women and Politics, Eagleton Institute of Politics, Rutgers University

1993; McDermott 1997; Sanbonmatsu 2002; Sanbonmatsu and Dolan 2009). Voters also prefer women candidates who are wives and mothers (Teele, Kalla, and Rosenbluth 2018) and who present traditionally feminine traits.[15] This becomes particularly challenging for Republican women, whose party is viewed by voters as more competent on "masculine" issues (Winter 2010) like national security and crime (Petrocik 1996; Petrocik et al. 2003; Huddy and Terkildsen 1993). The disconnect between what voters expect of women candidates and what they expect of Republican candidates makes it especially challenging for Republican women to win elections—and, in particular, to convince primary voters that they are conservative enough (King and Matland 2003; Schneider and Bos 2016).[16]

Ideological barriers in primary elections are compounded by cultural barriers that are specific to GOP politics, resulting in less overall structural support for Republican women candidates. Republican Party culture, and in particular the party's aversion to "identity politics" (Freeman 1986; Grossmann and Hopkins 2015; 2016; Wineinger and Nugent 2020), gives Republican women access to fewer identity-based resources (Crowder-Meyer and Cooperman 2018; Elder 2012; 2021; Kitchens and Swers 2016). For instance, while women's organizations such as EMILY's List help fund Democratic women candidates, Crowder-Meyer and Cooperman (2018) find that Republican women's organizations are largely ineffective, in part due to the fact that party donors care more about a candidate's conservative ideology than her gender. This effect is compounded for women of color, who, on the Democratic side of the aisle, have benefitted from their intersecting identities (Bejarano 2013; Elder 2020; Smooth 2006) and have driven overall increases in women's representation (Carew 2016; Hardy-Fanta et al. 2006). On the Republican side of aisle, women of color have been dismally underrepresented, with a record five serving in the 117th Congress.[17]

Even after being elected, Republican women face unique challenges to staying in office. While electoral vulnerability causes congresswomen in both parties to devote more effort than men to representing their constituents (Lazarus and Steigerwalt 2018), Republican women are also under particular pressure to demonstrate party loyalty. As Lawless and Pearson (2008) find, for example, Republican women are more likely than Republican men to field a primary challenger. Essentially, women in the GOP face electoral opposition from outside and within their own party and must work harder to credential themselves as conservatives.

This electoral terrain has implications not only for the number of Republican women in Congress, but also the ideological characteristics of those women. While Republican women in the electorate tend to be more moderate, on average, than Republican men (Barnes and Cassese 2017), many moderate Republican women opt out of running for Congress due to these partisan and ideological constraints (Thomsen 2015; 2017). Thus, the Republican women who *are* elected to Congress have been increasingly conservative (Frederick 2009; 2013). Figure 1.3 shows the average ideology of House members by gender and party over time. While Republican congresswomen were significantly less conservative than their male Republican colleagues in the 1980s and early 1990s, there is no longer a statistical gender difference in the ideologies of House Republicans.

That GOP women in the House are more conservative and more ideologically aligned with their male colleagues highlights the need to examine changes in the way Republican congresswomen represent women. While political scientists have long acknowledged the significance of conservatism in American politics, feminist scholars have at times portrayed conservative women as political pawns or victims of "false consciousness" (Dworkin 1983, 17). Yet those who study conservative women activists have consistently found that they, like feminist activists, possess a gender consciousness. Rebecca Klatch, for instance, notes that socially conservative women are well

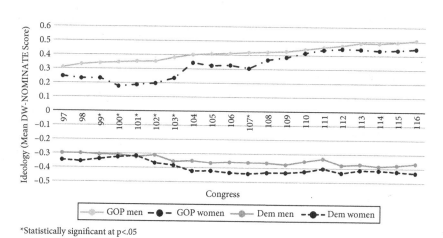

*Statistically significant at p<.05

Figure 1.3 Mean Ideology of Members in the House by Gender and Party, 97th–116th Congresses (1981–2021)

Data source: Lewis, Jeffrey B., Keith Poole, Howard Rosenthal, Adam Boche, Aaron Rudkin, and Luke Sonnet (2019). *Voteview: Congressional Roll-Call Votes Database*. https://voteview.com/

aware of their interests as women and have often worked to defend those interests (Klatch 1987, 10). Indeed, conservative women have organized collectively around their shared gendered experiences (Gurin and Townsend 1986) and have "framed their policy goals in terms of women's interests" (Schreiber 2002, 331). These conservative women's groups have been influential throughout American history, particularly when it comes to mobilizing political opposition to feminist policies. Discussing conservative women's activism against social welfare policies in the years following the ratification of the 19th Amendment, Kristen Delegard (2012) writes, "In a lesson that would be repeated many times over the course of the twentieth century, progressive women discovered how difficult it was to exercise political influence in the face of female foes who rallied to defeat subversion under the banner 'It takes women to fight women'" (221).

The historical effectiveness of conservative women activists suggests feminists should take seriously the impact of increasingly conservative women elected to Congress (see also Carroll and Liebowitz 2003). As Reingold and Swers (2011) contend, "The increased polarization of the political parties and the expanding number of conservative Republican women at the national and state level require us to examine how gendered life experiences and political ideologies shape legislators' competing definitions of women's interests/issues" (433). Indeed, in order to understand the development of competing definitions of women's interests and to fully capture the evolution of women's representation in Congress, Republican women must not be regarded as mere pawns. Instead, it is important to examine the intricacies of intraparty gender dynamics and to begin with the premise that conservative Republican women are legitimate political actors with agency. Rather than relying on a defined set of "women's issues," I begin this book with an analysis of Republican congresswomen's rhetoric to best understand how they conceptualize women's interests and how they claim to work on behalf of women.

Rhetoric as Representation

As polarization and competition have intensified in Congress, so has the importance of party communication and messaging strategies. Interparty competition, in particular, has caused individual members to focus on fundraising and reelection campaigns (Heberlig and Larson 2012; Lee 2016).

Collectively, congressional parties have devoted more resources to communications and public relations staff—especially when they are in the minority (Lee 2016) or when they disagree with the president (Malecha and Reagan 2012). These institutional changes and recent technological advances have led congressional scholars to more closely examine the way representatives communicate not only with their own constituents (Fenno 1978; Fridkin and Kenney 2014; Grimmer 2013), but also with the public more broadly (Lipinksi 2004; Meinke 2016; Malecha and Reagan 2012; Sellers 2010). "Communication," Patrick Sellers (2010) writes, "is central to politicians' work, particularly in the U.S. Congress" (1).

Studies of congressional communication have shown that the rhetoric of individual members is increasingly partisan (Lipinksi 2004), in part because party leaders work to shape and develop national party messaging strategies (Malecha and Reagan 2012). Notably, these messaging efforts are not the same on both sides of the aisle. In her analysis of senators' Twitter activity, Annelise Russell (2018) illustrates the asymmetry of partisan communication, finding that Republican senators are more likely than their Democratic counterparts to engage in explicitly partisan rhetoric. These findings are consistent with the claim that party polarization is driven more so by the rightward shift of the GOP than by the leftward shift of Democrats (Mann and Ornstein 2012; Skocpol and Williamson 2012).

Communication differences also exist at the intersection of gender and partisanship. Women in Congress are more likely than men to participate in floor speeches (Pearson and Dancey 2011a) and to reference women in those speeches (Pearson and Dancey 2011b; Osborn and Mendez 2010; Shogan 2001). Colleen Shogan's (2001) analysis of "woman-invoked rhetoric" in House floor speeches during the 105th Congress (1999–2001) showed that, while Republican and Democratic congresswomen invoked women in their speeches at similar frequencies, they tended to speak about different issues. For instance, Republican women more often discussed the ways in which tax, business, and pension law affect working women, while Democratic women were more focused on funding for state welfare programs (Shogan 2001). While these analyses provide valuable insight into the way representatives speak for women in the context of their parties, there has yet to be an in-depth, qualitative study of (1) changes in the nature of this gendered rhetoric over time or (2) the politics of women as party messengers.

I argue that these questions are especially important to consider within the realm of GOP politics, given Republican women's overrepresentation in Conference leadership positions. A major role of the House Republican Conference—comprising a chair, vice chair, and secretary—is to help create and disseminate party messages (Lee 2016; Malecha and Reagan 2012). In the 99th Congress (1985–1987), Lynn Morley Martin was elected the first female vice chair of the Conference, holding that position for two terms. It took a decade for the second woman to be elected to Conference leadership in 1995; however, since then, women have held top Conference leadership roles in every Congress, including chair in the five most recent Congresses (see Figure 1.4). Indeed, as Kanthak and Krause (2012) find, Republican women are four times more likely than Democratic women to be elected to these types of leadership positions in their respective party caucuses.

That Republican women are more frequently found in party messaging roles raises questions not only about changes in the gendered and partisan nature of congressional communication, but also about the ways in which we study women's representation. As previously discussed, gender politics literature has often focused on the way descriptive representation affects substantive representation. That is, do women represent women? More recently, critics of this approach have urged scholars to "focus not on when women make a difference but on *how* the substantive representation of women occurs" (Childs and Krook 2006; emphasis added).

Michael Saward's (2006) concept of "representative claims-making" is a useful tool for expanding studies of women's representation. Saward argues that political elites have the potential to shape public interests through the claims they make, emphasizing a more dynamic process of political

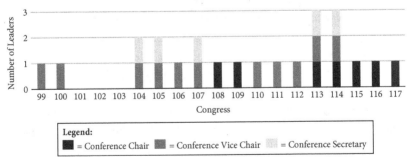

Figure 1.4 Number and Position of Female House Republican Conference Leaders, 99th–117th Congresses (1985–-2023)

Note: In the 117th Congress, Rep. Liz Cheney (R-WY) was replaced as in the middle congressional session by Rep. Elise Stefanik (R-NY), who would become the fourth woman to chair the House Republican Conference.

representation. Thus, rather than defining women's representation as the enactment of specific "interests" that have been assumed a priori, we should instead view "the politician as maker of representations" (Saward 2010, 16). In other words, how do representatives *claim* to act for women? Beginning with this question gives us the opportunity "to uncover patterns in representation that would have remained hidden in traditional studies" (de Wilde 2013) and to expand our understandings of who can substantively represent women and what, exactly, that entails (Celis et al. 2008).

Examining *conservative* claims about women, for example, can paint a more complex picture of the relationship between ideology and women's interests (Celis and Childs 2012; 2018). In this book, I begin with an analysis of the way Republican congresswomen speak as and on behalf of women: which issues do they discuss, what types of claims do they make, and how has this evolved over time? Understanding, first and foremost, changes in rhetoric allows me to then delve deeper into Republican women's mechanisms of representation in Congress. By pairing my rhetorical analysis with an in-depth examination of the institutional and interpersonal dynamics Republican women navigate, I begin to reveal the process through which gendered representative claims become part of a unified party message.

A Partisan-Gender Identity

I contend that increased ideological cohesion among Republican women, in the context of a competitive political landscape, affects the way Republican congresswomen represent women *and* the way they work to advance their own interests as women in the party. In her analysis of women's representation in Congress, Michele Swers (2002) finds that Republican women were more partisan in the 104th Congress (1995–1997) after Republicans gained control of the House. Needing to credential themselves as ideologically conservative and aligned with the goals of party leadership, Republican women were less likely to deviate from their party's positions on women's issues than they had been in the previous Congress (Swers 2002). In a later piece, Swers and Larson (2005) illustrated the diverse views of Republican women in the 108th Congress (2003–2005), identifying three Republican women "archetypes": (1) the socially conservative woman, (2) the woman who denies gender differences, and (3) the feminist woman (125–128). The socially conservative woman and feminist woman both embrace their identities as women and claim to act in the interests of women, though the socially conservative woman does so from a distinctly conservative standpoint in which her roles as a mother and wife are emphasized. The woman who denies gender differences denies the existence of distinct women's interests or, at least, chooses not to focus on them (Swers and Larson 2005).

Increasingly, evidence of this ideological diversity among House Republican women has been waning. As Danielle Thomsen (2015) demonstrates, a more polarized electoral terrain in which potential candidates evaluate their "fit" with one party or the other helps to explain why "one of these archetypes––the conservative Republican woman––can succeed in an increasingly conservative and homogeneous Republican Party" (315). The creation of the Republican Women's Policy Committee in 2012—a caucus in which all Republican women in the House were members—and the prevalence of press conferences led exclusively by Republican women provide further evidence that the GOP is comprised not merely of conservative, gender-blind Republican women, but of conservative women who acknowledge the significance of their gender identity.

I delve deeper into this concept throughout the book, exploring the recognition and mobilization of what I call a *partisan-gender identity*. More specifically, I examine the extent to which Republican congresswomen explicitly identify and work together as partisan women, and how this has changed over time. Just as ideological cohesion and interparty competition produces electoral incentives for partisans to work together against the other party (Aldrich and Rohde 1997; 2000; Koger and Lebo 2017; Lee 2009; 2016), I argue that it can also incentivize congresswomen to work at the intersection of their partisan and gender identities. As Melody Valdini (2019) has demonstrated in her cross-national analysis, women's inclusion and power within political parties increases when party leaders are convinced that women are electorally valuable to the party. Especially in a political landscape where Democratic messaging is gendered, polarization lessens the incentive for Republican women to work with women across the aisle and strengthens the incentive to mobilize around their partisan-gender identity. Doing so functions to simultaneously undercut Democratic messaging and convince party leaders that women are an asset to the party.

Because my ultimate goal is to deepen our understandings of *how*—not just if and when (Childs and Krook 2006; also see Beckwith 2014)—women are represented in an environment of heightened party polarization and competition, I focus my analysis on rhetoric and institutional gender dynamics rather than legislative output. Examining changes in the way Republican women speak, identify, and work as women can paint a more accurate picture of women's congressional representation. An in-depth analysis of the way women navigate the institutional and cultural norms of the GOP can also deepen our understanding of women's consistent underrepresentation in the Republican Party and suggest potential ways to address it.

Methodology

This book examines the evolution of Republican women's representation, focusing on Republican congresswomen's use of gendered rhetoric and their attempts to gain influence within the GOP. First, I examine how growing party polarization and competition has affected the way Republican congresswomen speak for and organize as women. While an analysis of shifts in representational behavior is in itself an important endeavor, the overarching goal of this project is to deepen scholarly understandings of institutional gender dynamics within the GOP and Congress more generally. Thus, I use a multimethod approach in which qualitative and quantitative analyses of congressional floor speeches are supplemented with case studies of women's caucuses and female Conference leaders. In-person interviews with women members of Congress are also a fundamental aspect of this project, as they work to unveil the motivations behind the use of gendered rhetoric, as well as the personal relationships and institutional opportunities/constraints Republican women must navigate. My findings reveal that while Republican congresswomen increasingly communicate and work collectively as *partisan women*, party leaders still function as gatekeepers in ways that both expand and limit the institutional power of Republican women.

A Comparison of Two Congressional Eras

I compare the behavior and experiences of Republican congresswomen in two congressional eras, comprised of four Congresses: the 103rd/104th Congresses (1993–1997) and the 113th/114th Congresses (2013–2017). I chose to study these periods for several reasons. First, lawmakers were working in similar political environments. In the 104th, 113th, and 114th Congresses, Republicans controlled the House with a Democratic president in the White House.[18] That Democrats held the majority in the 103rd Congress also allows me to better isolate the effects of party competition, which I discuss further in the next paragraph. Another important characteristic of these periods is the relevance of gendered issues—and the willingness of Republican leadership to promote women in their party as a result. In both congressional eras, Republican leaders were forced to reckon with a widening gender gap in presidential elections, as well as overt criticisms of the Republican Party as "anti-woman."[19] These gendered landscapes, which I detail throughout the book, give me the chance to delve deeper into the role party leaders play in advancing women's congressional representation within certain contexts.

Second, comparing these periods allows me to analyze the effects of increasing party competition, as well as ideological cohesion among Republican women in Congress. As discussed previously, the transition from the 103rd to the 104th Congress marks the transition into a more competitive congressional environment. The 1994 election gave Republicans control of the House for the first time in four decades, incentivizing members of both parties to continue to compete for control of the government. It is also in this election that we begin to see an increase in the number of ideologically conservative Republican women in Congress (see Figure 1.3). But while the average conservatism of House Republican women increased, the range of individual ideologies and issue positions among Republican women in the 104th Congress were still considerably more diverse than in the later Congresses. For example, Figure 1.5 shows the individual and mean DW-NOMINATE scores of House Republican women in each Congress; the range of DW-NOMINATE scores was .815 in the 104th Congress compared to .431 and .460 in the 113th and 114th Congresses, respectively. A comparison of these two congressional eras, then, helps unveil the gendered implications of interparty competition, as well as the increased conservatism and ideological cohesion among Republican women.

Finally, researchers at the Center for American Women and Politics (CAWP) at the Eagleton Institute of Politics at Rutgers University conducted extensive interviews with women members of Congress in the 103rd, 104th, and 114th Congresses. Access to these transcripts affords me a more detailed, behind-the-scenes understanding of the motivations for various forms of representational behavior. In the following section, I elaborate on the methodology as well as on my role in conducting these interviews during the 114th Congress.

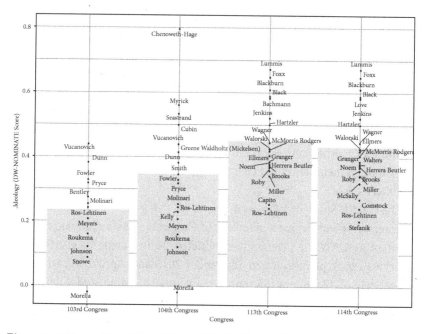

Figure 1.5 House Republican Women's Individual and Mean Ideology by Congress

Data source: Lewis, Jeffrey B., Keith Poole, Howard Rosenthal, Adam Boche, Aaron Rudkin, and Luke Sonnet (2019). *Voteview: Congressional Roll-Call Votes Database.* https://voteview.com/

My comparison of the 103rd/104th and 113th/114th Congresses focuses on members of the House of Representatives, rather than the Senate, for two main reasons. First, the House functions under relatively rigid debate rules compared to the Senate.[20] This helps provide consistency across cases and makes it easier to pinpoint institutional factors that may shape political rhetoric. Second, the larger number[21] of Republican women in the House compared to the Senate, while still difficult to examine statistically, provides a better opportunity to analyze variations in rhetoric and behavior.

Interviews with Women Members of Congress

This project relies heavily on elite interviews with congresswomen conducted as part of two larger studies at CAWP. The CAWP Study of Women in the 103rd and 104th Congresses[22] included a total of 82 semi-structured interviews with women members of Congress. The first round of interviews was conducted between June and October 1995 with 43 of the 55 women who had served in the 103rd Congress (36 representatives, 6 senators, and 1 delegate—a response rate of 78 percent). The second round of interviews took place between October 1997 and July 1998 with 39 of the 58 women who had served in the 104th Congress (35 representatives, 3 senators, and 1 delegate—a response rate of 67 percent). Some interviews were conducted by phone, but most were conducted in person and ranged in length from about 15 minutes to one hour. Each interview was recorded and done on the record, though members could choose to go off the record at any point during the interview.

The CAWP Study of Women in the 114th Congress[23] included a total of 83 interviews with women members of Congress.[24] As a graduate research assistant at CAWP, I personally conducted 24 in-person interviews. The interviews took place between September 2015 and April 2017, with a response rate of 77 percent (68 representatives, 13 senators, and 2 delegates). Almost all the interviews were conducted in person on Capitol Hill, although a few were conducted by phone to accommodate members' schedules. The semi-structured interviews ranged from 12 to 77 minutes in length, with the average interview lasting 29 minutes. All interviews were once again conducted on the record, though members could choose to go off the record at any point.

Interviews with Democratic women and Republican senators were helpful in providing additional institutional context and a better understanding of the interpersonal relationships among women in Congress. However, as my intention in this book is to expand our knowledge of the experiences of *House Republican women*, I focused my analyses primarily on those interviews. The response rates among Republican women in the House of Representatives were 100 percent (12 of 12) in the 103rd Congress, 65 percent (11 of 17) in the 104th Congress, and 73 percent (16 of 22) in the 114th Congress (see Appendix A for a full list of House Republican women interviewees). General questions in both periods focused on representational goals, policy priorities and achievements, party polarization, and perceptions of gender dynamics within Congress. Other questions were more individualized and tailored to members' specific legislative actions or leadership roles. In the 114th Congress interviews, we also asked Republican congresswomen about the creation and role of the Republican Women's Policy Committee, and whether and how they believe they approach conservative issues differently than their male Republican colleagues. These interviews, paired with content analyses and case studies, are incorporated throughout this book in various ways to inform my evaluations of institutional and interpersonal dynamics within Congress. In the methods section of each subsequent chapter, I detail the specific ways in which interview data were analyzed.

Content Analyses of Floor Speeches

The first step in understanding the evolution of Republican women's representation is to examine shifts in the way they claim to represent women. Using *The Congressional Record*, I collected every substantive floor speech given by each House Republican woman in the 103rd, 104th, 113th, and 114th Congresses. Every speech was considered to be substantive unless it pertained exclusively to congressional protocol. For example, constitutional authority statements, motions to adjourn, and committee elections were excluded from the analysis. In total, 3,979 substantive speeches were collected.

I apply Colleen Shogan's (2001) concept of "woman-invoked rhetoric" to determine when Republican congresswomen made claims about women. First, *NVivo* was used to extract speeches that contained variations of gendered key words, including variations of "women," "girls," "mother," "daughter," "grandmother," "wife," "female," and "gender." I also searched for words like "son," "husband," "spouse," and "children" to examine whether and how Republican congresswomen spoke about themselves as wives and mothers. I then read each speech that contained one or more of these words. Simply mentioning women did not qualify a speech as containing woman-invoked rhetoric. Rather, a speech with woman-invoked rhetoric was coded as such when a woman (1) claimed to represent women or girls in some way or (2) invoked her own identity as a woman to make a statement about the issue at hand. A total of 694 floor speeches given by Republican congresswomen contained woman-invoked rhetoric (17.4 percent of all floor speeches). These speeches were then examined quantitatively and qualitatively for shifts in policy priorities, speech type, and rhetorical frames. In Chapters 2 and 3, I elaborate on the methods used for each analysis.

While other forms of communication—like press releases or media interviews—are also important measures of public claims made by politicians, I chose to examine floor speeches for three main reasons. First, because most floor speeches are given during policy debates, I am better able to capture changes, if any, in the way Republican congresswomen conceptualize "women's issues." In which types of policy debates are women being invoked, and how has this changed over time? Second, floor speeches in the House are regulated by institutional rules, thus helping to limit variation in types and length of speeches among members. At the same time, distinguishing between types of speeches—debate, one-minute, or special order[25]—can also help reveal the motivations behind the use of woman-invoked rhetoric. For instance, one-minute and special order speeches have increasingly been used as party messaging tools (Gentzkow, Shapiro, and Taddy 2019; Harris 2005) and as a way for individual members to demonstrate party loyalty (Harris 2005; Pearson and Dancey 2011a; Pearson 2015). Thus, an analysis of floor speeches can be used to understand how, if at all, the rhetoric used by individual legislators aligns with broader party messaging tactics.

Finally, floor speeches have become significant forms of public political communication. Beyond legislative deliberation, floor speeches function as a mechanism for representative claims-making. The creation of C-SPAN in 1979 has given representatives a way to communicate directly to the public from the House floor, and party leaders have been able to take advantage of such technological advancements. Newt Gingrich (R-GA), elected speaker of the House in 1995, often encouraged rank-and-file Republicans to push a party message through special order speeches. As described by Frantzich and Sullivan (1996), "When asked whether he would be the Republican leader without C-SPAN, Gingrich . . . gave an uncharacteristic and unqualified one-word answer: 'No.' . . . C-SPAN provided a group of media-savvy House conservatives in the mid-1980s with a method of circumventing the more liberal press and winning a prime-time audience" (275). Even today, with television becoming less popular, representatives are able to effectively use C-SPAN footage of floor speeches on other mediums such as Facebook and Twitter.[26] Analyses of congressional floor speeches, then, can reveal *how* members of Congress are claiming to represent women as well as whether these are individual or collective messages.

In this book, I use the term "woman-invoked rhetoric" (Shogan 2001) rather than "representative claims-making" (Saward 2006) because my analysis is not limited only to *representative claims*: those which overtly represent a constituency. Also included are what I call *identity claims*: those in which women members invoke their own gender identity to speak *as* women. This distinction is important, particularly when examining the gendered claims made by Republican women, who must work within a party culture that ideologically rejects the notion of representation based on group identity, or "identity politics." By speaking as women,[27] rather than on behalf of women, Republicans may be better able to represent women within the confines of their party culture. That said, the overarching concept of representative claims-making—that claims made by political elites have the potential to shape public conceptualizations of women's interests—is still central to my project, and I often discuss the implications of woman-invoked rhetoric in those terms.

Findings from this analysis, described further in Chapters 2 and 3, reveal notable shifts in the use of woman-invoked rhetoric on the House floor. In particular, I show that, compared to those in the early 1990s, Republican congresswomen in the later Congresses more frequently engage in explicitly *partisan* woman-invoked rhetoric—gendered claims that closely align with Republican policies, messaging strategies, and culture. Such findings inform my methodological approach for Chapters 4 and 5, which I discuss next.

Case Studies: Women's Caucuses and Conference Leaders

The second half of this book focuses on the way Republican congresswomen navigate intraparty politics. In my analysis of congressional floor speeches, I find evidence that Republican congresswomen are more likely than in the 1990s to speak explicitly and collectively as *Republican* women. In several speeches, representatives referenced their membership in the Republican Women's Policy Committee (RWPC), established in 2012 as the first and only Republican women's caucus in Congress. In contrast, women in the earlier Congresses rarely spoke as partisan women and, in fact, would reference their membership in the bipartisan Congressional Caucus for Women's Issues (CCWI). This particular finding provided initial evidence of the increasing recognition of a *partisan-gender identity* among Republican congresswomen. Thus, in Chapter 4, I explore the development and eventual institutionalization of this partisan-gender identity through case studies of the CCWI and the RWPC.

Originally founded as the Congresswomen's Caucus in 1979, the CCWI is a bipartisan, bicameral congressional member organization (CMO) dedicated to working on legislation that improves the lives of women. While the CCWI still exists today, increasing polarization and institutional changes have limited the effectiveness of the caucus in addressing issues that are more substantive than symbolic[28] (Gertzog 2004). Meanwhile, Democratic and Republican women in the House have created their own partisan caucuses: the Democratic Women's Caucus (formerly the Democratic Women's Working Group until March 2019) and the RWPC. While the intricacies of a partisan-gender identity on both sides of the aisle are important to understand, this book continues to focus specifically on Republican women in order to deepen scholarly understandings of Republican Party culture and identity politics on the Right. Through in-depth analyses of elite interviews, media coverage, and primary and secondary sources from the National Archives and the Library of Congress, I investigate the politics of the CCWI and RWPC. By focusing on Republican women's collective action and the ways they have navigated ideological tensions between their partisan and gender identities, I am able to disentangle the complex relationship between Republican congresswomen and male party leaders in an increasingly competitive and polarized institution. My findings, detailed in Chapter 4, show that Republican congresswomen view themselves as *partisan women*— with experiences distinct from those of Democratic women and Republican men—and that they have taken advantage of political opportunities to organize collectively around that identity. The opportunities and constraints they have encountered from male party leaders further reveal the ways in which Republican Party culture limits women's role within the GOP primarily to loyal messengers.

Given the formal collective organization of Republican women in the House, the increasingly consistent overrepresentation of women in Republican Conference leadership positions, and the focus on women as party messengers, my final analysis examines the evolving role of women as Conference leaders. I conduct case studies of three female House Republican Conference leaders: Susan Molinari (R-NY), vice chair in the 104th Congress; Jennifer Dunn (R-WA), vice chair in the 105th Congress; and Cathy McMorris Rodgers (R-WA), chair in the 113th and 114th Congresses. I again rely on interviews, news articles, and archival sources to analyze each woman's (1) pathway to leadership, (2) gendered goals and priorities, and (3) experiences in attempting to carry out those goals.

While Dunn was not in leadership in the 103rd or 104th Congresses, I include her in this analysis for two reasons. First, there were no women in Republican leadership positions during the 103rd Congress. Second, in her interview with CAWP, McMorris Rodgers explicitly cited Dunn as a role model and trailblazer for her own leadership goals. The personal and ideological similarities between Dunn and McMorris Rodgers can help pinpoint institutional reasons for any discrepancies between their individual leadership experiences. The overarching goal of these case studies is to understand the evolving role of women as Conference leaders and to underscore changes in the way the voices of Republican congresswomen are amplified by the GOP.

Outline of the Book

The first objective of this project is to examine how institutional changes in Congress have affected the way Republican congresswomen speak as and on behalf of women. In Chapters 2 and 3 I analyze the floor speeches of Republican women in the House of Representatives to determine shifts in the use of woman-invoked rhetoric. In Chapter 2 I focus on the issues that members discuss when engaging in woman-invoked rhetoric, as well as the positions they take on those issues. I also explore the types of speeches being made—one-minute, special order, or debate—and the various narratives within those speeches. Findings reveal a shift toward woman-invoked rhetoric that is increasingly in line with official Republican Party policy positions and messaging strategies.

In Chapter 3 I examine more closely changes in the types of claims made by Republican women, as well as the rhetorical frames being implemented. I demonstrate that Republican congresswomen increasingly speak as and on behalf of women within the confines of their party culture. For example, as members of a party that explicitly touts "family values" and rejects what is often referred to as "identity politics," Republican women in recent Congresses are more often speaking about themselves as mothers, rather than claiming to represent women as a whole. Taken together, Chapters 2 and 3 highlight a shift toward the use of *partisan woman-invoked rhetoric—* gendered claims that align with Republican policies, messaging strategies, and culture. In each of these chapters, I explain why ideological polarization and interparty competition are likely explanations for this shift.

In Chapters 4 and 5 I take a closer look at changes in the intraparty gender dynamics of the House GOP and how Republican women navigate those dynamics. Chapter 4 specifically focuses on the collective action of Republican congresswomen. Through case studies of the CCWI and the RWPC,

I examine the way Republican women have negotiated tensions between their gender and partisan identities over time. I demonstrate how institutional and political changes intensified the recognition of a partisan-gender identity among Republican women beginning in 1995. I further show how Republican women collectively organized around this partisan-gender identity to create the RWPC in 2012. I also show the various challenges faced by Republican congresswomen and the significance of male party leaders as gatekeepers.

In Chapter 5 I compare the experiences of three female Republican Conference leaders: Susan Molinari, Jennifer Dunn, and Cathy McMorris Rodgers. Once again using in-depth case studies, I highlight similarities in each woman's pathway to office—particularly, the importance of male party leaders in encouraging and endorsing women as Conference leaders. I also illustrate how ideological cohesion among Republican women, along with the creation of the RWPC, has made it possible for recent female Conference leaders to amplify a collective, gendered message.

I concludes the book with an overview in Chapter 6 of the way Republican women's representation has evolved over time, as well as the theoretical and potential electoral implications of such changes. In examining how Republican women navigate the political and gender dynamics of the House GOP in a highly partisan era, I complicate the narrative of women's underrepresentation in Republican Party politics. In particular, I point out previously overlooked gendered tensions within the GOP, showing that Republican congresswomen work to represent women by at times pushing back against party leadership and at other times embracing their roles as loyal partisans. Gaining more substantive power in future Congresses, I argue, depends not solely on recruiting women candidates but also on changing the cultural norms that have limited Republican women primarily to party messaging roles.

2

Speaking for Women as Republicans

Partisan Woman-Invoked Rhetoric

In a 2015 special order speech given on the House floor, Representative Renee Ellmers (R-NC) criticized President Obama's recent implementation of the Iran nuclear deal and his decision to reduce military troop levels. As Ellmers saw it, the Joint Comprehensive Plan of Action was a "bad deal" and a troop reduction "as threats continue to grow overseas" was not in the country's best interest.[1] But while her positions on national security were in line with those of her male Republican colleagues at the time, the premise of her speech was different—and explicitly gendered. "Today," she said, "I stand with my fellow members of the Republican Women's Policy Committee to discuss an issue of concern that's on the mind of every American, especially moms."[2]

Seven other Republican congresswomen joined Ellmers in this special order on national security, also discussing the issue from a gendered standpoint. In several ways, their speeches signal a shift in the way Republican congresswomen claim to represent women. First, this focus on national security is in line with Republican policies and policy positions. National security is not a conventional women's issue and, certainly, taking hawkish positions on such issues is not typically considered one of the ways women represent women. And yet, here we see Republican women standing together *as women* to criticize the Democratic president and defend their party's call for a stronger military presence.

Second, the nature of special order speeches is important to consider. Since the 1990s, special orders have commonly been used by individual members and party leaders alike as a way to broadcast a unified party message (Gentzkow, Shapiro, and Taddy 2019; Harris 2005; Rocca 2007). These speeches are given at the end of the day, and while members can speak on any topic they choose, they are typically reserved in advance through party leadership.[3] That these speeches on national security were given in a special

Gendering the GOP. Catherine N. Wineinger, Oxford University Press. © Oxford University Press 2022.
DOI: 10.1093/oso/9780197556542.003.0002

order suggests this gendered rhetoric may be in line with a broader GOP messaging effort.

Finally, the emphasis in Ellmers' speech on a specific type of woman—mothers—aligns her rhetoric with the gendered cultural norms of her party. As explained further in Chapter 3, the Republican Party's formal rejection of "identity politics" makes the use of gendered representative claims—speaking "on behalf" of women as a group—more challenging for Republican women than for Democratic women. The importance the party places on family values and traditional gender roles also creates a tension in terms of how Republican women in the public sphere talk about women's interests (see Schreiber 2016). In speaking as a mother, then, Ellmers is able to represent women within the confines of the cultural values of the GOP.

In this chapter and the following chapter, I show that this shift in rhetoric is not an isolated phenomenon. On the contrary, I find that an environment of increasing party polarization and competition has led to the use of gendered rhetoric that is not only more conservative, but also more explicitly and implicitly *partisan*. I apply Colleen Shogan's (2001) concept of woman-invoked rhetoric to examine shifts in the way Republican congresswomen speak as and on behalf of women. Comparing House Republican women's floor speeches in the 103rd/104th (1993–1997) Congresses to those in the 113th/114th (2013–2017) Congresses, this chapter focuses specifically on changes in the types of issues Republican women discuss and the types of speeches they make. Chapter 3 looks more closely at the claims being made within these speeches.

Demonstrating the evolution of woman-invoked rhetoric on the House floor sheds light on the gendered effects of congressional polarization. In particular, I find that Republican congresswomen's woman-invoked rhetoric has become increasingly aligned with the party's policy positions, messaging tactics, and cultural norms. While not solely confined to one era, these characteristics are more prevalent in recent speeches and point to a general shift in the way Republican women approach women's representation. The politics behind this shift and what it can tell us about Republican women's role in the party are explored further in the remainder of the book.

Data and Methods

This chapter draws on data from congressional floor speeches and elite interviews with women members of Congress. As detailed in Chapter 1,

I used the *Congressional Record* to extract every substantive floor speech given by House Republican women in the 103rd, 104th, 113th, and 114th Congresses. I then applied Colleen Shogan's (2001) concept of "woman-invoked rhetoric" to identify speeches in which congresswomen (1) claim to represent women or girls or (2) invoke their own identity as a woman to make a statement about a particular issue. A total of 694 floor speeches given by Republican congresswomen contained woman-invoked rhetoric (17.4 percent of all floor speeches). Figure 2.1 shows the percentage of Republican women's speeches that contain woman-invoked rhetoric in each Congress. Notably, there has been no significant change in the frequency of woman-invoked speeches, despite the presence of a more homogenously conservative group of Republican congresswomen in the later Congresses.

To explore the implications of party polarization on woman-invoked rhetoric, I analyze changes in when and how such rhetoric is used. I begin with a descriptive quantitative analysis that examines changes in who is engaging in woman-invoked rhetoric, the issues that are discussed in woman-invoked speeches, and the types of speeches that are made. In coding for issue areas, I distinguished between those that are considered to be conventional women's issues and those that are not.[4] This is particularly important to consider in the context of the Republican Party, which "owns" issues that are not conventional women's issues—such as national security, crime, and economics (Petrocik 1996; Petrocik et al. 2003; Winter 2010). A shift toward

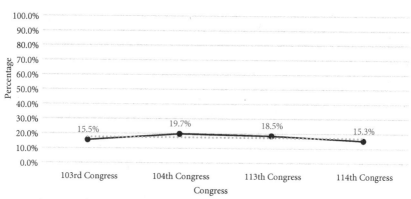

N = 134 of 862 in 103rd; 234 of 1,189 in 104th; 178 of 963 in 113th; 148 of 965 in 114th

Figure 2.1 Percentage of Republican Women's House Floor Speeches Containing Woman-Invoked Rhetoric

discussing these types of issues would demonstrate a shift toward rhetoric that more closely aligns with GOP policy priorities.

My decision to analyze speech type stems from the partisan function of different types of speeches. Indeed, just as special orders have been used to promote cohesive party messages (Gentzkow, Shapiro, and Taddy 2018; Pearson 2015; Rocca 2007), one-minute speeches are given most frequently by those who are disadvantaged within Congress—junior members, members of the minority party, women, etc.—often as a way to demonstrate party loyalty (Maltzman and Sigelman 1996; Harris 2005; Morris 2001; Pearson and Dancey 2011a; Pearson 2015). Thus, an increase in such speeches among Republican women may signal a shift toward woman-invoked rhetoric that more closely aligns with party messaging strategies.

Of course, a thorough examination of rhetorical changes requires an in-depth reading of these speeches. I therefore supplement this quantitative look at floor speech characteristics with a qualitative content analysis. In case studies of three policy areas—abortion, health, and foreign policy—I uncover shifts in the gendered policy frames used by Republican congress-women. A qualitative reading of one-minute and special order speeches also allows for a more detailed analysis of how these speeches are used to represent women in the context of party politics.

Finally, interviews with women members of Congress provide additional context for these speeches and, importantly, help disentangle the relationship between woman-invoked rhetoric and women's representational behavior.[5] Interview questions about the unique perspectives women bring to Congress enable me to explore the way Republican congresswomen approach the concept of "women's issues." Republican women's discussions of specific policy areas also provide insight into their decisions to invoke women (or not) in their floor speeches.

"All Issues Are Women's Issues": The Limits of Woman-Invoked Rhetoric

While floor speeches and other public claims made by political elites can be important mechanisms for representation (Celis et al. 2008; Celis and Childs 2012; Saward 2006; Shogan 2001), it is helpful to first examine the relationship between woman-invoked rhetoric and congresswomen's conceptualizations of "women's issues." Interviews with women members can deepen our understanding of the representational function and purpose of floor speech rhetoric for women in the Republican Party. In particular, it is necessary to recognize the limits of such rhetoric as a measurement of women's representation.

When asked about the difference women make in Congress, Republican women often argue that, while they bring an important perspective to the policymaking table, that perspective is not necessarily issue-specific. On the contrary, as Nancy Johnson (R-CT) put it in her 1995 interview, "Women's issues are all the issues. There are no distinctly women's issues."[6] In 2016, Ann Wagner (R-MO) made a similar claim, saying, "I'm not a believer in women's issues. I think all issues are women's issues. We just may come at them from a different perspective and, from living our lives and the complexity of it all, we may have a different approach to so many different issues."[7]

This tendency to reject the notion of a specific set of women's issues while still placing political value in gendered life experiences is not limited to congresswomen on one side of the aisle. Democratic and Republican women alike have made the claim that "all issues are women's issues" (Carroll 2002; Dittmar, Sanbonmatsu, and Carroll 2018). But this claim must also be understood in the context of party politics. The policy priorities of the two parties, for instance, present different challenges for Democrats and Republicans as they work to simultaneously represent women and be taken seriously as political actors.

On the Democratic side, politicians prioritize (and are viewed as most competent on) issues like health care, education, and welfare services—issues that are typically thought of as "women's issues" (Petrocik 1996; Petrocik et al. 2003; Winter 2010). Working on conventional women's issues, then, puts Democratic congresswomen in line with their party's legislative agenda. When Democratic women reject the notion of "women's issues," they often argue that the issues they work on are of national importance and should not simply be viewed as issues affecting women. For example, Rosa DeLauro (D-CT) was adamant in her 1995 interview that issues like abortion and health care should not be pigeonholed as "women's issues":

There are many women in this body who will fight like hell for a woman's right to choose. Now clearly, maybe the women have a more basic interest in that. But there again, if you don't have men and women voting on that issue in this place, you cannot win it. So it is not just a narrowly defined women's issue. It's a national issue. Health care is a national issue. Does it make sense to include women in the equation when we're doing research at the National Institutes of Health? Yes. But that's not a "women's issue." That's a national issue . . . And I'll tell you, in this body, I think that one of the things that has hurt women the most is defining women's issues and [saying] that women come here to work on women's issues. And I won't be a part of it. I will not be a part of it.[8]

Karen Thurman (D-FL) also argued that she is not simply representing women when she works on issues that affect women, saying, "I would like to think that by supporting women, I am also supporting their families—I mean, male, female, whatever."[9]

In contrast, the issues "owned" (Petrocik 1996; Petrocik et al. 2003) by Republicans—crime, national security, the economy—are stereotypically "masculine" (Winter 2010) and not typically viewed as "women's issues." Thus, when asked to specify which issues are important to them as women, many Republican congresswomen rejected the concept of "women's issues" while arguing that traditional Republican issues directly impact the lives of women. Kay Granger (R-TX), who served as chair of the Appropriation Committee's State-Foreign Operations Subcommittee from 2011–2017 and chair of the Defense Subcommittee from 2017–2019, said that national security has always been one of her top priorities. She argued that defense issues are important to women, especially as more women enter the military: "I love defense because I go to the bases all over the world. But every time, it's more women, every time. And I'll say, what made you join the Navy? And it's so interesting to hear their reasons and what they're doing."[10] In the 103rd Congress, Helen Delich Bentley (R-MD) said that she focused "on the issue of jobs" and "fair trade" because she believed "all economic issues are women's issues as well."[11] Similarly, Tillie Fowler (R-FL), a member of the Armed Services Committee in the 103rd Congress, argued that "defense is a women's issue."[12] Notably, despite their claims that these issues are important to them as women, none of these three representatives invoked women in their floor speeches when speaking on these issues.

Also important to consider is the fact that the claim "all issues are women's issues" has often functioned as a way for Republican women to distinguish themselves from Democratic women. When asked in her 1998 interview about the ways Republican women differed from Democratic women, Sue Myrick (R-NC) said, "We don't just single out specific issues. I mean, we are very concerned about fiscal matters, as I said, the education issues, the crime and violence issues. All of those affect women very dramatically."[13] Martha Roby (R-AL) responded similarly in 2016:

[Republican women] don't believe that there are issues that are women's issues. The same things that are important to our male colleagues are important to us. . . Energy is important. We have members that serve on eight committees that can talk about trade and tax reform. . . You have women that have served in the military that can talk about issues from that perspective.[14]

In this particular take, we see Republican women emphasizing Republican policy priorities while challenging the idea that Democratic women are better suited to represent women.

These interviews with women members across congressional eras illustrate two main points about the relationship between "women's issues" and woman-invoked rhetoric. First, while women in both parties acknowledge that they bring important life experiences as women to every issue, woman-invoked rhetoric cannot capture all of these gendered perspectives. In the Republican Party especially, women may bring important perspectives to the policymaking process on issues like national security or tax reform without ever explicitly mentioning women. An analysis of woman-invoked rhetoric should therefore not be the only measure of women's representation in Congress. Second, and relatedly, the disconnect between what some Republican congresswomen claim in interviews to be "women's issues" and their lack of woman-invoked rhetoric in floor speeches related to those issues suggests that such rhetoric should be viewed not simply as a genuine belief about what is beneficial for women, but also as a political decision. Indeed, the decision of whether to engage in woman-invoked rhetoric must be understood in the context of party politics and the broader political environment.

The goal of this analysis, then, is not to determine the validity of Republican women's claims. That is, I do not seek to judge whether or not Republican congresswomen are *actually* acting in the best interests of women, though that is an important endeavor (see Celis and Childs 2018). Rather, my goal is to delve deeper into the claims made by Republican women, to explore the evolution of these claims, and, most importantly, to understand the politics behind this evolution. While woman-invoked rhetoric is a limited measure of women's representation, it nevertheless provides important insights into the evolving role of women in party politics. In what follows, I present changes in the way

Republican congresswomen speak as and on behalf of women and explain how party polarization and competition have likely driven these changes.

When Is Woman-Invoked Rhetoric Used?

While the frequency of woman-invoked speeches given by Republican women has remained consistent over time, my analysis reveals changes in the characteristics and content of these speeches. First, I find a shift in *who* is engaging in woman-invoked rhetoric. Figure 2.2 shows the relationship between Republican congresswomen's individual ideology and the total number of woman-invoked speeches they gave in each Congress. I find a strong negative correlation between conservative ideology and woman-invoked speeches in both the 103rd and 104th Congresses.[15] No such correlation exists in the 113th and 114th Congresses. In other words, the gendered claims put forth by Republican congresswomen in the 1990s were coming disproportionately from moderate voices. Today, that is no longer the case; it is a more homogenous group of conservative women who are making these claims.

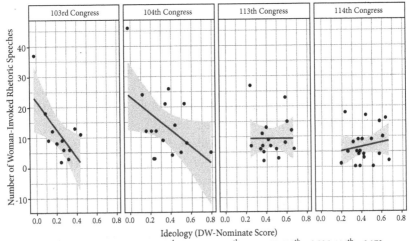

Pearson's correlation for each Congress: 103rd = −0.644**; 104th = −0.472*; 113th = 0.006; 114th = 0.172
**Statistically significant at p<.05
*Statistically significant at p<.10

Figure 2.2 Relationship between Republican Congresswomen's Ideology and Total Number of Woman-Invoked Speeches

Data source: Lewis, Jeffrey B., Keith Poole, Howard Rosenthal, Adam Boche, Aaron Rudkin, and Luke Sonnet (2018). *Voteview: Congressional Roll-Call Votes Database.* https://voteview.com/

Table 2.1 Top Three Issues Discussed in Woman-Invoked Speeches

103rd/104th Congresses (1993–1997)	113th/114th Congresses (2013–2017)
Welfare: 15.8%	Abortion: 19.6%
Health: 15.5%	Commemorative: 16.0%
Abortion: 12.0%	Health: 15.6%
$N = 2,051$	$N = 1,928$

One might expect that this ideological shift has had an effect on the types of issues discussed these speeches. However, I find that the issues are remarkably similar in both congressional eras. Table 2.1 shows the top three issues discussed in Republican women's woman-invoked speeches during the 103rd/104th Congresses and 113th/114th Congresses. These three issues were also the only issues that individually constituted over 10 percent of all woman-invoked speeches in those eras (for a complete list of issues, see Appendix B).

There are two important points to take away regarding these top issues. First, in both eras, Republican congresswomen were most likely to invoke women when speaking about conventional women's issues. Welfare, health, and abortion have all been labeled "women's issues" by scholars, as they directly impact the lives of women or are associated with women's roles as caregivers (see Chapter 1 for a more in-depth discussion of "women's issues"). A closer look at issue areas shows that *un*conventional women's issues—those which are viewed as more "masculine" and not typically associated with women—were discussed at similar rates in both eras, although they were slightly more prevalent in the earlier congresses (see Figure 2.3). Thus, generally speaking, it is not the case that Republican women are increasingly likely to speak about "masculine" Republican-owned issues like crime, the economy, and national security. That they are speaking largely on issues of traditional importance to women, even in an intensely polarized environment, raises questions about how these claims have changed over time. In particular, how has Republican congresswomen's framing of women's issues evolved, and what role does party politics play in shaping those frames?

In the following section, I present findings from my qualitative analysis of changes in issue framing. I focus in particular on abortion and health, given

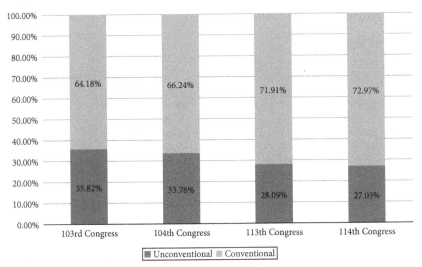

N = 134 in 103rd; 234 in 104th; 178 in 113th; 148 in 114th

Figure 2.3 Percentages of Woman-Invoked Speeches Pertaining to Conventional versus Unconventional Women's Issues

that these issues were both among the top three issues discussed in woman-invoked speeches in each congressional era. Also important to consider is how the framing of *un*conventional women's issues has changed over time. In both congressional eras, the most frequently discussed unconventional women's issues were those related to foreign policy.[16] Foreign affairs (defined as issues dealing with other countries, excluding national defense/military issues) was the top issue in the 103rd/104th Congresses, making up 7.6 percent of woman-invoked speeches. In the 113th/114th Congresses, national security (defined as issues related specifically to the military or national defense) was the top unconventional women's issue, comprising 5.8 percent of these speeches. Indeed, as Sara Angevine (2017) finds, women in Congress, regardless of party, are more likely than their male counterparts to introduce "women's foreign policy" legislation. Given this, I conducted a third case study of foreign policy rhetoric to better understand changes over time. These case studies shed light on the way woman-invoked rhetoric has evolved to more closely align with GOP policy stances.

The second takeaway from this analysis is that differences in the legislative agenda and political environment affect the way Republican women invoke women in their speeches. In particular, this can help explain why welfare and commemorative speeches were among the top three issues in their re-spective eras (see Table 2.1). In the 1990s, welfare reform was at the top of the legislative agenda. The Personal Responsibility and Work Opportunity Reconciliation Act (PRWORA), a priority in the Republican "Contract with America,"[17] passed a Republican-controlled Congress and was signed into law by President Clinton in 1996. The prominence of welfare reform as a po-litical and legislative issue is probably one reason that we see it among the top three issues discussed in woman-invoked speeches at this time.

But the context of these speeches must also be considered. For instance, the more moderate, senior Republican women of the 104th Congress—most significantly, Representatives Nancy Johnson (R-CT), Connie Morella (R-MD), and Olympia Snowe (R-ME)—fought to include provisions for child care, child support, and child protection in PRWORA (Casey and Carroll 2001). That these provisions centered on women's experiences helps to ex-plain why we see woman-invoked rhetoric most frequently used in speeches relating to welfare during this era. Importantly, while Republican women overwhelmingly supported the general principle of welfare reform, they also worked "to temper or moderate some of the harsher effects of the proposed legislation and . . . to expand the legislation in a way that many feminists would find desirable" (Casey and Carroll 2001, 130). Woman-invoked rhet-oric, then, was used often in welfare debates because it was on the legisla-tive agenda *and* because more moderate Republican congresswomen were pushing back against the stringent policies of their party.

In contrast to the 1990s, we see *commemorative* speeches among the top three issues in the 113th/114th Congresses (see Table 2.1). I labeled speeches "commemorative" when claims symbolically represented women but were not directly connected to any piece of substantive legislation, or when the leg-islation was symbolic in nature. Examples include support for a women's or-ganization, praise for women veterans, recognition of women's achievements, etc. The relatively large percentage of commemorative speeches in the later congresses raises questions about changes in the characteristics of woman-invoked rhetoric. Indeed, nearly all commemorative speeches were one-minutes or special orders. Given that these types of speeches are used regularly by members to demonstrate party loyalty or promote a unified party message, this signals a potential shift toward woman-invoked rhetoric that more closely aligns with official party messaging strategies.

In further support of this thesis, my analysis of speech *type* across these four Congresses reveals that Republican women in recent Congresses are

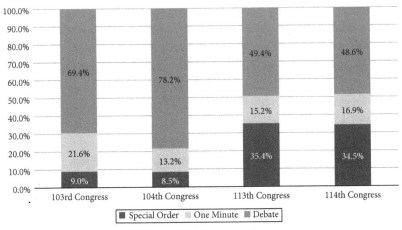

N = 134 in 103rd; 234 in 104th; 178 in 113th; 148 in 114th

Figure 2.4 Types of Woman-Invoked Speeches by Congress

using woman-invoked rhetoric less often in policy debates and more frequently in one-minute and special order speeches. Figure 2.4 shows that the
percentage of woman-invoked special order speeches has more than tripled
in the past two decades. In addition, commemorative speeches constitute an
increasingly large percentage of woman-invoked one-minute speeches: In
the 114th Congress, the majority of these speeches were commemorative
(see Figure 2.5).

In what follows, I show how party competition, paired with the presence of
a more cohesively conservative group of Republican women, has shaped the
evolution of woman-invoked rhetoric in the House. Through a qualitative
analysis of commemorative speeches and comparative case studies of policy
speeches, I demonstrate how woman-invoked rhetoric among Republican
congresswomen has become more explicitly partisan over time.

Aligning with GOP Messaging Tactics and Policy Positions

While there has been little change over time in the types of issues Republican
congresswomen discuss, a qualitative analysis of these issues nevertheless reveals
important shifts. I focus my analysis on four main issue areas: commemorative, abortion, health, and foreign policy. As described in the previous section,
abortion[18] and health policies have consistently been among the top three issues

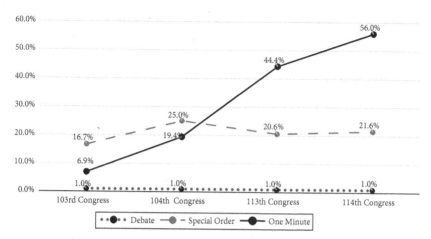

Figure 2.5 "Commemorative" Speeches as a Percentage of Type of Woman-Invoked Speech

discussed in speeches containing woman-invoked rhetoric, together making up about one-third of these speeches. Among unconventional women's issues, foreign policy issues have been the top priority in each congressional era.

I find that when Republican women in recent Congresses invoke women in commemorative speeches, they often do so in ways that align with broader party messaging tactics. I also find significant shifts in the way top policies are framed, with Republican congresswomen increasingly engaging in woman-invoked rhetoric that is consistent with their party's policy platform. Importantly, party messages and rhetoric in support of party policies are not necessarily mutually exclusive; in many cases, lawmakers frame their support of specific policies in ways that are also in line with the party's messaging strategies. While I am able to tease this out in some cases, it is more difficult to do in other cases. Nevertheless, I show that woman-invoked rhetoric among Republican congresswomen has shifted in ways that more explicitly align with GOP messaging tactics *and* policy positions—sometimes distinctly and sometimes simultaneously.

Winning Women with Commemorative Speeches

After significant losses in the 2012 general election, including Mitt Romney's loss to incumbent President Barack Obama, the Republican Party engaged in some self-reflection. This post-election practice is a normal aspect of electoral politics; it's a time in which "political observers, parties, and politicians try to draw a lesson from recent elections to inform their decision-making about the next one" (Masket 2020, 38). In March of 2013, the Republican National Committee (RNC) released its "autopsy report," titled the *Growth and Opportunity Project*. The narrative the GOP told itself was that it was not doing enough to reach out to women and racial minorities; it needed to advance a "brand of conservatism" that "invites and inspires new people" to join the party.[19] And it laid out suggestions on how to do just that.

Among these recommendations were general messaging strategies like, "We need to do a better job connecting people to our policies."[20] But there were more gender-specific tactics as well. For instance, one gendered recommendation was to "use Women's History Month as an opportunity to remind voters of the Republicans Party's historical role in advancing the women's rights movement."[21]

The growing number of woman-invoked commemorative speeches in recent years signals in itself a prioritization of these types of symbolic outreach efforts. Whereas commemorative speeches comprised only 4.3 percent of all woman-invoked speeches in the 103rd/104th Congresses, that number jumped to 16 percent in the 113th/114th Congresses. Republican congresswomen frequently used one-minute speeches to honor women's organizations in their districts or to recognize women's achievements. In the later Congresses, though, they also used rhetoric that was in explicit alignment with the recommendations and language of the RNC's *Growth and Opportunity Project*.

In 2016, Cynthia Lummis (R-WY) scheduled a special order on the topic of Women's History Month. She was joined by two female and three male Republican colleagues—Virginia Foxx (R-NC), Renee Ellmers (R-NC), Ken Buck (R-CO), Matt Salmon (R-AZ), and Steve King (R-IA). Lummis opened the special order:

> This month of March we are blessed with the opportunity to discuss the opportunities particularly presented by the Republican Party and the philosophies of the Republican Party as they relate to women, women's history and women's future and the opportunity to be involved in building women up and providing opportunities in the future, an opportunity culture that is shared by men and women to make sure that our homeland is safe and secure, to make sure that our families are in an environment that will be uplifting. These are some of the topics we will be discussing today.[22]

For the remaining 60 minutes of the speech, the Republican representatives emphasized their party's commitment to women. That Lummis and her colleagues discussed Women's History Month in a way that highlighted the GOP's "opportunity culture" for women suggests that these speeches were part of the party's broader messaging effort to attract women voters.

Exploring changes in the use of woman-invoked rhetoric among Republican congresswomen can enhance our understanding of the gendered effects of party polarization. The increasing use of special order speeches, the large percentage of commemorative speeches, and the alignment of these speeches with established party messaging strategies illustrate that Republican congresswomen are not only more ideologically conservative, but are also more *partisan* in the way they speak about women. In the remainder of this chapter, I present findings from case studies of the most frequently discussed issues, demonstrating that this shift to a *partisan woman-invoked rhetoric* can be seen in the discussions of specific policies as well.

Reframing Abortion: From Women's Decision to Women's Protection

While abortion has always been a controversial topic, the gendered framing of this issue by Republican congresswomen has evolved significantly over the past two decades. For one thing, many congresswomen in the early 1990s explicitly supported abortion rights. Barbara Vucanovich (R-NV) notes this in her CAWP interview: "In the 103rd Congress, there were very few of us who were pro-life women."[23] Indeed, several Republican women in this earlier era advocated on the House floor for access to abortion. Marge Roukema (R-NJ) emphasized her support for the Freedom of Access to Clinic Entrances Act in a floor speech, saying, "It is absolutely vital to protect a woman's ability to exercise her constitutional right to an abortion."[24] In support of the same bill, Connie Morella (R-MD) said that "women must be able to safely and privately obtain medical services from health clinics."[25] Using rhetoric that is similar to that of feminist activists today,[26] Morella notably described a protester who murdered a women's clinic doctor as "anti-choice" rather than "pro-life."[27]

Some of the congresswomen who did hold anti-abortion views resented the fact that abortion was even discussed in the House of Representatives. In her interview with CAWP, Helen Bentley (R-MD) said, "I don't think it's an issue that belongs on the floor of Congress. I don't think it's an issue that belongs in political circles. And even though I was pro-life basically, I repeatedly told our people that we didn't need that issue tacked on every bill. I felt it did more people harm than it was good."[28] Even as the 1994 election brought more women with anti-abortion views into the House, many of these conservative congresswomen were hesitant to engage on this particular issue. For example, when asked in an interview how she would describe her role in the abortion debate, Barbara Vucanovich (R-NV) responded, "Very reluctant. You know, I don't like to get up and be confrontational. But somebody had to speak . . . On the Republican side, Ileana [Ros-Lehtinen] is pro-life, but she would never speak on the issue. She would always vote for the issue, but she wouldn't speak on it."[29] Indeed, only two (fewer than 1 percent) of Ros-Lehtinen's 359 total speeches in the 103rd, 104th, 113th, and 114th Congresses were related to abortion, and only one of those included woman-invoked rhetoric. Sue Myrick (R-NC) responded similarly to the same question: "Pretty much I just voted. I'm a pro-life person, I always have been, so I support that position. The concern I've always had on that issue is that it's a no-win issue."[30]

These interviews with women members reveal what an analysis of floor speeches alone cannot: many conservative Republican women felt that engaging in abortion debates was unproductive, despite holding policy positions that were consistent with the national party's stances at the time. The 1992 Republican Party platform read:

> We believe the unborn child has a fundamental individual right to life which cannot be infringed. We therefore reaffirm our support for a human life amendment to the Constitution, and we endorse legislation to make clear that the Fourteenth Amendment's protections apply to unborn children. We oppose using public revenues for abortion and will not fund organizations which advocate it. We commend those who provide alternatives to abortion by meeting the needs of mothers and offering adoption services. We reaffirm our support for appointment of judges who respect traditional family values and the sanctity of innocent human life.[31]

That moderate Republican women were most outspoken on this issue also means that the abortion narrative being put forth by women in the party explicitly deviated from official party stances.

That said, there were instances of more conservative, anti-abortion women engaging in woman-invoked rhetoric when speaking on abortion. In these cases, women tended to invoke their own identities as mothers or grandmothers. For example, Linda Smith (R-WA) supported the Partial-Birth Abortion Ban Act of 1996 in a floor speech: "As a mother and grandmother, it is mind boggling to imagine having labor induced, to be giving birth, only to have the opportunity to be a mother stopped in midstream."[32] Less often, anti-abortion Republican women talked about protecting women from pro-abortion rights legislation. In her support of the Partial-Birth Abortion Ban Act, Representative Andrea Seastrand (R-CA) said in a floor speech, "Mr. Speaker, today this body of Representatives decides one of the most profound moral debates in the history of our Nation. Our children will look upon this day to see if we stood for principle. Will we vote to *defend and protect the women and future children of this Nation?* Will we vote for principle over political party?" [emphasis added].[33] This protection framework, used by only the most conservative women in the 1990s, dominated the abortion debate 20 years later.

Republican congresswomen in the 113th and 114th Congresses are not only more ideologically conservative; they are also more homogenous in their policy stances. In contrast to Republican women in the 1990s, every Republican woman in these later Congresses held anti-abortion policy positions and identified as "pro-life." This is consistent with the shift Kelly Rolfes-Haase and Michele Swers (2021) find in their study of abortion voting in the US House over time. They argue that "the changing nature of the party coalitions and increasing power of social conservatives in the Republican Party" have contributed to Republican women voting more consistently with their party on abortion issues since the 1990s (Rolfes-Haase and Swers 2021, 26). This difference in the ideological composition of Republican women has contributed to a shift in woman-invoked abortion rhetoric. (In Chapter 4, I also discuss how ideological cohesion on abortion issues has helped build and strengthen Republican women's coalitions).

In 2011, an unlicensed Philadelphia abortion provider, Kermit Gosnell, made national headlines when he was convicted of murder and involuntary manslaughter.[34] Outcry ensued from both ends of the political spectrum as details of his illegal and unethical abortion practices were revealed. Democrats used this case as an argument for greater access to safe abortion, while Republicans used it to support stricter regulations. Advocating for the Pain-Capable Unborn Child Protection Act, which would prohibit abortions after 20 weeks of pregnancy, Michele Bachmann (R-MN) argued in a floor speech that the bill "not only protects the unborn, it protects the mom against the lethal practices of abortionists like Gosnell. And women deserve better than abortion."[35]

This protection framework was seen throughout abortion debates in the 113th and 114th Congresses.[36] For instance, calling for the defunding of Planned Parenthood in a 2013 floor speech, Vicky Hartzler (R-MO) argued that abortion is harmful not only to "babies," but to women as well:

> Planned Parenthood ended the beating hearts of these innocent victims while *deluding vulnerable women* that their choice wouldn't have any harmful consequences, and they did so with taxpayer funding, over $500 million in 2011. This must stop. Abortion does have consequences. It destroys babies. *It harms women physically and emotionally*, and it harms men, too.[37] [emphasis added]

Ann Wagner (R-MO) made a similar claim about Planned Parenthood in a 2015 floor speech, saying, "We must protect women and unborn children from these dangerous procedures that are designed to increase revenue for this group and profit from the destruction innocent life."[38] And Martha Roby (R-AL), who describes herself as "unapologetically pro-life," told me in her CAWP interview that abortion "has very harmful effects on the woman who made that decision."[39] She said in a 2014 floor speech: "Recently, important legislative actions have been taken to defend the unborn and protect women from the brutality of late-term abortions. These include measures to tighten restrictions and raise health and safety standards for abortion providers."[40]

This intertwining of anti-abortion stances and claims to protect women is consistent with the policy positions and rhetorical strategy of the national Republican Party. The GOP's 2012 party platform takes the same anti-abortion position it did in 1992, with the addition of a clause that centers women: "We affirm the dignity of women by protecting the sanctity of human life. Numerous studies have shown that abortion endangers the health and wellbeing of women, and we stand firmly against it."[41] This finding is also consistent with recent research at the state level, which has shown that conservative Republican women are active proponents of anti-abortion legislation—and in particular, bills that frame anti-abortion policies as "pro-women" (Reingold et al. 2021; Roberti 2017).

In addition to changes in rhetoric, there has also been a shift in women's desire to engage in abortion rights debates. Unlike the Republican women who held anti-abortion views in the 103rd and 104th Congresses, many of those in the 113th and 114th Congresses believed they should be the ones delivering this message to the public. Cathy McMorris Rodgers (R-WA), House Republican Conference Chair at the time, had been a strong advocate for changing the messengers of the party to better relate to women voters on every issue, including abortion. In her interview, she stated, "Anyone who finds themselves in a position where they are even considering an abortion is in a very difficult situation. And so, from a woman's perspective, it's very important that we're a part in leading that discussion."[42] Renee Ellmers (R-NC) further discussed Republican women's role in the abortion debate in terms of party strategy:

> When an older man is leading on an issue that affects women, it just doesn't connect. It tends to cause people to question, "Do they even understand that this is a woman's issue?" Now, I maintain, and so do all my colleagues, that every issue is a woman's issue . . . But [abortion is] specific to women and our bodies . . . The perception is: "A man is up there telling me what I should be doing with my body." And that has never gone over well. And those are things that, I think, in the Republican Party, we should be looking to change. And so, it is very important that women are out there having the discussions.[43]

Republican women in these more recent Congresses are working in a political environment in which gendered attacks on the GOP are of concern to party elites, and in which their individual policy stances on abortion align with those of the party. It is perhaps unsurprising, then, that compared to the Republican women in the 103rd/104th Congress, the more homogenously anti-abortion women in the 113th/114th Congresses have engaged in woman-invoked rhetoric that explicitly aligns with their party's abortion policy positions and frames. That Republican congresswomen view themselves as party messengers on this issue further suggests there has been an evolution not only in the claims made by Republican women, but also in their relationship to the party's broader electoral goals. This concept is explored further in the remainder of the book.

Reframing Health: From Women's Health to Women's Economic Empowerment

Health is another area in which Republican congresswomen have consistently talked about women, with health speeches accounting for 15 percent of woman-invoked speeches in both congressional periods. When coding for "health" issues, I included issues directly related to health (such as cancer research funding) as well as issues related to health care reform (such as the repeal of the Affordable Care Act). Just as with the abortion issue, I find there are notable changes in rhetoric over time.

Under the broader umbrella of health issues, health care reform was a salient topic during both of these congressional eras. Proposed by the Clinton administration, the Health Security Act was introduced in Congress in November 1993 and defeated nearly a year later in September 1994. The health care proposal was the product of a task force chaired by then-First Lady Hillary Clinton (causing many Republicans to refer to it as "HillaryCare"), and it was a hotly debated issue in the 103rd Congress. Nearly two decades later, health care reform passed in the form of the Patient Protection and Affordable Care Act (also known as "ObamaCare"). In response, Republican members of the House have attempted to repeal or reform it numerous times. Given that health care legislation was most salient in the 103rd and 113th Congresses (Rocco and Haeder 2018), I focus my analysis of the changes in health rhetoric during these two Congresses.

In both the 103rd and 113th Congresses, Republican women denounced the Democratic health care plans and talked specifically about the negative economic impact these pieces of legislation would have on women. Nancy Johnson (R-CT) argued against the employer mandate provision in the Clinton health plan, saying in a floor speech, "For women, this mandate will mean isolation, it will mean dead-end jobs, it will mean stagnation. For women, that bifurcated premium structure is terminal to their dreams."[44] Jan Meyers (R-KS) further emphasized what she viewed as an economic hardship for women business-owners:

Mr. Speaker, as the ranking member of the Small Business Committee, I am concerned about the harm we will inflict on the 6.5 million women-owned small businesses if we endorse President Clinton's employer mandate as a part of health care reform. Women collectively employ more people in the United States than the Fortune 500 companies employ worldwide . . . We should assist our small women-owned businesses, not burden them with further mandates.[45]

A similar economic frame was used by Republican women throughout the 113th Congress to highlight the gendered implications of the Affordable Care Act. Yet, notably, this later rhetoric also included references to a "war on women."

In the months leading up to the 2012 election, Democratic politicians and feminist activists frequently accused Republicans of engaging in a "war on women." Recognizing this as an effective tactic, Republicans developed a strategy to defend themselves against such rhetoric. The RNC's 2013 autopsy report provided lawmakers with this recommendation:

> Republicans should develop a more aggressive response to Democrat rhetoric regarding a so-called "war on women." In 2012, the Republican response to this attack was muddled, and too often the attack went undefended altogether. We need to actively combat this, better prepare our surrogates, and not stand idly by while the Democrats pigeonhole us using false attacks. There are plenty of liberal policies that negatively impact women, and it is incumbent upon the party to expose those and relentlessly attack Democrats using that framework.[46]

Indeed, many Republican women in this era have used this tactic when engaging in health care debates. Diane Black (R-TN), for example, argued against a specific employer mandate provision that defined full-time employees as those who work 30 hours per week. She said in a floor speech, "For all the talk about the supposed 'war on women,' it is ObamaCare that is waging a war against female workers. That is why I am proud to stand in support of women across this country to repeal this arbitrary, 30-hour, full-time workweek."[47] Marsha Blackburn (R-TN) agreed: "I have to tell you, it really is a war on jobs. It is a war on women . . . 63 percent of those affected by the adverse impact of the President's health care law are women."[48] This finding suggests that Republican congresswomen are not only making policy arguments in their speeches related to health; they are also actively engaged in responding to gendered attacks against their party as a whole.

Moreover, while a gendered economic frame is present in the health speeches from both congressional eras, I also find this frame is much more prevalent in the 113th Congress (see Figure 2.6). This discrepancy likely

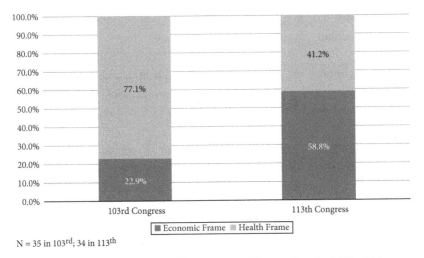

N = 35 in 103rd; 34 in 113th

Figure 2.6 Economic versus Health Frames in Woman-Invoked "Health" Speeches: 103rd and 113th Congresses

exists for two main reasons. First, in addition to financial implications, women in the 103rd Congress emphasized quality of care while women in the 113th Congress stressed economic choice and empowerment. Deborah Pryce (R-OH) notes in her 1995 interview that Republican congresswomen "firmly believed that the Clinton health care plan was a negative, not just for the country, but for women in particular. If you look at the fact that you had one physician and only one, and most families have a pediatrician and an OB/GYN and a general [physician] . . . We felt it was very negative. From what I can remember of it, we encouraged others to make floor statements to that effect."[49] And indeed, Republican congresswomen did frame their speeches in those terms. In a floor speech, Nancy Johnson (R-CT) said

> Most doctors believe that women need to have a baseline mammogram at the age of 35 and should have one every year thereafter from the age of 40 on. Now, the document to which my colleague referred, the President's health plan, denies women coverage for mammograms until they reach age 50 and then provides every 2 years until age 65. Many, many women in America enjoy much better insurance benefits than that.[50]

Emphasizing government intrusion into the patient-physician relationship was consistent with the general messaging strategies of the GOP in 1993

(Skocpol 1996; Winter 2005). Still, the focus on quality of care and women's health experiences places this frame in alignment with conventional interpretations of "women's issues" in ways we do not see as often in later Congresses.

The woman-invoked health care rhetoric used in the 113th Congress often framed women as the financial decision-makers of their home. Elise Stefanik (R-NY), for example, underscored in an interview the importance of listening to women's perspectives on health care reform:

> Eighty percent of healthcare decisions are made by women, whether it's for their spouse, whether it's for their kids or their elderly parents. And we see this even on the constituent services basis when oftentimes if an elderly constituent is struggling working through the bureaucracy it's sometimes the daughter or daughter-in-law making the phone call more often than not.[51]

This statistic was repeatedly used in debates on the House floor to argue that the Affordable Care Act undermined women's financial choices. Renee Ellmers (R-NC) said in a floor speech:

> Nationwide, women in this country make the health care decisions. Over 80 percent of the health care decisions that are made are made by women. That means that wives, mothers, or single women who are choosing health care coverage for themselves have now been told by the President and the Democrats who voted for this bill, and who knew full well that you wouldn't be able to keep your health care plan if you liked it: Do you know what? What you chose for you and your family—what was affordable to you—is not adequate, and we know better than you do for your family.[52]

This rhetorical shift from *quality of care* to *economic empowerment* is consistent with shifts in the GOP's health care messaging more broadly. The 2012 Republican Party platform, for example, placed emphasis on efforts to "empower consumer choice" in health care.[53] That Republican congresswomen have worked to gender this narrative is notable and, as discussed further in Chapter 4, can be attributed to a collective effort among Republican women to ensure that their party is viewed as welcoming to women.

A second reason economic frames were more prevalent in the 113th Congress is that Republican congresswomen discussed the topic of health care reform more frequently in their woman-invoked health speeches than they did in the 103rd Congress. Figure 2.7 shows that fewer than 30 percent of the woman-invoked health speeches in the 103rd Congress were related to health care reform, compared to over 70 percent in the 113th Congress. Instead, Republican women emphasized other health issues. For example, Olympia Snowe (R-ME) spoke in support of the Minority Health Improvement Act of 1994, arguing that "For far too long, at the Federal level, women's health has been neglected."[54] Sharing the same sentiment, Connie Morella (R-MD) underscored the importance of congressional action on women's health, saying in a floor speech, "Without leadership from Congress, women's needs in the HIV epidemic will continue to be given less priority, and women's programs will continue to be underfunded . . . We are running out of time for a generation of young women—we cannot afford to wait."[55] While women in the 113th Congress spoke of women's health concerns, such as breast cancer and lupus research funding, these types of speeches were overshadowed by discussions of health care reform (see Figure 2.7).

Intensifying polarization and party competition have created an institutional environment in which parties are focused on gaining (or retaining) control of government. The continued effort to repeal and replace the Affordable Care Act functioned less as a legitimate policy position and more as a symbolic campaign gesture for the minority party Republicans

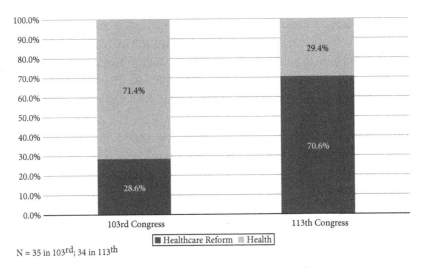

N = 35 in 103rd; 34 in 113th

Figure 2.7 Percentage of Woman-Invoked "Health" Speeches Pertaining to Healthcare Reform: 103rd and 113th Congresses

in the 113th Congress, who were unlikely to get such legislation signed into law (Lee 2016; Rocco and Haeder 2018). That the topic of Republican congresswomen's woman-invoked health speeches focused primarily on health care reform in the 113th Congress—and that many of these speeches contained overt "war on women" rhetoric—indicates an alignment with broader party tactics. In general, this analysis reveals the growing use of gendered narratives that align with the economic and health care policies and messages of the Republican Party.[56]

Reframing Foreign Policy: From Women's Rights to Security Moms

Among "unconventional" women's issues, changes in the frequency and framing of foreign policy also support the idea that Republican congresswomen are increasingly engaging in partisan woman-invoked rhetoric. Again, I split foreign policy into two more specific topics: foreign affairs and national security. Foreign affairs are those issues which engage other countries, excluding national defense or military issues. National security issues are those which are specifically related to the military or national defense. In what follows, I reveal the evolution of woman-invoked foreign policy rhetoric over the past two decades, focusing first on foreign affairs and then on national security.

In the 1990s, when Republican women invoked women in foreign affairs speeches, they typically did so to bring light to conventional women's issues within the realm of foreign policy. These more moderate congresswomen advocated for women's literacy; fought against female genital mutilation; and condemned the United States' global gag rule, "which prohibits aid to foreign nongovernmental organizations that engage in abortion services or advocacy with non-US funds" (Barot and Cohen 2015). For instance, Jan Meyers (R-KS) spoke out against the defunding of the United Nations Population Fund (UNFPA) in a 1993 floor speech:

Defunding of UNFPA has not prevented a single coerced abortion in Communist China. What it has prevented is the provision of voluntary family planning services to thousands and millions of women in poor countries. It has prevented poor women from acquiring the knowledge and the ability to have only the number of children they want, when they want them. It has prevented women from getting the information they needed to save their lives, as a pregnancy killed them.[57]

Indeed, in the 103rd/104th Congresses, conventional women's issues were discussed in 24 of the 28 (85.7 percent) woman-invoked foreign affairs speeches—and abortion was specifically referenced in 21 (75 percent) of them. The centrality of the abortion debate in foreign affairs speeches and the deep divide between pro- and anti-abortion Republican women in the House suggests that there was no collective gendered narrative put forth by Republican congresswomen on the issue of foreign affairs. For example, while anti-abortion women were less vocal on this issue, they would at times use their floor speeches to take the opposite stance on foreign affairs issues as their Republican colleagues who supported abortion rights. In a 1995 floor speech, Andrea Seastrand (R-CA) used the issue of sex-selective abortion to condemn foreign governments, arguing, "The Chinese population control policy forces women to have abortions. I can think of few established policies that are more antiwoman or policies that are making women victims."[58] In the later Congresses, we see a shift in the way foreign affairs issues are framed, as well as a more cohesive message from Republican congresswomen on foreign policy issues more generally.

In the 113th and 114th Congresses, none of the 12 woman-invoked foreign affairs speeches were related to conventional women's issues. Instead, these speeches were in line with Republican Party policy stances and were used mainly to criticize the actions of the Democratic president and the United Nations (UN). For example, Ileana Ros-Lehtinen (R-FL), condemned President Obama's recent visit to Cuba, arguing that women there are still victims of human rights violations:

In December 2015, President Obama said in an interview that he would go to Cuba only when the human rights situation on the island had improved. Well, Mr. Speaker, this is what human rights looks like on the island, the valiant Ladies in White, who walk peacefully in Cuba to their church—and you see one being dragged away in the lower corner. This is what happens to them every week in Castro's Cuba. They are harassed. They are beaten. This is not what an improved human rights situation looks like at all, Mr. President.[59]

And in a 2015 speech, Virginia Foxx spoke out against a UN resolution that condemned the actions of the Israeli government: "Well, last week, the United Nations really went off the deep end when its Commission on the Status of Women adopted a resolution that singles out and condemns Israel for violating the rights of women. That's right . . . It accused the only country in the Middle East that fully respects the rights of women with violating the rights of women."[60] What we see here, then, is a shift toward woman-invoked foreign affairs rhetoric that is less focused on conventional women's issues like abortion access and more focused on explicit Republican policy stances—including a condemnation of shifting US-Cuba relations and strong support of Israel.

More often, Republican congresswomen in the later Congresses invoked women in foreign policy speeches that dealt specifically with national security. In these speeches, Republican women often defended or supported military intervention by demonstrating how certain governments and terrorist organizations hurt women. Mia Love (R-UT), for instance, said in a 2015 speech, "Iran is a snake in the grass. Its leaders have made it very clear that they want to implement sharia law, not freedom. Iran does not value human life the way we do. They have actually shown that they are willing to support terrorists. They have shown that they are willing to hurt their own women and children."[61] This differs significantly from the rhetoric used in the earlier Congresses: only 1.9 percent of woman-invoked speeches in the 103rd and 104th Congresses pertained to national security, and the majority of those speeches (4 of 7) centered on supporting women in the military. For example, in support of the conference report on the National Defense Authorization Act, Tillie Fowler (R-FL) said in a 1993 speech: "There are a number of important achievements in this year's bill. We have provided a much-deserved cost-of-living increase to our service personnel, enhanced critical logistics capabilities, and moved forward on our next generation of submarines. I am also especially pleased that we have opened up many new opportunities to women in the military."[62]

Notably, one gendered national security narrative present in both congressional eras is the idea that defense issues are inherently important to women *as mothers*. In the 103rd and 104th Congresses, it was the most conservative Republican women who made this connection between security and motherhood. For example, Helen Chenoweth (R-ID) stated in a floor speech that President Clinton did not pass what she called the "mother's test":

I guess my major claim to fame is the fact that I am a mother. I am a mother of a military man who would respond to the command of his Commander in Chief, because that is the way he has been raised. But my heart breaks to think of mothers across this Nation having to let their sons and daughters go because of a President who does not understand what his role is and the role of the military, his responsibility as Commander in Chief; because, since the beginning of civilization, mothers have been willing to send their sons off to war to protect the interests of the country or the tribe or the community, to preserve the peace and tranquility of their existence, to make sure that freedom and liberty will reign for their future generation. That silent mother's test.[63]

With the increase in ideologically conservative women elected to Congress, this motherhood narrative became more prominent in the 113th and 114th Congresses. During the special order on national security described at the beginning of this chapter, Marsha Blackburn (R-TN) said, "Madam Speaker, when you talk about issues that are women's issues, right now national security is at the top of the heap. As we have talked about soccer moms and Walmart moms and all of these other iterations and descriptions during the years, right now we are looking at a category of security moms because the issue of security is what mothers are talking about."[64] In her 2015 interview with CAWP, Kristi Noem (R-SD) delved deeper into the reasoning behind her focus on national security, arguing that women bring an important perspective to this issue specifically because they are mothers:

Every mom in the country, their number one priority is that their kids are safe. And that is central to the discussion that we need to have when it comes to national security and our military. And that perspective has to always be interjected into these conversations that we have, whether we are talking about a new next generation bomber or if we are talking about adequately training and equipping our military. That mom's perspective should be in that discussion, too. And it's always made it a much more fruitful conversation.[65]

This shift to a focus on "security moms" also shines light on the effects of party competition. As Susan J. Carroll (2008) notes, the "security mom"— a supposedly new, post-September 11th female voter—garnered national media attention during the George W. Bush administration and the 2004 presidential election. According to media reports, security moms were the swing voters candidates needed to sway; they were white, married mothers concerned about future terrorist attacks and their children's safety. However, as Carroll (2008) finds, the claim that security moms were swing voters was largely unfounded. Ideologically conservative and solidly Republican, the security mom voted overwhelmingly for Bush in the 2004 election. Nevertheless, the portrayal of this group of women as swing voters gave Bush an opportunity "to appear to be responsive to women voters without making specific commitments that he might have had to follow through on once elected" (Carroll 2008, 87). As congressional Republicans today compete for control of government and work to defend their party against claims of a Republican "war on women," speaking as and on behalf of security moms allows them to advocate for conservative policies while simultaneously claiming to represent women.

Importantly, women in the 113th/114th Congresses were not simply speaking differently than women in the 103rd/104th Congresses about foreign policy issues—they were also speaking collectively, as women. First, the narratives they used were increasingly consistent with one another and with the positions of the Republican Party more broadly. Second, several of the national security speeches were part of the 2015 RWPC special order, in which seven[66] Republican congresswomen joined Renee Ellmers to make a collective argument about why conservative stances on national security are important to women. In Chapter 4, I elaborate on the significance of the RWPC and its role in building and advancing a unified, gendered voice among Republican congresswomen. Overall, this analysis of foreign policy speeches supports the notion that the woman-invoked rhetoric used by Republican congresswomen is increasingly partisan.

Conclusion

In this chapter I examined changes in the gendered claims made by House Republican congresswomen over the course of two decades. My quantitative data show there has been little change over time in both the frequency with which Republican congresswomen invoke women in their floor speeches and the issues discussed in those speeches. Nevertheless, a qualitative analysis of speeches and interviews with members reveals the emergence of what I call partisan woman-invoked rhetoric among Republican congresswomen.

Specifically, I show that the rhetoric used by Republican congresswomen is increasingly aligned with their party's policy platform and gendered messaging tactics.

I find, for instance, a growing use of special order speeches as well as a tendency to use one-minute speeches to symbolically commemorate women, which is consistent with the national party's strategic recommendations for reaching out to women voters. Moreover, I show that the rhetoric used by Republican congresswomen in abortion, health, and foreign policy debates has become more consistent with the policy platform and messaging strategies of the GOP. Finally, as the Republican women elected to Congress have become more ideologically homogenous, they are also more unified in the messages they put forth.

This is not to say, of course, that individual women in the 1990s did not engage in partisan rhetoric. Certainly, as members of a political party, both Republican and Democratic women have incentives to engage in rhetoric that is consistent with both their own ideology and their party's brand. However, my analysis highlights significant changes over time. Womanhood is now more explicitly and frequently invoked in Republican women's speeches as a way to advocate for conservative policy stances and undermine gendered Democratic attacks on the GOP. In the following chapter, I continue my analysis of partisan woman-invoked rhetoric and demonstrate how the claims made by Republican congresswomen align more closely with the cultural norms of the Republican Party.

3

Culturally Speaking

Motherhood Rhetoric and Identity Claims

American political parties, like most institutions, have their own internal cultural norms. Contrary to the notion that the Republican and Democratic parties are mirror images of one another, literature on party culture has shown that they are in fact two different entities with distinct rules and dynamics (Freeman 1986; 1987; Grossmann and Hopkins 2015; 2016). Cultural differences between the parties stem from differences in their electoral base: whereas Republicans garner most of their support from "social majorities or pluralities such as white voters, Protestants, suburbanites, and (heterosexual) married voters," the Democratic Party comprises a coalition of "racial, religious, economic, and sexual minorities" (Grossmann and Hopkins 2015, 125–126).

The demographics of these coalitions shape current party culture, but they are also the result decades of political activism and decisions made by party elites. The racial realignment of the political parties started in the late 1930s and 1940s, with activists and voters beginning to merge economic liberalism and support for civil rights with the Democratic Party (Schickler 2016). As Eric Schickler (2016) argues, "The pressure built over time became difficult to suppress as grassroots civil rights activists forced the issue to the top of the nation's political agenda" (174). National party elites eventually responded with new electoral strategies. Beginning with the candidacy of Barry Goldwater in 1964, the Republican Party focused specifically on courting white southern voters.

But as Angie Maxwell and Todd Shields (2019) demonstrate in *The Long Southern Strategy*, it was the combination of a rejection of civil rights *and* an embrace of the antifeminist and Christian Right movements that eventually allowed Republicans to gain control of the South. Indeed, white women—as activists and voters—were fundamental to the transformation of the culture of the Republican Party (Maxwell and Shields 2019; McRae 2018; Nickerson 2012). Since the 1980s, the GOP has consistently

Gendering the GOP. Catherine N. Wineinger, Oxford University Press. © Oxford University Press 2022. DOI: 10.1093/oso/9780197556542.003.0003

adopted antifeminist policies and emphasized "family values" in its national platform (Alphonso 2018; Elder and Greene 2012; Wolbrecht 2000). Increasingly, social identities like race, ethnicity, and religion have become associated with partisan affiliation—with white, Christian voters feeling particularly attached to the Republican Party (Mason 2018; Mason and Wronski 2018).

As a result of these coalitional shifts, differences exist in the value the parties place on social identities and the way they approach group interests. Grossmann and Hopkins (2015; 2016) argue that the Democratic Party's coalition of social groups gives party elites incentives to appeal to group interests through the promotion of specific policies. Republicans, on the other hand, have a more hierarchical structure and emphasize ideological purity. The party's embrace of the conservative movement means GOP elites tend to focus more on broad, ideological principles—like personal responsibility, limited government, and moral traditionalism—while rejecting the premise that members of different social groups have specific policy interests (Freeman 1986; Grossmann and Hopkins 2015; 2016).

Certainly, these concepts are not always clear-cut. For instance, as previously discussed, "identity politics" is evident in the Republican Party's appeals to a white, Christian base (Jardina 2019; Mason and Wronski 2018). Beyond white identity politics, tension also exists in the way the GOP approaches the interests of marginalized groups. For instance, as Freeman (1986) notes, while the Republican Party "officially ignores group characteristics, . . . it is obvious that it does pay attention to them when it feels the need to cater to the interest of the voting public in a particular group" (336). Scholars have shown, for example, that the GOP will showcase women and racial minorities as speakers at their national convention to present the image of appealing to certain groups of voters (Fauntroy 2007; Fraga and Leal 2004; Freeman 1986; 1993; Och 2018; Philpot 2007; Sanbonmatsu 2004). In Congress, too, Republican women have been tapped by party leadership to speak on topics believed to attract women voters.

From a messaging standpoint, this tension between the Republican Party's explicit rejection of identity politics and its desire to mobilize women voters presents a challenge for Republican congresswomen. On the one hand, their gender identity is at times viewed as an asset to the party, with the potential to undercut gendered Democratic attacks and help close the gender gap. On the other hand, emphasizing gender identity can be a turn-off to a conservative base that denounces identity politics and values ideological purity (see Crowder-Meyer and Cooperman 2018).

One way Republican women have addressed this tension is by embracing traditional gender roles and conservative conceptualizations of femininity by focusing on their experiences as mothers (see Wineinger 2021). Perhaps the most well-known example of this is Sarah Palin's use of motherhood rhetoric. Palin, 2008 Republican vice presidential nominee and the face of the Tea Party movement, frequently referred to herself as a tough "hockey mom" and a "mama grizzly" who would fiercely defend her cubs. In doing so, Palin spoke to voters in a way that centered her own, individual experiences as a mother and presented those mothering experiences as vital to the realm of conservative politics and policymaking. This is also consistent with findings that show conservative Republican women in Congress generally approach women's issues from the standpoint of traditional gender roles and religious values (Swers and Larson 2005). While not necessarily a conscious political decision, the use of individualized narratives and motherhood rhetoric allows Republican women to work within the confines of their party's culture—one that simultaneously rejects group identity politics and embraces white, Christian constructions of womanhood.

In Chapter 2, I uncovered the growing use of partisan woman-invoked rhetoric among Republican women in Congress. Compared to the 1990s, the gendered rhetoric deployed in Republican congresswomen's floor speeches has become more explicitly aligned with the policy platform and messaging strategies of the Republican Party. I further illustrated how ideological cohesion among Republican women and increasing party competition between Democrats and Republicans has fueled this change in rhetoric.

This chapter continues my analysis of partisan woman-invoked rhetoric, showing how Republican congresswomen's rhetoric has evolved to conform to their party culture. By exploring the types of claims made in woman-invoked speeches—that is, *how* women are invoked—I find that Republican women are more likely than in the 1990s to speak about themselves as women and mothers. Given the GOP's emphasis on traditional gender roles (Barnes and Cassese 2017; Elder 2020), family values (Alphonso 2018; Cooper 2017), and individualism (Freeman 1986; Grossmann and Hopkins 2015; 2016), this shift in rhetoric places Republican women in line with the cultural values of their party.

The Politics of Conservative Motherhood

In her now infamous speech at the 2008 Republican National Convention, Alaska Governor Sarah Palin accepted the vice-presidential nomination, saying, "I was just your average hockey mom and signed up for the PTA."[1] On the convention floor, women cheered, waving paper signs with "Hockey Moms 4 Palin" written in red and blue paint. Palin pointed to the signs and continued, "I love those hockey moms. You know, they say the difference between a hockey mom and a pit bull? Lipstick."[2] The crowd erupted in laughter and applause.

Sarah Palin was new to the national stage when John McCain selected her as his running mate. But by the time they lost the general election in November, Palin had become a force in American politics. The Tea Party movement—a conservative backlash to the election of President Barack Obama—embraced Palin as she helped mobilize the activists and candidates who would bring a Tea Party wave to Congress in the 2010 midterms.

Central to Palin's politics has always been her identity as a mother. Speaking in 2010 to members of the Susan B. Anthony List, an anti-abortion women's organization, Palin compared conservative mothers to "the mama grizzly bears that rise up on their hind legs when somebody's coming to attack their cubs."[3] "You thought pit bulls were tough?" she said, "You don't want to mess with the mama grizzlies."[4] As Ronnee Schreiber (2016) has observed, Palin's presentation of motherhood has resonated with conservative women activists, who must grapple with their ideological belief in traditional gender roles while simultaneously being politically engaged in the public sphere. Tea Party women activists, many of them stay-at-home-moms who felt called to political action for the first time in their lives, also frequently deployed "mama grizzly" language in their calls for limited government and conservative economic policies (Beail and Longworth 2013; Deckman 2016).

Yet while Palin's "mama grizzly" rhetoric gained notable media attention, her emphasis on motherhood is not a new phenomenon in politics. In fact, motherhood has been a tool for women in movement politics on both the left and the right. Feminist women, while critical of an essentialist definition of motherhood, have nevertheless utilized common mothering experiences to engage in political action (Fabj 1993; Stearney 1994). On the Right, women have often been driven explicitly by their desire to preserve traditional heterosexual gender roles and white constructions of "family values" (McRae 2018; Nickerson 2012; Rymph 2006).

Political engagement by white conservative mothers has shaped the history of conservative politics. Michelle Nickerson (2012), for instance, details the politics of what she calls "housewife populism"—a post-war conservatism that "valorized mothers and wives for virtues imparted by their political marginality, especially selflessness, anonymity, and militancy on behalf of their families" (30). These antecedents of prominent conservative mothers like Phyllis Schlafly, Sarah Palin, and Michele Bachmann laid the groundwork for the current policies and rhetoric emphasized by conservative activists and party elites alike. Indeed, both social and economic conservatives in Republican Party politics have supported policies that underscore "family values" and promote women as caregivers in the home (Barnes and Cassese 2018; Cooper 2017; Schreiber 2012).

As the Republican Party develops strategies to reach out to women voters, it is important to consider the role that Republican congresswomen play in constructing and delivering a pro-woman message. Thus far, I have demonstrated that Republican women in Congress have increasingly engaged in rhetoric that aligns with the gendered messaging goals and policy priorities of the party. Given the historical importance of motherhood in conservative politics and the growing number of conservative women elected to Congress, I argue that understanding changes in motherhood rhetoric provides further insight into the effects of ideological polarization and the role that women play in the Republican Party.

Data and Methods

Continuing my analysis from Chapter 2, I use congressional floor speech data and elite interviews to explore the growing use of partisan woman-invoked rhetoric among Republican congresswomen. Using my original dataset of Republican congresswomen's House floor speeches, I analyze changes in woman-invoked rhetoric from the 103rd/104th Congresses (1993–1997) to the 113th/114th Congresses (2013–2017). Again, woman-invoked rhetoric (Shogan 2001) was only coded as such when a congresswoman (1) claimed to represent women or girls in some way or (2) invoked her own identity as a woman to make a statement about the issue at hand. The dataset comprises a total 694 woman-invoked speeches. In this Chapter, I focus specifically on shifts in the way Republican women (1) engage in motherhood rhetoric and (2) invoke their own gender identity or experiences in their speeches.

First, I read and coded each woman-invoked speech for the use of motherhood rhetoric. Motherhood rhetoric was considered to be used if the member claimed to represent mothers or identified as a mother in her speech. Of the 694 woman-invoked speeches, 244 (35percent) were coded as motherhood speeches. Additionally, I coded each motherhood speech as containing a *representative* claim (speaking on behalf of mothers), an *identity* claim (speaking as a mother), or both.

Next, given of the rise of the Tea Party in 2010 (Blum 2020; Skocpol and Williamson 2012; Deckman 2016), I coded for the use of "mama grizzly" rhetoric to examine the relationship between ideology and motherhood rhetoric. Melissa Deckman (2016) outlines four main rhetorical frames used by "mama grizzlies" in the Tea Party era: (1) *generational theft*: mothers feel an obligation to protect their children from the burden of national debt; (2) *limited government as family protection*: mothers emphasize the detrimental effects they believe big government has had on their families; (3) *kitchen table conservatives*: women claim that, as mothers who are often in charge of their family budgets, they can best discuss the need for fiscal discipline in Washington; (4) *right to bear arms*: women make claims about the use of guns as family protection. Based on these descriptions, I read each motherhood speech to determine which, if any, "mama grizzly" frames were deployed. Across all four Congresses, a total of 139 speeches contained mama grizzly rhetoric.

Finally, to get a better sense of whether and how Republican congresswomen speak in ways that align with the GOP's rejection of group identity politics, I analyzed the changes in the types of claims made in woman-invoked speeches. To do so, I read and coded each woman-invoked speech once again as containing *representative* claims (claiming to represent women), *identity* claims (speaking as a woman), or both. In total, 433 (62.4 percent) of all woman-invoked speeches contained only representative claims, 142 (20.5 percent) contained only identity claims, and 119 (17.1 percent) contained both.

As in Chapter 2, this analysis is paired with in-depth, qualitative readings of speeches and interview transcripts to help uncover more subtle changes in the way Republican congresswomen engage in woman-invoked rhetoric.[5] For this chapter, I used interviews with Democratic and Republican congresswomen to explore the relationship between their experiences as mothers and their role as lawmakers. Interviews with Republican congresswomen, in particular, provided insight into the way they grapple with the tension between rejecting identity politics and valuing the legislative contributions women make in Congress.

The Significance of Motherhood on Both Sides of the Aisle

Just as motherhood has played a significant role for women in both feminist and conservative movements, it has also been an important political identity for Democratic and Republican women in Congress. Indeed, interviews with women members suggest that simply counting the number of motherhood speeches cannot tell us whether and how Republican congresswomen's woman-invoked rhetoric aligns with party culture. In both congressional eras, women across the ideological spectrum pointed to their experiences as mothers to demonstrate their belief that women bring necessary perspectives to the legislative process, have more collaborative leadership styles than their male counterparts, and are better able to accomplish their legislative goals. Next I offer evidence from interviews that shows how motherhood can function as a legislative asset for women members. This insight is important for understanding that, while motherhood can operate as a partisan mechanism for women's representation, it can also create bipartisan bonds between women members. How Republican women's rhetoric has evolved to nurture these two functions is explored throughout this chapter.

A Mother's Perspective

First, women on both sides of the aisle have said in interviews that their distinct experiences as mothers give them unique insights into which types of policies should be introduced and prioritized. During the 103rd Congress, Eva Clayton (D-NC) pointed to dealing with the challenges of child care as a shared experience among mothers: "Being married and with a family, childcare usually falls [more] to the responsibility of the mother than . . . [to] the father, and I think all of them [mothers] . . . know the hassle and the frustration and the anxiety they go through of trying to find a secure place for their children . . . I think all mothers, rich or poor, identify."[6] Lois Frankel (D-FL) in the 114th Congress agreed that motherhood is a distinctly gendered perspective and that this perspective is important to bring to the policymaking table: "We bring perspectives that men don't have . . . Just being a mother is a different perspective, and it's a different perspective than being a father."[7]

Republican women have made similar claims about the distinct perspective that women bring as a result of their experiences as mothers. For example, Jennifer Dunn (R-WA) said during the 104th Congress that being a single mother has given her expertise from which even men in her own party could learn. She contended, "I've been a single mother for 20 years, since my kids were six and eight. So there are issues I understand and can interpret for my male colleagues. I have become a resource that they turn to on certain votes to say, 'Is this really something we want to do or something we don't want to do?'"[8] To Kay Granger (R-TX) in the 114th Congress, being a single mother has also given her an important perspective on economic policies: "When you're talking about financial issues, we're breadwinners, we take care of our parents, we work and make decisions in business. And so to be known that way, to really stand out there, I think it's just extremely important."[9] And Vicky Hartzler (R-MO), also in the 114th Congress, argued that being a mother and experiencing pregnancy makes it especially necessary for women to not only work on certain issues, but speak out on those issues. Adamantly anti-abortion, Hartzler said in her 2016 interview that "women, by nature, many of them are mothers and have dealt with pregnancy, so that's why . . . it's a natural fit for women to share their perspective on [pro-life issues]."[10]

For many women members, the perspective they bring as mothers is viewed as an asset in the realm of policymaking. Indeed, motherhood has given congresswomen a specific gender lens through which to understand and analyze legislation. It is perhaps why, as Lisa Bryant and Julia Hellwege (2019) have found, working mothers in Congress have formed their own "Moms in the House" caucus and are more likely to introduce legislation pertaining to women and children. And while mothering perspectives undoubtedly vary and can be used in explicitly partisan ways, it is also true that women on both sides of the aisle see these perspectives as unique to women.

A Common Bond

Beyond legislation, women members have also noted that motherhood is a common bond that many women in Congress share, making it easier to both get along with each other on a personal level and work across party lines on a professional level. Cheri Bustos (D-IL), in the 114th Congress, said, "I've got a group of six members. We were all elected at the same time, we are all moms, and we get together at least once every couple weeks for dinner where we talk about everything from our husbands to our kids to our grandkids to legislation."[11] As representatives like Grace Meng (D-NY) and Cathy McMorris Rodgers (R-WA) have noted, the shared experience of motherhood gives women a desire to provide one another with moral support—both within and across parties. Meng notes the mentorship she has received from a fellow Democrat, Diana DeGette (D-CO), saying, "She started in Congress as a mom with two young children, so she always gives me advice."[12] And McMorris Rodgers, then-chair of the House Republican Conference, told us about the support she received from her Democratic colleagues: "I was single when I was elected to Congress and then I got married and then I had the kids, so I was the fifth woman to ever give birth. And Debbie Wasserman Schultz and Carolyn Maloney hosted a baby shower for me."[13]

In addition to emotional support, motherhood has also been a common bond that has motivated Democratic and Republican women to work together on various policies. For example, while not exclusive to mothers in Congress, several women members from both sides of the aisle have taken an annual Mother's Day trip to Afghanistan. "Through that," McMorris Rodgers stated, "I've worked with Donna Edwards [Democrat of Maryland] on an Afghan women's task force in focusing on the importance of mentorship and supporting women in Afghanistan."[14] Human trafficking is another issue that has garnered bipartisan support in the 114th Congress, especially from women who have argued that this issue is particularly important to them as mothers. When asked in an interview about her work on human trafficking legislation, Krisi Noem (R-SD) said, "Well, I'm a mom . . . No mom can comprehend that happening to their child. And there's a lot of these kids that don't have anybody fighting for them."[15] While legislators work across the aisle for a variety of reasons, it is clear that motherhood is one place women members can find common ground in Congress.

Working Like a Mother

Finally, both Democratic and Republican women members have claimed that women are more likely than men to focus on solving problems and getting things done in Congress. Some attribute this gender difference to the fact that this is also how women operate as mothers. When asked if she thought women made a difference in the 114th Congress, Alma Adams (D-NC) responded:

> I think we bring a perspective that the guys just don't bring. Many of us are mothers and grandmothers and so we reason all the time with our children and our grandchildren and that kind of thing. Men just kind of let you go on. I see it with my grandchildren, even now. They would rather go to get it from Dad because he's not going to deal so much with the reasoning. I watch my daughter, and they would rather go to their Daddy because Mom is going to scrutinize it and look very closely.[16]

Marsha Blackburn (R-TN) argued that the Republican women in the 114th Congress were "the leaders of the Get-'er-Done Caucus."[17] She went on,

> I have always been a coalition builder. I seek to include people . . . That is much more a female type leadership. I've got this little term I've always used [that] goes back to when my children were little. They would say, "Why did you tell me to do this?" And I would say, "Because I'm the mommy, that's why." And then, I started telling [my colleagues] I was the chief-momma-in-charge. And I felt like, you know, maybe we're at a time where the institution kind of needs that: the chief-momma-in-charge type mindset.[18]

These interviews suggest that motherhood shapes how congresswomen on both sides of the aisle view their roles as legislators. Many members attribute their ability to get along, work together, and accomplish policy goals to their experiences as mothers. For both Democrats and Republicans, motherhood plays a role in helping women navigate institutional norms and make a difference within Congress.

Still, I maintain that examining how Republican women deploy motherhood rhetoric in their floor speeches can deepen our understanding not only of congresswomen's experiences as mothers, but also the evolving relationship between motherhood and partisan politics. Motherhood has the potential to simultaneously operate as a bipartisan bond between Democrats and Republicans and as a partisan tool for Republican women. Focusing on shifts in motherhood rhetoric can provide insights into the role of women in Republican Party politics. In particular, I analyze how Republican congresswomen may perpetuate specific constructions of motherhood in ways that allow them to conform to GOP culture and gain legitimacy within their party.

Republican Motherhood Rhetoric on the Floor:
Changes over Time

Among Republican congresswomen, I find that a significant percentage of woman-invoked speeches contained motherhood claims. In both congressional eras, statements in which congresswomen either claimed to represent mothers or referenced their personal identity as a mother comprised over 30 percent of all woman-invoked speeches. Overall, that proportion did increase in the last two decades from 31 percent in the 103rd/104th Congresses to 39.9 percent in the 113th/114th Congresses.

A closer look at motherhood rhetoric in each of these four Congresses reveals two important details. First, unlike woman-invoked rhetoric more generally, which was more commonly used by moderate Republican women in the 1990s (see Figure 2.2 in Chapter 2), *motherhood* rhetoric in the 1990s was deployed by women across the political spectrum—including the more conservative women. Figure 3.1 shows the correlation between congresswomen's ideology and number of motherhood speeches. I find there is no statistical or substantive correlation in any of the four Congresses,

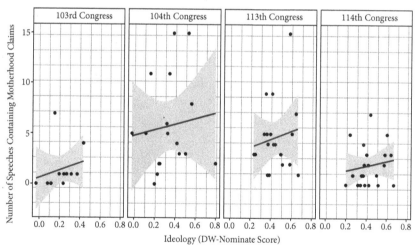

Pearson's correlation for each Congress:
103rd = 0.230, p = 0.47; 104th = 0.114, p = 0.66; 113th = 0.137, p = 0.58; 114th = 0.149, p = 0.51.

Figure 3.1 Relationship between Republican Congresswomen's Ideology and Total Number of Motherhood Speeches in Each Congress

Data source: Lewis, Jeffrey B., Keith Poole, Howard Rosenthal, Adam Boche, Aaron Rudkin, and Luke Sonnet (2018). *Voteview: Congressional Roll-Call Votes Database.*

suggesting that motherhood speeches were not given disproportionately by moderate women during the 103rd and 104th Congresses. Thus, engaging in motherhood rhetoric may be one gendered avenue that ideologically conservative women are more comfortable taking.

Second, the frequency of motherhood rhetoric has not been consistent across all four Congresses. In particular, motherhood speeches comprised only 11.9 percent of the total woman-invoked speeches given by Republican women in the 103rd Congress. That number nearly quadrupled to 41.9 percent in the 104th Congress (see Figure 3.2). In the following section, I take a closer look at these speeches to help explain the significant rise in motherhood claims between the 103rd and 104th Congresses—and what that can tell us about the role of gender in Republican Party politics at the time.

Representing "Welfare Mothers" in the 1990s

To understand the sharp increase in motherhood rhetoric from the 103rd to the 104th Congress, I first examined the issues that were discussed in these speeches. In both the 103rd and 104th Congresses, welfare was the most frequently discussed issue in motherhood speeches, making up 25 percent and 36.7 percent of all motherhood speeches, respectively. Welfare was not a prevalent topic in the 113th or 114th Congresses. Given that welfare

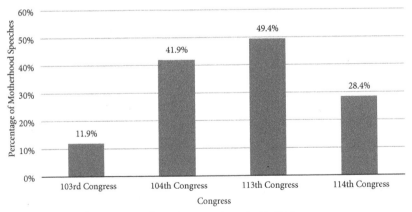

N = 16 of 134 in 103rd; 98 of 234 in 104th; 88 of 178 in 113th; 42 of 148 in 114th

Figure 3.2 Percentage of Woman-Invoked Speeches Containing Motherhood Claims

reform was at the top of the legislative agenda as the Republican majority took control in the 104th Congress, it makes sense that motherhood rhetoric increased with the rise of welfare speeches more generally.

This finding is supported by previous research on the gendered aspects of the welfare reform debates of the 1990s. First, as detailed in Chapter 2, while moderate Republican congresswomen were overwhelmingly supportive of welfare reform, they also introduced provisions that would increase federal childcare subsidies and strengthen child support laws (Casey and Carroll 2001). In advocating for welfare reform, I find that Republican congresswomen spoke most often on *behalf* of women, rather than *as* women. Of the 40 motherhood speeches related to welfare in the 103rd and 104th Congresses, 28 (70 percent) contained only representative claims.[19]

More specifically, Republican congresswomen talked about empowering women by getting them off public assistance. In one floor speech, Jennifer Dunn (R-WA) told a story of meeting with mothers in her district, saying, "The welfare mothers whom I met with last weekend in my district at a Head Start meeting told me that the welfare system, or AFDC, is a negative system that pulls people down and robs them of their self-esteem, and too often devalues them and their ability to be productive members of our community."[20] In a similar fashion, Susan Molinari (R-NY) said in a 1994 floor speech that welfare reform would "enable" mothers to "feel good" about themselves.[21] And Barbara Vucanovich, (R-NV) argued that the Personal Responsibility and Work Opportunity Reconciliation Act of 1996 takes "handouts" away from "prisoners and noncitizens who have imposed on our system" and "promotes work and helps mothers on welfare by providing job training and child care they need to achieve this goal."[22] This message of government assistance as inherently oppressive to mothers was the philosophical premise on which Republican congresswomen linked gender and welfare reform in the 1990s.

Importantly, discussions of "welfare mothers" by politicians in the 1980s and 1990s were explicitly and implicitly racialized (Abramovitz 2006; Gilens 1999; Hancock 2004; Foster 2008; Sparks 2003). Support for welfare reform was largely fueled by narratives "of the raced-gendered welfare queen who promiscuously gives birth to multiple children in order to receive more benefits and avoid working" (Reingold and Smith 2012, 135). Republican Congressman E. Clay Shaw, Jr. of Florida painted a picture of irresponsible teen mothers on welfare, saying they were "children you wouldn't leave your cat with on a weekend."[23] As described by Mary Hawkesworth (2003),

Democratic congresswomen of color worked hard to combat these narratives, as they "perceived the attack on single mothers at the heart of welfare reform proposals as an attack on the black family, an attack that resurrected pathological theories of poverty" (542).

Indeed, engaging in similarly racist language, Republican congresswomen often claimed to represent mothers by punishing negligent "deadbeat dads." Marge Roukema (R-NJ) argued in a floor speech, "Mr. Speaker, here is new evidence that we must address: The disgrace of deadbeat dads, and some moms, who can afford to, but do not pay child support is forcing mothers into endless, debasing legal battles just to get the support to which their children are legally and morally entitled."[24] Likewise, Connie Morella (R-MD) said she had been working on "critical provisions" that would "finally crack down on deadbeat parents by enacting penalties with real teeth and establishing Federal registries to help track deadbeats."[25] While purporting to support mothers on public assistance, these policies perpetuated the racial stereotype that low-income fathers—who are disproportionately people of color—are lazy and irresponsible rather than living within a racist system of poverty (Murphy 2005). In these ways, the gendered claims of Republican women were in line with the broader racial narratives of the GOP, including the dog whistle politics that has come to define the party's appeal to white voters (Lopez 2015).

In other ways, though, Republican congresswomen pushed party leaders on policy, advocating for provisions that would assist mothers on welfare with childcare costs (Casey and Carroll 2001). Tillie Fowler (R-FL) said, "There is nothing compassionate about our current welfare system. The bill we are considering today . . . provides child care for welfare mothers who want to work."[26] And Deborah Pryce (R-OH) argued, "It is clear that lack of affordable quality child care is a primary obstacle to employment for many parents, especially single mothers. If we are going to require work, and we should, our Nation's children must not be forgotten." While punitive measures were still part of their platform, Republican women's bipartisan effort to increase funding for mothers on government assistance diverged from the GOP's original welfare reform agenda.

These types of representative claims were used throughout motherhood speeches in the 1990s, although some of the more conservative Republican women elected to the 104th Congress also engaged in identity claims. These women used their own experiences as single mothers to endorse a "pull-yourself-up-by-your-bootstraps" approach to welfare reform, which once again ignored the racial realities of poverty. For example, Sue Kelly (R-NY) and Helen Chenoweth (R-ID), both elected in 1994, argued that they understood first-hand the struggles of making ends meet and the empowering feeling of bringing home a paycheck. Chenoweth said in a floor speech, "Mr. Speaker, as a woman who raised two teenage children . . . [as] a single parent, . . . my income was at the poverty level. But sometimes to get through life it takes a bit of a struggle and sometimes to realize all you can be takes a bit of a struggle."[27] And Kelly noted, "As working women and mothers, who among us does not remember earning their first paycheck, meeting that first payroll, or the pride of seeing our own child bring home their first paycheck? It is this sort of restoration of self-esteem that we must achieve."[28]

In sum, the sharp rise in motherhood speeches from the 103rd to the 104th Congress can be explained, in part, by the fact that welfare reform dominated the Republican legislative agenda in the 104th Congress. While a few newly elected women invoked their identity as mothers, the motherhood rhetoric during this time was most frequently used to represent mothers as a group. Additionally, Republican congresswomen were not putting forth a consistent party message; while some claims aligned with the raced-gendered narrative of party, others diverged from that narrative. This could be seen, in particular, through the push for more moderate child care policy proposals that were developed and endorsed by women in the bipartisan CCWI.[29]

Speaking on Behalf of Mothers: Representative Claims

Even outside of the welfare reform debate, Republican congresswomen in the 1990s often claimed to represent the interests of mothers by speaking on behalf of them as a group. This section details the evolution of *representative* motherhood claims among Republican congresswomen. Figure 3.3 shows the breakdown of motherhood speeches in each Congress by type of claim. I find a decrease in the use of representative claims over time, with only 9.5 percent of the 42 motherhood speeches in the 114th Congress containing strictly representative claims.

A qualitative analysis of these speeches also unveils other changes in the way Republican congresswomen claim to act on behalf of mothers. First, I find that representative motherhood rhetoric has become increasingly partisan. In the earlier Congresses, Republican women most often supported bipartisan provisions aimed at mothers. Examples include childcare and

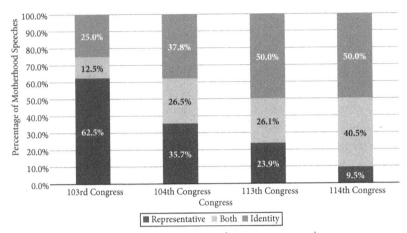

Note: 103rd Congress: N = 16; 104th Congress: N = 98; 113th Congress: N = 88; 114th Congress: N = 42

Figure 3.3 Types of Claims in Motherhood Speeches

child support, as previously discussed, but also issues like family leave and postpartum care. For example, Marge Roukema (R-NJ) advocated for family leave while condemning Republicans who opposed it: "In these harsh economic times and with health costs soaring, are you going to tell a pregnant woman or the mother of a child dying of leukemia to, 'Go find another job, if you can?' Are these family values?"[30] Connie Morella (R-MD) also supported a bipartisan provision to ensure that health insurance companies cover postpartum care. She said in a floor speech,

> As managed care becomes increasingly prevalent, we are seeing mothers and their newborns in and out of the hospital in as short a time as 12 hours. Many illnesses in newborns are not detectable until the first 48 hours. Those first 2 days are absolutely critical. Guidelines of the American Pediatric Association and ACOG specify that mothers should stay in the hospital for 48 hours for normal delivery and 96 for cesarean delivery. This provision would ensure that this happens.[31]

Motherhood speeches containing strictly representative claims in the later Congresses were fewer in number but also more partisan in content. The largest percentage of these speeches (32 percent) were related to health, probably because the Affordable Care Act was such a prominent issue at that time. As detailed in Chapter 2, speeches related to health in the 113th Congress focused largely on attacking the president's health care plan. In a floor speech, Shelley Moore Capito (R-WV) emphasized that the individual mandate in the Affordable Care Act would be especially harmful to mothers: "We need to make it easier for businesses to hire full-time employees, not harder, but the ACA's mandate and the administration's repeated delays have only created more uncertainty for businesses and moms throughout this country." Mothers were also discussed in other particularly partisan issues, like immigration. For instance, Michele Bachmann (R-MN) explicitly condemned President Obama in a special order speech, saying,

> I believe the next population most hurt is actually the legal Hispanic population in the United States. It's their wages that are suppressed. So if you're thinking of a Hispanic mother who's working as a hotel maid, if we have legalization, she could be competing with seven other people who are vying for her job as well . . . What we're looking at is hurting the job prospects of those who are the most vulnerable. And that's one thing that we've seen from the President's policies.[32]

Another notable change is that Republican women in recent Congresses are more likely to use specific constituent examples, claiming to represent the women—or, in many cases, one particular woman—in their district. For example, Susan Brooks (R-IN) criticized the president's policies, using a specific example from one of her constituents. She said, "Barbara from Indianapolis recently logged on to my Web site to share her ObamaCare story, which is about her choices. She's a single mom trying to give her daughter the gift of a college education in a tough economy. President Obama's holiday gift to her, however, was a $200 increase in her monthly premium."[33] Candice Miller (R-MI) similarly stated, "I will just give you one example—a vivid example—of many, many that we got, especially women who have contacted my office. This is from a mother named Tracy in Macomb County, Michigan." Miller went on to tell the story of a mother in her district who had seen her daughter's work hours cut due to provisions in the Affordable Care Act.

The incorporation of these types of constituent examples occurred much more frequently in the 113th and 114th Congresses. Compared to about 6 percent of the representative motherhood speeches in the 1990s, nearly one-third of these speeches in the later Congresses contained specific examples. Whatever the intentions, this shift in the way Republican congresswomen speak on behalf of mothers signals a greater alignment with Republican

Party culture. By using specific examples of mothers in their floor speeches, Republican congresswomen can claim to be reaching out to women and embracing family values while stopping short of engaging in "identity politics" as they recognize it. In claiming to be responding to specific constituents in their districts, Republican congresswomen avoid lumping all women into a category with specific group interests.

Speaking as Mothers: Identity Claims

Whereas Republican congresswomen in the 1990s were more likely to utilize representative motherhood claims, those in the later Congresses more frequently invoked their own identities as mothers. In the 113th and 114th Congresses, identity claims were used in 76.1 percent and 95.5 percent of Republican congresswomen's motherhood speeches, respectively. In what follows, I examine shifts in the use of identity claims and discuss what these claims can teach us about the evolving nature of Republican women's representation.

An in-depth look at these speeches shows that Republican congresswomen are using their motherhood experiences to take conservative stances on a broader range of policy areas. In the 103rd and 104th Congresses, Republican women invoked their identity as mothers to discuss issues directly related to parenting, like adoption or family leave. Linda Smith (R-WA) spoke in favor of the Adoption Promotion and Stability Act, which would provide tax benefits to adoptive parents: "As a mother and grandmother, I can tell you that adoption creates families where we would otherwise have children languishing in foster care and couples denied a heartfelt desire to raise a family."[34] And Tillie Fowler (R-FL) advocated for a bill that would provide compensatory time off to employees, saying in a floor speech, "As a working mother, I learned the hard way that you can't be in two places at once. Whether it is due to a Little League game; a case of chicken pox; a visit to the doctor or caring for an elderly parent—sometimes the needs of a family require a flexible working schedule."[35]

Most frequently, however, identity claims in the earlier Congresses were used by the most conservative women to talk about economic issues like taxes and the budget. Andrea Seastrand (R-CA), for example, supported a constitutional amendment requiring a supermajority vote to increase taxes, saying, "I will tell you, my 26-year-old who is just entering the job market, my daughter who is 24, are anxious, like your children and grandchildren, are anxious for us to do this tonight."[36] Another common way ideologically conservative women invoked their motherhood in the 1990s was through claims that the national debt would have a detrimental impact on their children and grandchildren. Sue Myrick (R-NC) argued in a floor speech, "As a mother of five and grandmother of six, almost seven, I have a moral obligation to balance this budget for them because I want my kids and grandkids to have a better future, to have more opportunity than I have. But, how can that happen if they start out with this great mountain of debt on their backs?"[37] Interestingly, this rhetoric is consistent with what scholars of the Tea Party have deemed "mama grizzly" rhetoric (see Deckman 2016). In the following section, I explore if and how mama grizzly rhetoric was utilized in Congress prior to and after the Tea Party movement.

In the 113th and 114th Congresses, Republican women were more likely to invoke their own motherhood in their floor speeches. Moreover, they did so on issues ranging from education and human trafficking, to gun rights and immigration, to energy and national security. In these later Congresses, a total of 16 issue areas were discussed in the motherhood speeches containing identity claims; this is compared to just eight issue areas in the earlier Congresses.[38] Virginia Foxx (R-NC), for example, argued against federal overreach in education, saying, "Mr. Speaker, my background as an educator, school board member, mother, and grandmother reinforces my belief that students are best served when people at the local level are in control of education decisions."[39] Marsha Blackburn (R-TN) used her white motherhood to engage in racial dog whistling (Lopez 2015) and advocate for the enhanced enforcement of immigration laws: "How are we going to be certain that we are safe in our homes, in our communities? How do I know that my children are going to be safe at school? . . . These are questions of concern to so many moms who, like me, worry about their children and their grandchildren."[40] And Kristi Noem (R-SD) spoke in support of gun rights, saying that firearms have always been a part of her heritage and that she hoped to have "the opportunity to enjoy it . . . with my own kids and with my husband, Brian."[41]

The growing tendency of Republican women to speak *as* mothers signals a shift to rhetoric that is more closely aligned with the cultural norms of their party. By invoking their own individual experiences and identities as mothers, GOP women are able to speak for women in a way that allows them to relate conservative issues to women voters while upholding the party's raced-gendered narratives and ideological principles of individualism, family values, and traditional gender roles.

Mama Grizzlies in the House

Sarah Palin's "mama grizzly" rhetoric certainly inspired conservative and Republican women activists across the country. Conservative mothers who had never previously been involved in politics were suddenly prominent players in the Tea Party movement that would lead to a Republican takeover of the House of Representatives in 2010. Given the significance of Palin and the Tea Party, one might assume that mama grizzly frames would be found primarily in more recent Congresses. Indeed, Melissa Deckman (2016) has argued that the mama grizzly rhetoric used by members of Congress is a result of Tea Party influence. She writes, "The emphasis on motherhood appeals, for example, when calling for Congress to cut its spending and reduce the debt . . . takes a page out of the rhetorical playbook first used by Tea Party women" (Deckman 2016, 52).

Yet despite this perception, my findings reveal that this deployment of motherhood by Republican congresswomen in fact predates the Tea Party movement. Speeches that contained "mama grizzly" rhetorical frames, as defined by Deckman, were actually *more* prevalent in the motherhood speeches of the 1990s. In the 103rd/104th Congresses, 14.9 percent of motherhood speeches contained mama grizzly rhetoric, compared to 13.8 percent in the 113th/114th Congresses. Sue Myrick (R-NC), for instance, invoked her motherhood in a 1995 floor speech while advocating for a balanced budget:

> I want my kids to have the same opportunity to succeed that I have enjoyed in this generation. We are looking today at a national debt of $4.8 trillion. What this vote on the balanced budget means is very simply that Sarah and my new grandchild, No. 7, who is going to be born in December, will not have to pay $187,000 just to cover the interest on the debt alone through their lifetimes. We cannot go on literally mortgaging our children and our grandchildren's future, and saddling them with this huge mountain of debt.[42]

That said, a qualitative reading of these speeches shows significant shifts in content over time. These changes suggest that, while these rhetorical frames are not new, the *way* they are deployed by Republican congresswomen is probably influenced by the Tea Party specifically and polarization more generally.

Figure 3.4 shows the types of mama grizzly frames deployed in each congressional era. "Generational theft," a term originally coined by Sarah Palin, is one motherhood frame used by Tea Party women activists and Republican congresswomen alike. As described by Deckman (2016), this frame is rooted in the idea that conservative mothers must "save children from the large debt burden that they face" (121). Indeed, this was the most common frame used by women in the 103rd/104th Congresses, comprising 82.3 percent of their mama grizzly speeches. Like Myrick, Andrea Seastrand (R-CA) also called for a balanced budget, saying it "would definitely mean that we would have a future free of debt. We as mothers would bequeath to our children a future of greater opportunity and a government of increased virtue and vitality."[43] And Linda Smith (R-WA), like her many of her colleagues, described federal spending as *moral* issue, saying, "As a grandmother of six young children,

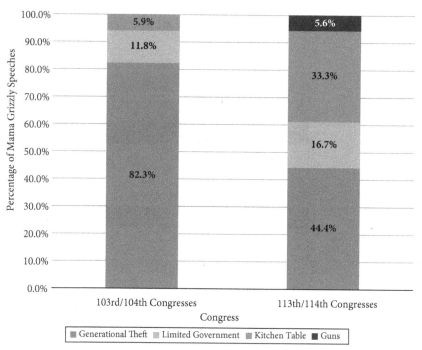

Note: N = 17 in 103rd/104th Congresses; N = 18 in 113th/114th Congresses

Figure 3.4 Types of Mama Grizzly Frames in Each Congressional Era

I only have to think of their future tax rates to realize what will happen if we do not get Federal spending under control. We have no moral right to depend on tax increases in the future to fund the Federal spending today."[44]

This rhetorical frame is consistent with the "generational theft" frame that Republican congresswomen have invoked more recently. For example, Martha Roby (R-AL), said in a 2013 floor speech, "We are spending well beyond our means—we have $17 trillion in debt and our 4th year with over $1 trillion deficit. My kids, Margaret and George, are the reason that I'm here. Why I'm fighting is for that generation that's going to carry this burden after we're all gone."[45] Marsha Blackburn (R-TN) made a similar claim about her motivation to address the national debt, saying, "Mr. Chairman, it is why it is important for us to have a budget that balances in 10 years. I have to tell you, as a mom and a grandmom, I look a lot at what is happening to our children and our grandchildren"[46] Still, while mama grizzly rhetoric framed as "generational theft" has been used long before Tea Party women stepped into the political spotlight, there are notable differences in who is using mama grizzly rhetoric and which type of mama grizzly frames are being deployed.

As illustrated in Figure 3.5, women who engage in mama grizzly rhetoric have been, on average, more conservative than all other House Republican

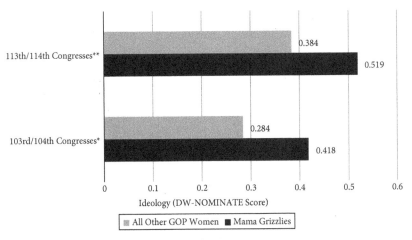

*Statistically significant at p<0.10. **Statistically significant at p<0.01.

Figure 3.5 Average Ideology of All Republican Congresswomen versus Average Ideology of Mama Grizzlies

Data Source: Lewis, Jeffrey B., Keith Poole, Howard Rosenthal, Adam Boche, Aaron Rudkin, and Luke Sonnet (2018). *Voteview: Congressional Roll-Call Votes Database*. https://voteview.com/

women. In both congressional eras, the mean DW-NOMINATE score of women who used mama grizzly rhetoric was statistically greater than the mean DW-NOMINATE score of the Republican women who did not engage in mama grizzly rhetoric. One difference is that, in the later Congresses, these speeches were given by a larger percentage of the women. In the 103rd/104th Congresses, 6 of the 19 (32 percent) Republican women used mama grizzly rhetoric compared to 12 of the 24 (50 percent) Republican women in the 113th/114th Congresses. This also suggests that as Republican congresswomen become both more conservative and more ideologically cohesive, they become more unified in their rhetoric as well.

One significant shift in rhetoric is the increasing use of the "limited government as family protection" frame, in which mothers emphasize the detrimental effects they believe big government has had on their families (Deckman 2016). While some Republican women deployed this rhetorical frame in the 103rd/104th Congresses, the overwhelming majority of mama grizzly speeches in this era were framed as "generational theft." In the 113th/114th Congress, the "limited government" frame is used in a larger percentage of speeches (see Figure 3.4). For instance, Mia Love (R-UT) condemned what she viewed as federal overreach in the education system, saying, "As a mayor and mainly as a mother—I have three children in public schools—I have found that the best solutions are found at the most local level. This amendment puts a larger footprint in the hands of the Federal Government and gives more power to the Federal Government."[47] And Virginia Foxx (R-NC) argued that "as a mother, a woman, and individual of prayer," she supported a measure that would protect her constituents "from a massive Federal overreach being perpetrated by the [Environmental Protection Agency]."[48] This critique of government regulation can also be seen in recent mama grizzly discussions of gun rights, which were nonexistent in the 103rd/104th Congresses (see Figure 3.4). For example, Vicky Hartzler (R-MO) opposed gun control legislation, citing her daughter's right to self-protection: "My daughter, we've had a lot of fun with her, teaching her how to shoot a gun and going out also in our pasture . . . But just as importantly as it being enjoyable, I think just being familiar with guns and for the potential of having self-protection is so important, as well."[49]

Another change in mama grizzly rhetoric since the 1990s is the growing use of the "kitchen table conservatives" frame, in which conservative women argue that mothers, who are often in charge of their family budgets, are best qualified to talk about the need for fiscal discipline in Washington.

Deckman (2016) turns to Jenny Beth Martin, co-founder of the Tea Party Patriots, as an example of such rhetoric: "We are the ones, oftentimes, in the houses and families, who are balancing the checkbooks and buying the groceries ... When it comes to their own personal family checkbook, women are the ones who pay such close attention to it. And we are saying we want the government to do the same thing" (118).

As shown in Figure 3.5, this frame existed in one-third of mama grizzly speeches in the 113th/114th Congresses, compared to only 5.9 percent in the 103rd/104th Congresses. Virginia Foxx (R-NC), for example, argued in a floor speech that the family budgeting she engaged in at home should also be mandatory for the federal government: "Mr. Speaker, we have all had hands-on experience balancing a budget, sitting at the kitchen table long after the kids have gone to bed shuffling through bills and pay stubs. We all know the feeling. In my family, balancing our budget isn't just a priority, it is a requirement. We must view America's budget the same way."[50] And Diane Black (R-NC) stressed in a 2015 floor speech, "Long before I served on the Budget Committee, I got a crash course on budgeting 101 as a single working mother. And in those years, I raised three children on a nurse's salary, teaching me how to live within my means and stretch my dollars."[51]

Changes in mama grizzly rhetoric demonstrate another way in which motherhood rhetoric has shifted to more closely align with Republican Party culture. By explicitly arguing that their expertise in conservative policy is rooted in their individual experiences as mothers in the private sphere, Republican congresswomen are able to speak to and as women while simultaneously upholding Republican principles of individualism and traditional gender roles.

Speaking as Republican Women: The Growing Use of Identity Claims

Thus far, the rhetorical changes highlighted in this chapter have focused specifically on motherhood rhetoric due to the historical and continued significance of motherhood in conservative politics. In this section, I examine changes in the use of identity claims more broadly, showing that women are more likely than in the 1990s to speak *as* women rather than on behalf of women. Figure 3.6 shows the types of claims used in Republican

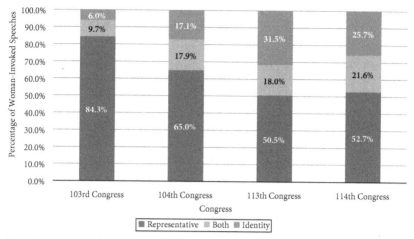

Note: N = 134 in 103rd; 234 in 104th; 178 in 113th; 148 in 114th

Figure 3.6 Types of Claims in Woman-Invoked Speeches

congresswomen's woman-invoked speeches by Congress. I find a decrease in the proportion of speeches containing only representative claims and an increase in the percentage of speeches containing only identity claims. The average percentage of woman-invoked speeches in which only identity claims are used more than doubles from 13 percent in the 103rd/104th Congresses to 29.1 percent in the 113th/114th Congress.

To better understand the relationship between ideology and the use of identity claims, I calculated each member's "Woman Identity Score" by dividing the number of speeches in which they only used identity claims by their total number of woman-invoked speeches.[52] Figure 3.7 shows the correlation between Republican congresswomen's "Woman Identity Scores" and DW-NOMINATE scores. In the 104th Congress, there is a substantively positive and statistically significant correlation between the use of identity claims and ideology, with conservative women more likely to invoke their own identity than moderate women. In the later Congresses, no such correlation exists. Thus, as Republican congresswomen have become more conservative and more ideologically cohesive over time, they have been more likely to use identity claims in their speeches. In the following section, I present results from a qualitative reading of these speeches to highlight other changes in the way Republican congresswomen invoke their womanhood.

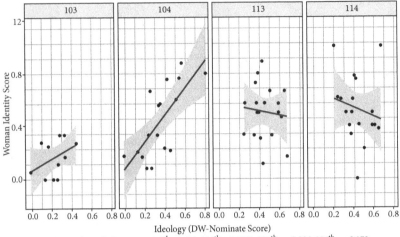

Pearson's correlation for each Congress: 103rd = 0.422; 104th = 0.718*; 113th = –0.096; 114th = –0.178
*Statistically significant at p<.01

Figure 3.7 Relationship between Republican Congresswomen's Ideology and "Woman Identity Score"

Data source: Lewis, Jeffrey B., Keith Poole, Howard Rosenthal, Adam Boche, Aaron Rudkin, and Luke Sonnet (2018). *Voteview: Congressional Roll-Call Votes Database*

The Significance of Being a Woman

The first notable change in identity claims is an increase in members claiming to be the first women to do something and recognizing the significance of that achievement. An example of this from the 103rd/104th Congresses can be seen in Helen Delich Bentley's (R-MD) speech on the death of Richard Nixon. She says, "Mr. Speaker, I was privileged to know him as his first major woman appointee."[53]

Republican women made these claims much more frequently in the 113th/114th Congresses. For instance, Michele Bachmann (R-MN) announced in 2014 that she would not seek re-election, saying, "It has been the privilege and the honor of a lifetime for me to serve as a Member of the United States Congress, serving as the first woman ever elected from the State of Minnesota in the capacity of being a Republican."[54] Kay Granger (R-TX) recalled her appointment to the Defense Appropriations Subcommittee, saying, "As one of the first women ever to serve on the subcommittee, I wasn't sure how I would be treated."[55] Ileana Ros-Lehtinen (R-FL) talked about playing in annual

Congressional Baseball Game, mentioning that she "actually became the first woman to get on base in this traditional game."[56]

Though few of these claims were substantive in terms of policy, this shift in rhetoric nevertheless signals an acknowledgement by Republican women that it is important to recognize the achievements of women, including their own. This can be attributed, perhaps, to a changing political environment in which breaking glass ceilings has become something to celebrate publicly—especially for a Republican Party that is working to reach out to female voters and demonstrate its commitment to women's leadership. The prominence of Democratic women "firsts" such as presidential candidate Hillary Clinton and Speaker Nancy Pelosi also provide partisan incentives for Republican women to highlight themselves as trailblazers.

From Congresswomen to Republican Women

Another rhetorical change is the shift from invoking a bipartisan gender identity to invoking an explicitly partisan one. Olympia Snowe (R-ME) chaired the bipartisan Congressional Caucus for Women's Issues (CCWI) in the 103rd Congress. In a 1994 floor speech, she emphasized that role, saying, "The Congressional Caucus for Women's Issues, which I cochair with my colleague, [Democratic] Representative Pat Schroeder, has aggressively pursued the issue of applying Federal laws to Congress."[57] Connie Morella (R-MD), chair of the CCWI in the 104th Congress, discussed the importance of child support enforcement laws, stressing the bipartisan work she was doing through the CCWI: "Mr. Chairman, as co-chair of the Congressional Caucus for Women's Issues, I have been working with my colleagues—particularly Representatives Johnson [R-CT], Roukema [R-NJ], Kennelly [D-CT], Norton [D-DC], and others—to fashion comprehensive legislation to strengthen our Nation's flimsy child support enforcement laws."[58]

In the 113th and 114th Congresses, the CCWI was chaired by Jaime Herrera Beutler (R-WA) and Kristi Noem (R-SD), respectively. Neither of them mentioned this role in any of their speeches on the House floor. Meanwhile, several Republican congresswomen did emphasize their identities as Republican women and, more specifically, their membership in the newly founded Republican Women's Policy Committee (RWPC). Virginia

Foxx (R-NC), for example, spoke as a member of the RWPC, criticizing President Obama and Democratic Senate leadership:

> Mr. Speaker, on Saturday, members of the Republican Women's Policy Committee sent an earnest letter to Senator Harry Reid, asking him to please put aside the partisanship for a second and to take the opportunity to enact commonsense legislation to help our kids; take up bipartisan House legislation to restore WIC; to open NIH; and to fund Head Start. Senator Reid has done nothing, though, and President Obama said that it's their way or the highway, to give them everything they want or get lost.[59]

During a special order scheduled by the RWPC, Diane Black (R-TN) said it was "an honor to be here and to be a part of today's Republican Women's Policy Committee on this Special Order on national security,"[60] and Martha McSally (R-AZ) appreciated the opportunity for "women in our Conference" to "speak about something that is vitally important to our communities."[61]

As they increasingly invoke a partisan-gender identity in their speeches, Republican congresswomen both distinguish themselves from Democratic women and defend themselves against the gender stereotype that Republican women are more liberal than Republican men. In doing so, they credential themselves as true conservatives while emphasizing that women are not a monolith, thus working to avoid the perception of engaging in group identity politics. Rhetorically pairing their gender identity with their partisan affiliation also allows Republican women to engage their womanhood without challenging GOP cultural norms that place party and ideology ahead of social identities like gender. In Chapter 4, I look more closely at the CCWI and the RWPC to better understand this evolution from "congresswomen" to "party women."

Relational Military Expertise

A final change to note is the use of a rhetorical frame in the 113th/114th Congresses that was not present in the 103rd/104th Congresses: what I call *relational military expertise*. In these speeches, Republican congresswomen used their personal relationship to a veteran or service member to demonstrate their expertise on issues pertaining to the military or foreign policy. An example of this can be seen in Michele Bachmann's (R-MN) praise of veterans. She said in a 2014 floor speech, "I am the daughter of a veteran, stepdaughter of a veteran, sister of a veteran, and I am so grateful because I recognize we would not be here today if it wasn't for our veterans, and I thank you for your service to our country because you answered the call."[62] Mimi Walters (R-CA) delivered a similar speech for Memorial Day, saying, "Mr. Speaker, as we approach Memorial Day, I wish to recognize our service members who have so bravely answered the call to defend our great Nation. As the daughter of a U.S. Marine, I am eternally grateful for the service and sacrifice our troops make, all in the name of freedom."[63]

Republican congresswomen used these types of identity claims to make more substantive arguments about legislation as well. For example, Diane Black (R-TN) said in a 2015 speech, "Madam Speaker, I rise today in strong support of the Hire More Heroes Act. In my home State of Tennessee, we have over 525,000 veterans who have served our country in both war and peace—veterans, people like my son, Steve, and my husband, Dave."[64] And Ileana Ros-Lehtinen (R-FL) argued in favor of the Vietnam Human Rights Act of 2013, saying,

My husband Dexter is a Vietnam combat veteran and former Army Ranger who was wounded defending the ideals of freedom and democracy—not just for Americans, but for all those who seek them. As the leading nation of the free world, the United States must stand with the Vietnamese people who are being brutally oppressed by their authoritarian government so that they may all live in a free and democratic country.[65]

Interviews with Republican congresswomen provide further insight into the connection between this type of relational rhetoric and Republican Party culture. Attempts to grapple with the tension between a belief in the importance of women's leadership and an ideological rejection of group identity politics point specifically to the significance of relational identities. For example, when asked which groups outside of her district she felt a commitment to represent, Kristi Noem (R-SD) said, "*I'm a mom* and the majority of voters in the county are women, so I think that I can always bring that perspective to the table [emphasis added]."[66] She immediately followed this up with, "It's not necessarily that I feel an obligation to always speak on behalf of other groups, but I do know that, that perspective needs to be interjected into every conversation."[67] Martha Roby (R-AL) told me, "I often get asked about being a woman in Congress, but it wasn't a factor in my decision [to run for office]."[68] Yet she also emphasized that "for [women] to have a seat at the table and be able to share an experience *as wives and mothers* is important [emphasis added]."[69]

Indeed, while Republican congresswomen are at times uncomfortable speaking on behalf of women or engaging in what they view as identity politics, they also acknowledge the importance of their gendered experiences as wives and mothers. Similarly, through the deployment of a *relational military expertise* frame, Republican congresswomen appear to be addressing ideological tensions within their party's culture. They are again using their roles in the private sphere—as wives and mothers—to credential themselves as experts on Republican-owned issues. In doing so, they relate conservative, "masculine" policies to women while conforming to the cultural norms of their party.

Conclusion

In Chapter 2, I showed that an increase in party competition and ideological cohesion among Republican women has led to an increase in woman-invoked rhetoric that more closely aligns with the policy positions and messaging strategies of the Republican Party. The gendered claims made by Republican women in recent Congresses contribute to what the RNC's *Growth and Opportunity Project* called, "a message demonstrating that [Republican] policies, principles, and vision address the concerns of female voters."[70] In this chapter, I find that the way Republican congresswomen invoked these claims also more closely aligns them with the culture of their party—including engaging in raced-gendered appeals to white women.

First, through an extensive analysis of motherhood rhetoric, I find that Republican congresswomen in recent years are more partisan in the way they represent mothers. Increasingly, Republican congresswomen directly criticize Democratic policies while claiming to act on behalf of mothers, thus touting conservative principles of "family values." Second, GOP congresswomen are speaking about women in ways that conform to their party's ideological rejection of "identity politics" and emphasis on individualism; this is seen both in the evolving use of *identity claims* and the shift to claiming to act on behalf of specific, individual constituents rather than women as a whole. Finally, my analysis of both mama grizzly rhetoric and identity claims more generally shows that, while "mama grizzlies" existed in both congressional eras, Republican congresswomen are increasingly using their experiences as wives and mothers to credential themselves when speaking on a wide range of Republican-owned issues like national security and economics. By highlighting the way their experiences in the private sphere are transferrable to the realm of policymaking, Republican congresswomen can speak for women in ways that adhere to the cultural norms of their party.

One apparent limitation of this book is that I do not compare the rhetoric of Republican congresswomen to that of Democratic congresswomen. After all, it may indeed be the case that Democratic women are also invoking women in their speeches in similar ways. Nevertheless, I assert that the partisan context of these claims matters. For Republican women, these changes in motherhood rhetoric and the increasing use of gendered identity claims give them the ability to speak for women within the confines of their specific party culture.

This shift to engaging in what I call partisan woman-invoked rhetoric may provide additional opportunities for women within Republican Party politics. In the following chapters, I analyze shifts in the way Republican congresswomen act collectively as women and how female Conference leaders are able to leverage these changes in rhetoric and collective action. By focusing on intraparty politics, I am able to delve deeper into the nuances of Republican women's congressional representation.

4

Institutionalizing a Partisan-Gender Identity

At an awards dinner hosted by the Independent Women's Forum in October 2012, Representative Mary Bono (R-CA) said, "You would think that I would argue with you about the conservative movement being clueless with talking to women, but I cannot argue with you because I agree with you."[1] Amidst claims of a Republican "war on women," Bono and her Republican women colleagues argued that their party needed to be more effective in the way it speaks to women across the country. Five months earlier, Bono founded the Republican Women's Policy Committee (RWPC)—a caucus comprised of all 24 Republican women in the House—to elevate women's voices within the GOP. It was the first time in congressional history that Republican women organized formally as a group.

In Chapters 2 and 3, I found a growing presence of partisan woman-invoked rhetoric among Republican women in the House of Representatives. That is, Republican congresswomen speak for women in an increasingly partisan manner, invoking gendered claims that align with GOP policy positions, messaging strategies, and culture. In this chapter, I delve deeper into the internal gender dynamics of the party by focusing on Republican women's desire and ability to organize as women. More specifically, I ask: (1) How do Republican congresswomen navigate tensions between their partisan and gender identities, and how has this changed over time? (2) How have congressional polarization and party competition affected the way Republican women organize collectively as women? To answer these questions, I trace the politics of congressional women's caucuses from the creation of the bipartisan Congressional Caucus for Women's Issues (CCWI) to the creation (and eventual disbanding) of the partisan RWPC.

The first half of this chapter explores Republican women's relationship to the CCWI. Focusing on caucus membership and participation, I show how various political and institutional changes have contributed to the recognition of a *partisan-gender identity* among Republican women. That is,

Gendering the GOP. Catherine N. Wineinger, Oxford University Press. © Oxford University Press 2022.
DOI: 10.1093/oso/9780197556542.003.0004

Republican congresswomen began to work explicitly at the intersection of their partisan and gender identities, distinguishing themselves from Democratic women and Republican men.[2]

The second half of the chapter examines the creation and accomplishments of the RWPC. Through this analysis of Republican women's collective action in the House, I show how congressional polarization has contributed to the *institutionalization* of a partisan-gender identity, in which Republican women formally advocate on behalf of their gender and party simultaneously. I further demonstrate that the use of partisan woman-invoked rhetoric is not simply a top-down strategy; rather, it is the result of a combination of Republican women's collective action and leadership's embrace of women as party messengers.

Women's Collective Action in Congress

In analyzing the institutionalization of a partisan-gender identity through the RWPC, I turn to Anna Mahoney's (2018) definition of an institutionalized group. Mahoney writes that institutionalization requires "a structure that enables the group to function and be recognized by other nonmembers as a group" (9). Within legislatures, members often choose to form institutionalized groups—also known as caucuses—in order to bring attention to their legislative interests. Formal caucuses in Congress, called Congressional Member Organizations (CMOs), must have an internal leadership structure and be registered with the House Committee on Administration.

In Congress and state legislatures, women have created bipartisan caucuses focusing on gendered interests, even despite some ideological disagreements about policy (Gertzog 2004; Holman and Mahoney 2018; Mahoney 2018). Mahoney (2018) describes the formation of women's caucuses as "collective action within institutions" (27). Consistent with social movement theory (McAdam, McCarthy, and Zald 1996; Olson 1965; Tarrow 1994), Mahoney finds that a combination of political opportunities, resources, and framing allows entrepreneurs to mobilize women as a group. She further argues that, as a result of varying political environments, women's caucuses can emerge for different reasons and pursue various goals.[3] For instance, when bipartisan women's caucuses are established in more polarized legislatures, they tend to focus less on policy and more on attaining social support and recognition for women within the institution (Mahoney 2018).

Susan Webb Hammond (1998) distinguishes between six types of caucuses in Congress. Among these are *intraparty caucuses* and *national constituency caucuses*.[4] The CCWI is an example of a national constituency caucus, as its membership is bipartisan and bicameral and works on a broad range of issues related to women. Intraparty caucuses, like the moderate Blue Dog Democrats or the conservative Freedom Caucus, are comprised of members from the same party who share similar ideologies. Yet as parties in Congress become increasingly polarized, caucuses like the Republican Women's Policy Committee—or, for that matter, the Democratic Women's Caucus[5]—do not fit neatly into Hammond's typology. This chapter thus seeks to understand how party polarization and competition have encouraged women in Congress to work together at the intersection of their gender and partisan identities.

Beyond that, this analysis focuses on the institutional and political factors that have both enabled and constrained Republican women's collective action in Congress. Working within a party culture that rejects group identity politics (Freeman 1986; Crowder-Meyer and Cooperman 2018; Grossmann and Hopkins 2016), prioritizes "masculine" issues like national security (Winter 2010), and advocates anti-feminist stances on conventional women's issues like abortion, Republican women have had to negotiate tensions between their gender and partisan identities in ways that Democratic women have not. By understanding changes in the way Republican congresswomen work collectively as women, I unveil some of the gendered implications of party polarization and competition that have been overlooked by congressional scholars.

Data and Methods

To examine the evolution of Republican congresswomen's desire and ability to work together as partisan women, I rely primarily on interviews conducted with women members of Congress in the 103rd, 104th, and 114th Congresses by the Center for American Women and Politics.[6] For this chapter, I look specifically at discussions related to the CCWI, the informal and formal gatherings of Republican women, the creation of the RWPC, and the role that the RWPC has played in elevating Republican women's voices within their party. These interviews provide valuable insight into changes in the way Republican congresswomen view their role in the party, their relationship with male leadership, their motivations to pursue women's collective action, and the challenges and opportunities they have encountered along the way. Interviews were supplemented with primary and secondary sources from the Library of Congress and the National Archives, news articles, and memoirs written by members of Congress and other political actors. These sources offered further insight into the political climate and provided additional context for the claims made by interviewees.

Gender versus Party: Tensions in a Bipartisan Women's Caucus

Conservative responses to the social movements of the 1960s and '70s presented a challenging environment for feminists involved in party politics. Throughout the 1970s, both Democratic and Republican feminists fought the rise of the New Right, which, among other things, sought to preserve traditional gender roles in its opposition to abortion rights and the Equal Rights Amendment. In response, the National Women's Political Caucus (NWPC) was created by activists in 1971 as a nonpartisan, grassroots organization dedicated to advancing feminist goals in the realm of electoral politics.

Although they all identified as feminists, Republican and Democratic women in the NWPC still viewed themselves as party women working within specific party cultures. Consistent with Freeman's (1986) analysis of cultural differences between the parties, Tanya Melich, Republican co-founder of the NWPC, wrote: "We had the same goals, but we were all finding our work on interparty problems to be strained and difficult within the NWPC. The Democrats had their way of doing things, and we had ours. We found them more disorganized and raucous; they found us more formal and staid. We tended to be less confrontational and more structured" (Melich 1996, 41). The NWPC thus formed separate partisan task forces as "a necessary recognition that feminists had to fight their own battles within their parties in their own ways" (Melich 1996, 41).

In Congress, too, Democratic and Republican women were simultaneously pursuing gendered policy goals while acknowledging their partisan identities and interests. While women in Congress had varying policy priorities and ideologies, they nevertheless recognized that they brought important gendered perspectives to the institution and were able to organize formally as women. In what follows, I trace the politics of the bipartisan congressional women's caucus, focusing specifically on the way Republican congresswomen have negotiated tensions between their gender and partisan identities. From the creation of the women's caucus in the 95th Congress (1977–1979) through the Republican Revolution in the 104th Congress (1995–1997), I analyze how changes in the political environment—including presidential administrations, congressional reforms, party control, and the composition of women in Congress—have affected Republican congresswomen's participation in the caucus. In doing so, I highlight a shift toward the recognition of a *partisan-gender identity*—an identity distinct from Democratic women and Republican men.

Organizing as Congresswomen: 1977–1993

Throughout the 1970s, both Democratic and Republican women were skeptical of the purpose and function of a caucus dedicated to women, fearing that attention to women's issues could be alienating and divisive. It was not until 1977 that Margaret Heckler (R-MA) and Elizabeth Holtzman (D-NY), two respected and experienced representatives, were able to garner sufficient support for the idea of a bipartisan, pluralistic women's caucus (Gertzog 2004). After several failed attempts, the Congresswomen's Caucus—as the CCWI was originally called—was officially established in the 95th Congress as a Legislative Service Organization (LSO) and co-chaired by Heckler and Holtzman. Fifteen of the 18 women members of Congress joined the caucus that year.

As Irwin Gertzog (2004) explains, a continued acknowledgement that women are not ideologically monolithic was of critical importance for the creation of the caucus. Bipartisanship was a survival strategy that was adopted and promoted by caucus leaders from the outset. As such, no member was forced to support a specific issue, and unanimous consent was required for all policy endorsements and actions. In the same vein, it was established from the beginning that the controversial issue of abortion would remain off the table.

Yet by the 1980s, partisan tensions had already begun to tear at the bipartisan fabric of the caucus. As the New Right gained steam in the American politics, the 1980 election brought with it a number of consequences for the Congresswomen's Caucus. Six caucus members lost their races that year. And, while five new Republican women were elected to Congress,[7] all of them refused to join the caucus. Calling the Equal Rights Amendment "irrelevant," the newly elected Republican senator from Florida, Paula Hawkins, said, "I don't believe in a women's caucus, black caucus or any special interest caucus."[8] She went on: "As women, we're all for equality – or superiority. But there are better ways to attack the problems which have come to be known as women's issues. Elect more women to the United States Senate. It's women's fault for not running for office."[9]

Even the more moderate Republican women took issue with the high membership dues and the fact that Representative Patricia (Pat) Schroeder of Colorado had replaced Holtzman as Democratic co-chair. Schroeder was an outspoken liberal who was vocal in her support of abortion rights and her criticism of Ronald Reagan. Freshman Republican representative, Lynn Martin of Illinois, made her case for not joining the Congresswomen's Caucus: "The dues were too high, and I don't need to pay that for a Pat Schroeder show."[10] Indeed, members were required to make an annual contribution of $2,500, and, in July of 1981, the Executive Committee repealed the unanimity rule, making it easier for the caucus to openly criticize the president's policies (Gertzog 2004, 22). For several Republican women, the cost of membership outweighed the benefits of joining the caucus, especially with Ronald Reagan as president.

President Reagan made clear his conservative stances on most issues, including those typically deemed "women's issues"; he was anti-abortion and opposed the Equal Rights Amendment. As such, congressional Republicans who had been elected on his coattails were reluctant to join groups and causes that could be seen as challenging the positions of the White House (Gertzog 2004, 21). For the newly-elected Republican women, that included the Congresswomen's Caucus, which was viewed by conservatives as a bastion for identity politics and liberal policy. By the 98th Congress (1983–1985), membership among House Republican women had fallen to just 33 percent (3 of the 9 women; Gertzog 2004, 25).

Congressional reforms to LSOs in 1981 also placed the Congresswomen's Caucus in a difficult situation. No longer able to raise funds from outside interest groups, caucus leaders were forced to find other means to finance the caucus. And so, officially renaming itself the Congressional Caucus for Women's Issues (CCWI) in 1982, the caucus expanded its membership to include men. By the end of the year, 100 congressmen—mostly Democrats—became dues-paying members of the CCWI. Among these congressmen was Democratic Speaker Thomas P. (Tip) O'Neill. Widely known as one of the most approachable leaders in the House, the Speaker met regularly with caucus members (Gertzog 2004, 24).

Indeed, establishing rapport with congressional leadership and presidential administrations was a strategic decision the caucus made in order to best represent women (Gertzog 2004). Yet, from the beginning, President Reagan and his advisers largely ignored the CCWI. While the caucus had maintained a successful working relationship with Democratic leadership and the Carter administration, it struggled to even receive responses to meeting invitations from the Reagan administration (Gertzog 2004).

The active distancing from the CCWI by the Republican administration and newly-elected Republican women in Congress highlights the complexity of collective action for women in the GOP. Many moderate Republican women, for instance, understood the unique perspectives that women could bring to the policymaking process. Three of the four[11] moderate Republican women who won their congressional elections in 1980 did so with the help of women's organizations (Gertzog 2004, 21). And while they may have, at times, disagreed with Democratic women on how to achieve gender equality, they nevertheless believed it was a cause worth pursuing. Representative Bobbi Fiedler (R-CA), who did not consider herself a feminist before coming to Washington, said that she felt a "special obligation" to represent women: "I began to realize that most men have very little real knowledge of the problems women face."[12] Marge Roukema (R-NJ) spoke of gender differences in economic prosperity, arguing, "There's a growing recognition that the reward for a lifetime of homemaking can be an old age of poverty."[13] Yet this recognition of gender inequality was not enough to overcome the political and electoral incentives *not* to join the CCWI.

President Reagan, despite rarely meeting with members of the women's caucus, advocated for Republican women's representation in elective office and discussed what he saw as the negative gendered implications of Democratic policies. At a 1984 fundraiser for Republican women candidates, Reagan argued that "big taxing and big spending" had "hit women especially hard":

The majority of elderly Americans are women, and they found their purchasing power eaten up by inflation. Working women saw taxes eat more of their paychecks. Homemakers found that double-digit inflation made it harder and harder to buy groceries and pay the bills. And the thousands of women who wanted to start their own businesses saw 21-percent prime interest rates slam shut the doors of opportunity.[14]

Importantly, though, Reagan valued women first and foremost as party loyalists[15] who could help the GOP close the gender gap that first emerged in the 1980 election.[16] To the women in the room that day, he said, "All of you are especially important, because you demonstrate the Republican commitment to American women . . . Republican women ought to increase their numbers at every level of elective office."[17]

In the early 1980s, then, it was not a lack of commitment to women that caused newly-elected Republican women to refuse membership into the women's caucus; it was a political calculation based on the institutional environment and political context. The election of Ronald Reagan as president, Pat Schroeder as Democratic co-chair of caucus, and the caucus's decision in 1981 to remove the unanimity rule and actively oppose White House policies all contributed to these decisions.

Even still, interest in the CCWI among Republican members gradually increased throughout the 1980s. While President George H. W. Bush was largely indifferent to the women's caucus, advisers in his administration did take time to meet with members, particularly on health-related issues (Gertzog 2004, 32). Aside from working on issues of importance to them, a major incentive to join the CCWI for Republican members, who were in the minority party at the time, included the ability to "learn from Democratic women members what majority party leaders were contemplating" (Gertzog 2004, 84). Between the 98th (1983–1985) and 102nd (1991–1993) Congresses, female Republican membership increased from 33 to 67 percent (6 of 9 Republican women), and male Republican membership increased from 5 to 8 percent (Gertzog 2004, 25).

The legislative success of the CCWI in the early 1990s is difficult to dispute. Republican and Democratic women worked together on issues related to women's health, violence against women, and childcare. When asked if Republican women were just as involved as Democratic women on issues related to women's health, Susan Molinari (R-NY) told CAWP:

Mm-hmm. And frankly, once you get to women's health, once you bring the issue up, men are too. Because while it may not be the first thing that triggers when you talk about breast cancer, every one of those guys has lost a wife, a sister, a cousin, to breast cancer, and is fearful that their daughter is going to be the one. So, once you bring those issues up, they are fairly bipartisan in their acceptance of it.[18]

As a legislative vehicle, the CCWI also played an important role in getting the Violence Against Women Act (VAWA) signed into law. Moderate Republican Representative Connie Morella, who chaired the CCWI's Task Force on Violence against Women, had this to say about the function of the caucus:

> We had strategy sessions. We also used women's groups. They were a great network for telling us what was happening on the Senate side, and maybe, 'We understand that so-and-so feels this way', and, 'This is the way to get through to so-and-so.' And then we asked all the members of the Caucus (and particularly those on the Task Force) to make sure that they spoke to them ... And I think it helped, I really do.[19]

Both Democratic and Republican women, through the CCWI, worked on gender-specific issues that could garner bipartisan support among their male colleagues. Yet despite clear moments of legislative success, the caucus continued to face partisan rifts into the 1990s and beyond. In what follows, I detail these dilemmas at the beginning of the Clinton administration and in the aftermath of the Republican takeover of the House, focusing on the perspectives and experiences of Republican congresswomen.

Clinton, Abortion, and Increasing Partisan Tensions: The 103rd Congress (1993–1995)

The initial decision by caucus leaders to keep the issue of abortion off the table was due to the controversial nature of the topic and to the fact that women on both sides of the aisle had varying policy stances. In fact, in 1977, six[20] of the 18 women in the House—three Republicans and three Democrats—voted in favor of the Hyde Amendment, which would prohibit the use of federal funds to finance abortion.[21] By 1993, though, abortion was becoming an increasingly partisan issue, with most Democratic women supporting abortion rights.[22] And while several moderate Republican women were also outspoken supporters of abortion rights, others identified as pro-life or preferred the issue to be kept off the legislative agenda altogether (see Chapter 2).

The 1992 election is commonly referred to as "The Year of the Woman." Leading into the 103rd Congress (1993–1995), women gained a total of 18 seats in the House and four seats in the Senate, bringing the total number of women to 48[23] and six, respectively.[24] Most of these gains were made by Democratic women: Republican women gained only three seats in the House, bringing their number to 12, or one-quarter of the total number of women in the House.[25] This partisan discrepancy among women in Congress, the election of President Bill Clinton, and a unified Democratic government encouraged CCWI leadership to reconsider their neutral stance on the issue of abortion (Gertzog 2004). At the first caucus meeting in 1993, following over a decade of Republican control of the White House and the appointment of conservative Justice Clarence Thomas to the Supreme Court, members voted to make the CCWI a pro-choice organization (Gertzog 204, 51).

With the abortion issue back on the table, anti-abortion Republican women distanced themselves from the CCWI. In an interview, Ileana Ros-Lehtinen (R-FL) said she refused to join the women's caucus because it "was really a pro-abortion group."[26] She argued that, by taking this stance, the CCWI "really limited itself, although [its members] would not agree. But everything was in terms of bashing the Republicans and advancing the abortion lobbyists' agenda. So it was really uncomfortable for me to participate."[27] Barbara Vucanovich (R-NV) expressed similar sentiments in her interview: "I have not specifically worked with the Congresswomen's Caucus . . . They are pro-choice, and it is part of their by-laws that if you are a member of the Congresswomen's Caucus you have to agree to that, and I don't."[28]

The issue of abortion was salient throughout the 103rd Congress. Among the specific legislation debated was the Freedom of Access to Clinic Entrances (FACE) bill, the Freedom of Choice Act (FOCA), and a reauthorization of the Hyde Amendment. Collectively, the CCWI opposed the Hyde Amendment and actively fought against it. However, Republican women who were more sympathetic to the cause also took issue with the CCWI's official stance. While Tillie Fowler (R-FL) was ultimately instrumental in working with Henry Hyde (R-IL) to include a rape and incest exception (Dodson et al. 1995), she felt the CCWI's opposition to the amendment illustrated the fact that the caucus was not welcoming to all women. "I felt that the caucus, which started out with the purpose [of being] a network for women members, became very politicized during the 103rd Congress," she said, "And I thought that was a minus for the caucus, really. And a lot of us quit going because of that. Some women viewed it as something they could use to speak for all women in the Congress, which was not the way it was to have been, and not the way I think it should be used."[29]

Even Republican women who explicitly identified as pro-choice were critical of the CCWI and its decision to support abortion rights. In an interview, Jennifer Dunn (R-WA) described how she arrived at her decision not to join the women's caucus:

> I was going to join because I thought it would be a good resource for me . . . And I found out they had taken a position on abortion. So I'm not going to join that group because I think it should be an inclusive group, and it should be for our use and that we shouldn't get into endorsing particular political points of view on some of these problems where our approaches are diverse. That keeps out people who are friends of mine, like Ileana Ros-Lehtinen—I want her to be able to join a group like that—or Helen Bentley, or Barbara Vucanovich. I want us to be able to all join that group.[30]

That Jennifer Dunn was concerned not about her own policy stances, but about the professional and political advancement of fellow Republican women, highlights the tension between partisan and gender identity for many Republican women in Congress—not only the most conservative ones. Republican women in the 103rd Congress were gender-conscious actors who wanted to work on "women's issues" and understood the benefits of joining a women's caucus. Yet ideological disagreements and partisan comradery kept some women from joining, despite those benefits. By the end of the 103rd Congress, CCWI membership had dropped to about 58 percent (7 of 12) among Republican congresswomen (Gertzog 2004).

Party Loyalty in the Republican Revolution: The 104th Congress (1995–1997)

The results of the 1994 midterm elections gave Republicans a majority in the House for the first time in four decades and ushered in a large freshman class of Republicans: the GOP gained 54 seats in the House and eight in the Senate. Notably, 11 women were elected to the House that year—seven Republicans and four Democrats—bringing the total number of Republican women in the House to 18.[31] On the heels of the historic 1992 election, the 1994 midterm marked what some analysts had deemed "the year of the Republican woman" (see Fox 1997, 15).

While some Republicans prior to the midterms were content with their status in the "permanent minority" (Connelly and Pitney 1994), others had been planning the "Republican Revolution." Tom DeLay (R-TX), majority whip in the 104th Congress, highlighted intraparty tensions in 1993 prior to the GOP's takeover: "We're having a struggle right now within the Republican Party . . . [between] those who think they're here to govern and those who think they're here to take over a majority. I am not among those here to govern. I am here to take over a majority from the Democrats" (Connelly and Pitney 1994, 62). Part of this winning strategy was to aggressively attack the Democratic president while proposing conservative policy alternatives. Six weeks before the midterm election, on September 27, 1994, over 300 congressional candidates stood on the steps of the Capitol to sign the Contract with America, a pledge to enact ten conservative bills that emphasized limited government, fiscal responsibility, and social welfare reform.

One consequence of the election results was that, rightly or wrongly, congressional Republicans in the 104th Congress believed they had a mandate from the American people to enact the Contract with America within their first 100 days in office (Fenno 1997). For newly elected Republican congresswomen, most of whom were more ideologically conservative than their senior counterparts, joining the CCWI was not on their list of priorities. On the contrary, many of them were overtly opposed to such a caucus and were determined to distinguish themselves from what conservative radio talk show host, Rush Limbaugh, called "the feminazis" (Gertzog 2004, 87). Of the seven freshmen Republican women, only one—Sue Kelly of New York—officially joined the caucus.

Beyond ideological differences, institutional changes also amplified the tension between gender and partisan identity for many Republican congresswomen. In the House, the majority party has the power to set the rules of the game (Cox and McCubbins 1993). In 1995, the Republicans of the 104th Congress elected Newt Gingrich (R-GA) Speaker of the House. Notoriously partisan in his approach to politics, Gingrich worked to restructure the House in a way that increased the power of party leaders and benefited Republicans. Among these reforms was the elimination of LSOs. As a result, the CCWI, along with other caucuses like the Congressional Black Caucus and the Democratic Study Group, no longer had office space or funding for staff. Pat Schroeder argued that the new Republican leadership was effectively establishing "a new gag rule for American women by seeking to silence the members of Congress who work on their behalf."[32] The subsequent ineffectiveness of the caucus, which reorganized itself as a Congressional Member Organization (CMO), had caused women on both sides of the aisle to work on issues outside of the CCWI. In an interview, Nancy Johnson (R-CT) noted: "My impression was that in the 104th Congress, the caucus was generally a small group of Democratic women meeting—and maybe Connie Morella [R-MD]."[33]

By restructuring the House and centralizing power in party leadership, Speaker Gingrich also incentivized party loyalty over gendered activism among Republican women. As Irwin Gertzog (2004) describes, "The increased distance Republican women placed between themselves and the caucus dovetailed with the designs of Newt Gingrich. The new Speaker sought actively to weaken the bonds GOP women had established with women Democrats, and to integrate them more fully into the Republican Party" (84). As Speaker, Gingrich imposed six-year term limits on committee chairmanships and weakened the seniority system, creating the House Steering Committee and giving Republican Party leaders power over committee appointments. "Under the new system," Gertzog (2004) writes, "a total of thirty-one votes would be distributed among Steering Committee members, with the Speaker's vote valued at six, and nine other GOP leaders casting ten more—a majority of the total votes. This meant that no Republican could be appointed to a committee without the approval of at least some party leaders" (60). Despite lacking seniority, Republican congresswomen were offered party leadership positions and appointed to powerful committees as a way to encourage party loyalty. In her interview with CAWP, Jan Meyers (R-KS), chair of the Small Business Committee in the 104th Congress, discussed how these appointments affected the relationship between Democratic and Republican women:

> We end up talking about the same issues, and in that way we are working together, [but] we don't get together and plan things particularly . . . Republican women [are] getting their feet on the ground in terms of leadership. I've got a chairmanship, Nancy [Johnson] has got a chairmanship, we've got a couple of people on Appropriations and a couple on Ways & Means. It's just kind of getting your feet on the ground in terms of legislative policy. And maybe the role of Republican women has changed just a little bit . . . the Republican women are a lot busier and a lot more involved with policy.[34]

In addition to formal leadership positions, Gingrich strengthened party loyalty by holding regularly scheduled meetings with Republican women. Tillie Fowler (R-FL) said in an interview, "We [the Republican women] meet with Newt about every other week . . . And really it was his suggestion. He said he wanted to find out what we were thinking, what our concerns were. No staff, just us and you, off-the-record meetings. And it has been great."[35] Indeed, Gingrich understood the importance of closing the gender gap and establishing rapport among Republican women (in Chapter 5, I talk more about the significance of Gingrich's support in Jennifer Dunn's pathway to Conference leadership). Access to the Democratic majority leadership had been a major incentive for Republican women to join the CCWI prior to the 104th Congress; by giving Republican congresswomen direct access to the Speaker, Gingrich effectively disincentivized membership in the CCWI and deepened the divide between Democratic and Republican women in the House (Gertzog 2004, 84). When asked in an interview whether there was any advantage to being a member of the women's caucus in the 104th Congress, Marge Roukema, moderate Republican of New Jersey, responded simply: "No."[36]

This strengthening of party loyalty can also be seen through the informal gatherings of Republican women. In the 104th and 105th Congresses, Republican women would get together for informal dinners, often at Representative Nancy Johnson's house. Jennifer Dunn (R-WA) told CAWP in a 1997 interview, "There is a dinner that we [the Republican women] can attend every Wednesday night . . . It is really a good support group. And we're going different directions. . . We all have our own interests . . . but we do have a lot in common, and we understand that and we work together on things."[37]

But working together as Republican women was not always easy. Republican congresswomen in the 1990s were not nearly as ideologically homogenous as they would be two decades later, and they often disagreed with each other in terms of policy. As Barbara Vucanovich (R-NV) noted in her interview, "You had very strong differences of opinions. . . Our Republican women had a very informal group where we would have dinner together, have a glass of wine, visit and so forth, and invariably we would get into some of those differences—I mean, in our party! And I don't respect them less, but you know, I would finally go home."[38] Still, institutional changes—including majority party status, the elimination of resources for the CCWI, and access to formal policymaking power—created incentives for beginning to identify and collaborate as partisan women.

Susan Molinari (R-NY) would later write in her memoir, "The tragedy of women's politics within the House was how frequently we were divided not by ideology, but by pure partisanship, by the pressures and politics from within our own caucuses" (Molinari 1998, 95). As discussed in Chapters 2 and 3, women in the 104th House were eventually able to accomplish some bipartisan policy goals through the CCWI, including the adoption of childcare and child support provisions within the Personal Responsibility and Work Opportunity Reconciliation Act of 1996. But the institutional changes ushered in during the 104th Congress resulted in increased party loyalty among Republican women and a shift toward the recognition of a partisan-gender identity. In the following section, I examine how polarization and changes in the political environment gave Republican women the opportunity and resources to organize formally at the intersection of their gender and partisan identities in way that has not previously been seen.

A Caucus of Their Own: Republican Women's Collective Action in the House

Navigating the tension between their gender and partisan identities, Republican congresswomen have at times chosen to work across party lines as women, and, at other times, have chosen party loyalty over their gendered interests. Yet since the 104th Congress (1995–1997), incentives to identify and work as Republican women—at the *intersection* of their partisan and gender identities—have become increasingly present. In what follows, I continue to trace the development of a partisan-gender identity along with the creation of the first and (so far) only Republican women's caucus: the Republican Women's Policy Committee (RWPC). I show that, while approval from party leadership plays a significant role, the formation of the RWPC was not merely a top-down decision made by party leaders; rather, Republican women view the attainment of institutional power as mutually beneficial for themselves and their party, and they have both taken advantage of opportunities and faced challenges in creating and maintaining their own caucus.

Anna Mahoney (2018) argues that women face unique collective action costs within legislative institutions. Along with typical organizational challenges like acquiring necessary time and resources (Olson 1965), women legislators must also navigate other formal and informal norms. For instance, party leaders can present obstacles for legislative collective action, especially if they perceive that action to contradict the norms and interests of the party (Mahoney 2018, 34). For Republican women, in particular, simply organizing around a social group identity challenges the cultural norms of the party (Freeman 1986; Mahoney 2018, 32). The institutional marginalization of women—exclusion from important leadership roles and the presence of gender biases, for example—also presents unique organizational obstacles for female legislators (Mahoney 2018, 32).

Nevertheless, these challenges can be overcome through various means. First, taking advantage of political opportunities when they arise is critically important. Through this analysis, I show how increased intraparty cohesion and interparty competition, within the context of a broader gendered political environment, has created opportunities for Republican congresswomen's mobilization. Women's acknowledgement of their own marginalization can also serve as motivation for collective action (Mahoney 2018). Indeed, despite a general rejection of identity politics among Republicans, I find that many Republican congresswomen recognize that they are uniquely disadvantaged in Congress and their party, and that this has been a motivating factor for the formation of the RWPC. Second, organizing successfully requires congresswomen to view a caucus as worthy of their time and resources. An effective caucus entrepreneur can help recruit potential members by framing caucus participation as worthwhile (Mahoney 2018). Finally, in the context of partisan politics, caucus members must also be able to frame their collective action in a way that does not alienate party leadership (Mahoney 2018). This analysis reveals how Republican congresswomen were successful in organizing around their partisan-gender identity *and* demonstrates the continuing power of male party leaders.

Party Politics and the Republican War on Women

The 1990s marked the beginning of an explicitly partisan use of the term "war on women."[39] Following the Republican takeover of Congress and the party's implementation of conservative policies, feminists increasingly claimed that the GOP was detrimental to women's rights. Tanya Melich, feminist activist and former Republican Party insider, titled her 1996 book *The Republican War against Women*. In it, she detailed the New Right's takeover of the Republican Party and demonstrated that the GOP's new electoral strategy involved a direct repudiation of the feminist and civil rights movements. Claims of a Republican "war on women" intensified during the George W. Bush administration, with feminists arguing that the administration's policies harmed women in the United States and abroad (Finlay 2006).

At the same time, the 2002 midterm elections brought even more ideologically conservative women into Congress. Unlike most midterms, in which the president's party typically loses congressional seats, Republicans gained seats in both chambers in the year following the September 11, 2001 terrorist attacks. Five freshmen Republican women entered the House in 2003, increasing the total number of House Republican women from 18 to 21.[40] The 108th Congress (2003–2005) also marked the beginning of Republican congresswomen's consistent ideological alignment with their Republican male colleagues; in every Congress since then, Republican men and women in the House have been "ideologically indistinguishable" (Frederick 2009).

When Democrats finally regained control of the House following the 2006 midterms, Nancy Pelosi (D-CA) was elected Speaker—the first woman in history to hold the gavel. And in 2008, Hillary Clinton ran a competitive race for the Democratic presidential nomination. This pro-woman image of the Democratic Party, paired with gendered critiques of the GOP, created a political environment in which Republicans felt they had to work to convince voters that they were not the anti-woman party they were accused of being. In what some saw as an attempt to attract women voters that had supported Clinton in the primary, 2008 Republican presidential nominee, John McCain, chose Alaska Governor Sarah Palin as his running mate. Republican women were quick to rally around Palin, defending her against what they claimed to be sexist attacks and pointing to her as evidence that Republicans were supportive of women in leadership positions. At a press conference in 2008, Republican women accused the media of unfairly attacking Palin and other conservative women. Representative Marsha Blackburn (R-TN) said, "The media continues to attack conservative women to seek a way to diminish their record and demonize their actions."[41]

Uniting around their partisan-gender identity, Republican women increasingly spoke as and on behalf of women in their party—and were often given media attention as a result (Lucas 2017). With a unified government in 2009, Democrats worked to push the Affordable Care Act (ACA) through Congress. Although ultimately unsuccessful in their attempts to kill the bill, the Republican women in Congress engaged in gendered claims-making while adamantly opposing health care reform. Cathy McMorris Rodgers, newly-elected vice chair of the House Republican Conference, organized press conferences with fellow female Republican colleagues, criticizing Democratic economic and health care policies. At one such conference, Shelley Moore Capito (R-WV) invoked her experience as a mother to argue that Republican women are uniquely positioned to understand the harmful consequences of the ACA:

> As mothers . . . we have that trained ear. So in the middle of the night, when you think your child's in distress, you put your ear to your child's chest . . . A mother's ear is very keen when we discover that we think one of our children's health is in danger . . . .And I think we, as the women in the Republican conference, have our ears listening to the distress of those concerned about Medicare, those who are concerned about access, those in the rural communities where I'm from, who are worried that their choices are going to be curtailed.[42]

At the same press conference, Michele Bachmann (R-MN) argued that women are concerned about the economic insecurity that would result from the ACA: "The number one concern of Americans, and particularly of women, is the idea of jobs . . . Women are very security-conscious about economics in their families; they feel it first before anyone."[43] These types of press conferences, led by Republican women, have continued throughout recent years.

Democratic claims of a Republican "war on women" skyrocketed after the 2010 midterm election, in which a conservative Tea Party wave once again gave Republicans control of the House; Democratic National Committee (DNC) chairwoman, Debbie Wasserman Schultz, began consistently using the term in 2011.[44] Controversial claims about women, rape, and abortion made by male Republican candidates like Todd Akin and Richard Mourdock further contributed to this environment,[45] and Republican women and party leaders worked to combat the image of an anti-woman GOP. Speaking for the women in her party, Marsha Blackburn said at a 2011 press conference:

> As you can see, we have a terrific group of women in our Republican conference . . . And I will remind you today that there have been no more fierce defenders of liberty and freedom in our nation's history than women . . . We're going to continue this fight . . . We are in a fight to protect

America's families from higher taxes and wasteful spending that has gone on for decades. And we are in a fight to protect our children's future.[46]

And during a 2012 press conference, the Republican women of the House attacked President Obama's contraceptive mandate, arguing that the violation of religious freedom was their main concern as conservative women.

This is the political environment in which Republican congresswomen would eventually create their own caucus, separate from the bipartisan women's caucus. In what follows, I demonstrate how this political landscape has created an awareness among Republican congresswomen of the political opportunities and obstacles they face specifically as women in their party. Moreover, I show how they have acquired the resources and developed the strategies necessary to form the Republican Women's Policy Committee. I argue that this was not simply a top-down decision made by party leaders, but rather, that Republican congresswomen have collectively organized to further their own interests in addition to the interests of their party.

Institutionalizing a Partisan-Gender Identity: Creating the RWPC

In 2012, the 24 House Republican women of the 112th Congress formed the Republican Women's Policy Committee (RWPC), an official CMO registered with the Committee on House Administration.[47] Almost immediately, Democrats attacked the group as a partisan show orchestrated by Republican leaders. Said Jennifer Crider, communications director for the Democratic Congressional Campaign Committee (DCCC): "It tells you everything you need to know about this political stunt, that House Republicans are forming a caucus in 2012 to give women a vote."[48]

In an era of heightened ideological polarization and party competition, Republican women have defended their party against claims of a Republican "war on women." Speaking explicitly as Republican women, they have used their gender identities to support conservative policy positions and legitimize the actions of their party (see Chapters 2 and 3 for examples of this occurring on the House floor as well). But their collective action in the House also demonstrates that Republican women are not simply defensive party loyalists. Working at the intersection of their gender and partisan identities, Republican congresswomen recognize their unique experiences and thus distinguish themselves not only from Democratic women, but from Republican men as well.

In talking with Republican congresswomen about their decision to form the RWPC, I find a belief that Republican women are often treated unfairly within and outside of their own party. Virginia Foxx (R-NC), for instance, believes Republican women's work has been downplayed by the media. In her interview, she reminded us that the first woman elected to Congress was a Republican and said, "Our involvement has been negated again by the media . . . And that's truly unfortunate because it's not that women have never . . . been an important part of the party. It's the perception of the public set up by the media."[49] Echoing that statement, Marsha Blackburn (R-TN) said that the media "has an incredible bias, it seems, against conservative women."[50] She went on: "I find it really quite interesting that conservative women can be accomplished [and] polished, and they are . . . not celebrated in the manner that liberal women are."[51] Arguing that they often face greater scrutiny than their Democratic female colleagues, Republican congress-women have distinguished their experiences from those of other women on the basis of ideology and partisanship.

At the same time, though, some Republican congresswomen have also pointed out the challenges they face as women within their party. For example, Blackburn also talked about the fact that women in the GOP are not treated as equals by some of their male colleagues. She said in her interview, "I think it should be noted that some conservative men do not view women as full and equal partners in the workplace. And I know for some men that is never going to change."[52] And when asked about the motivation for creating the RWPC, Cynthia Lummis (R-WY) pointed to Republican women's challenges in acquiring more legislative power within the institution: "I think that Republican women recognize that if we don't assert ourselves it isn't going to happen . . One of the significant reasons for the committee is how few Republican women were being appointed to conference committees . . . That was a major motivation and something that just didn't seem to be occurring to the Republican leadership who were men."[53] Republican congresswomen in recent years have argued that they face unique challenges at the intersection of their partisan and gender identities—that they are held to higher standards than Democratic women *and* Republican men. It is partly the recognition of this partisan-gender identity that has motivated Republican women to organize collectively in the House.

Of course, while an awareness of unfair treatment and unequal opportunity has been a motivating factor for some, not all Republican women believe that they face obstacles as women in their party. Ileana Ros-Lehtinen (R-FL), who served as a member of Congress from 1989–2019, was asked in a 2015 CAWP interview whether she thought women must overcome unique challenges within the GOP. "No," she said, "I'd say that would probably be true a while back. I just don't see it. I don't see it, I don't feel it, I don't sense it. Things have changed a lot . . . I mean, nobody says, 'Oh, you can't be on [the Committee on] Energy and Commerce because you're a woman.' That would be absurd. Of course they wouldn't say it, but would they think it? No, they wouldn't even think it."[54] Kay Granger (R-TX) also sees little evidence of active discrimination, though she did note the small number of women in the GOP compared to women in the Democratic Party. When asked if she saw any unique challenges for Republican women, she said, "I don't see it that way. There are more Democrat women than Republican women. I think that's it."[55] While Republican women vary in their views of discrimination, they nevertheless organized around a specific partisan-gender identity. One reason this was possible was the presence of an effective caucus entrepreneur: Representative Mary Bono of California.

Compared to collective action outside of Congress, forming a CMO in the House requires relatively few resources. The purpose of creating a CMO (rather than simply forming an informal, unregistered group) is to give members an opportunity to bring attention their specific cause by assigning personal staff to work on issues related to the CMO and discussing their CMO membership on their websites and in official House communications. As Virginia Foxx said when asked about the creation of the RWPC, "People form groups in order to get some recognition they think is not going to come any other way."[56] Registering a CMO requires a member to submit a letter to the Committee on House Administration explaining the purpose of the caucus and listing the names of its officers.[57] Because members cannot directly use their Members' Representational Allowance (MRA) on CMO activities or accept funds/services from external organizations,[58] the costs of joining a CMO are primarily limited to time and perceptions of legitimacy. That is, potential caucus members must view membership, first, as worthy of their time, and second, as a legitimate endeavor that does not alienate them from party leadership (Mahoney 2018).

The RWPC was formed in May of 2012, but Mary Bono (R-CA) had been discussing the idea with her colleagues for over a year. "It took a while to make sure that people were serious about this," Bono said, "to make sure it was really a good idea."[59] Though more ideologically moderate than many of her colleagues, Mary Bono was well respected in Congress. And while Bono was the chair and founder of the RWPC, the more conservative Marsha Blackburn (R-TN) was also working to bring Republican women on board. In an interview, Kristi Noem (R-SD) noted, "Mary Bono Mack and Marsha Blackburn were the two who really first brought it to the table and asked all the women if they would be interested in doing it."[60]

Through effective framing strategies (Mahoney 2018), Bono and Blackburn were eventually able to garner broad support for the RWPC: all 24 Republican women in the House officially joined the caucus, and party leaders, including Speaker John Boehner, were supportive of the effort. When asked about the motivation for creating the RWPC, Blackburn said in her interview, "This was an outgrowth of conversations we would have about there needing to be a female perspective . . . Our goal is to make certain that our colleagues realize there is a female perspective to these issues and they need to be mindful of that before they begin to talk about it."[61] Bono was even more critical of the GOP, telling a reporter that the caucus was born out of a "frustration" over Republican policies as well as some of the internal workings of the party, though she did not specify what those were.[62] Making a similar claim, Renee Ellmers (R-NC), chair of the RWPC in the 114th Congress (2015–2017) told me in an interview, "Some of the women members who had been here for a while, they had seen the way things worked and they really wanted . . . women in the conference to have more of a voice."[63] While reasons for joining the RWPC undoubtedly varied among Republican congresswomen, caucus entrepreneurs found ways to convince women members and male party leaders that the RWPC was important.

At first, Republican Party leaders responded to Bono's idea of a caucus with what she said was "a sort of glazed look in their eyes."[64] But as "war on women" rhetoric ramped up during the 2012 election and discussions of the gender gap became more prevalent, Bono said, "the leadership became a lot more interested in understanding the importance of what we're trying to do."[65] Indeed, by framing Republican women's collective action as a way to achieve the party's electoral goals, rather than as a criticism of the party, caucus entrepreneurs gained the support of party leaders and of women who might have been hesitant to join the group out of fear of not being viewed as loyal to the party.

The Republican women I spoke with about the RWPC pointed to their gender identity as being inherently beneficial for the party. In particular, they emphasized the important perspectives that women bring in reaching out to female voters and communicating the party's policies. Diane Black (R-TN) told me, "I believe that women look at issues differently than men do, and that's just the way we are. We come at things in a different way, and since 52 percent of the population is female, it behooves us to make sure that we have a woman's voice in the discussions."[66] Ann Wagner (R-MO) further emphasized women's ability to frame issues in a way that resonates with families:

> I believe that [Republicans] have to personalize our message, make our message much more Main Street . . . [Women] do it much better, especially in [the Committee on] Financial Services where so many of my male colleagues will talk in charts and graphs and numbers and swaps and derivatives and things. I want to talk about a family that is trying to save for their retirement and what it means to them, and [how] the policy we're passing . . . impacts that family and their future.[67]

Along the same lines, Elise Stefanik (R-NY) argued that Republican women "understand the importance of reaching out to women voters very effectively."[68] This frame—that organizing as Republican women can benefit the *party*—has been especially effective in an era of heightened interparty competition. As both parties place increased emphasis on messaging and campaigning, painting themselves as an electoral asset can help GOP women gain recognition and visibility within their party (see also Wineinger and Nugent 2020).

The fact that Republican congresswomen are more ideologically similar to one another and to their Republican male colleagues than they had been in the past has also made it easier to organize around shared interests. While Republican congresswomen in the early 1990s identified and often had informal dinners as partisan women, their ideological differences at times caused tensions and resulted in intraparty disputes.[69] Nevertheless, the existence of a partisan-gender identity—the recognition of a category "Republican women" that is different from Democratic women and Republican men—was beginning to emerge. As I have shown through an analysis of the creation of the RWPC, growing party polarization and competition, in the context of a gendered political environment, has created political opportunities for the institutionalization of this partisan-gender identity. In the following sections, I discuss the effectiveness of the RWPC as well as the continuing role of male party leaders as gatekeepers.

Elevating Women's Voices in the Party

Republican congresswomen joined the RWPC for various reasons. From interviews with Republican women in the 114th Congress (2015–2017), I have identified four main goals of the caucus. Through the RWPC, Republican women hoped to elevate their voices by working to (1) create a network of mentorship and support, (2) shape the messaging strategies of the party, (3) have a greater say in the development of GOP policies and legislation, and (4) acquire greater institutional power through committee chairmanships, positions on conference committees, etc. Overall, the RWPC has been an effective vehicle for most of these endeavors, although gaining substantive institutional power remains a challenge for Republican congresswomen.

Mary Bono originally envisioned the RWPC as a professional development tool for Republican women to gain opportunities within Congress. "What I then heard the most," Bono told a reporter in 2018, "was women just wanted some moral support for the job."[70] And indeed, the caucus became that source of support for many women. Renee Ellmers, then chair of the RWPC, told me in a 2015 interview, "We are there to support each other [through the] good and bad, whether it's a personal issue or whether it's a legislative issue. We want to help each other."[71] One way the RWPC supported the legislative efforts of Republican women was through the circulation of information, which gave them a chance to hear about—and ultimately support and amplify—the work of their female colleagues. As Cathy McMorris Rodgers (R-WA), said in her interview, "The Republican Women's Policy Committee has been a clearinghouse for identifying the legislation that we are working on; circulating it among the women; building support; highlighting press, media clips, [and] different interviews that the women may be doing; and just making sure that we are supporting them in those efforts."[72]

Another priority of the RWPC was to shape the communications strategy of the GOP—including making sure that women were visible and speaking out on a wide range of issues in a way that relates to women and families. In

Chapters 2 and 3, I found an increasing use of partisan woman-invoked rhetoric in the floor speeches of Republican congresswomen. Interviews with members show that this rhetoric is not simply a top-down effort by party leaders; through the collective action of Republican congresswomen, these gendered communication strategies are taken to the House floor. Members of the RWPC, for instance, have held meetings and conference calls to discuss upcoming legislation. "So if there's a bill that is coming to the floor," Kristi Noem (R-SD) said in an interview, "we will weigh in on it. If we do think it's a good idea, then we will make sure that some of the women are speaking on it. [The RWPC] gives us a forum to say, 'Hey, we need some more women to weigh in on this. Who wants to do that?' And we make sure we have all the bases covered."[73] According to Cathy McMorris Rodgers, "[RWPC chairwoman, Renee Ellmers,] will organize special orders on the House floor where we can go down and talk about a particular issue."[74] The institutionalization of a partisan-gender identity has thus contributed to the collective use of a partisan woman-invoked rhetoric on the House floor, in which Republican congresswomen speak as and on behalf of women from a partisan perspective.

A third goal of the RWPC was to have a greater say in the actual development of Republican policies and legislation. Many of the Republican congresswomen interviewees believe they have better access to party leaders as a result of the RWPC. Kristi Noem (R-SD) said that the caucus has "given us a little more of an opportunity to weigh in with leadership as a more unified group rather than [having] to all go forward and make decisions on our own."[75] Diane Black (R-TN) and Ileana Ros-Lehtinen (R-FL) both agreed with this, emphasizing that the RWPC has helped to elevate the voices of women within their conference. Black said, "I see a difference between when I came here five years ago and now, and my colleagues actually reaching out to us rather than us inserting ourselves. I have colleagues who actually reach out to me and say, 'What do you think about this?'"[76] Ros-Lehtinen discussed seeing a similar outcome, saying, "We have the ear of the leadership and that has been a big change. Before, when it was more ad hoc and not a real structure, we would have to knock on the door and . . . get an appointment, and by the time that happens the issue might have passed by the wayside. Now [that] we have a structured group, we have the ear of the leadership. [Speaker] Paul Ryan meets with us and that makes a big difference."[77]

As a result, there have been times when Republican congresswomen have been able to substantively alter Republican legislation. One case that garnered considerable media attention was the Pain-Capable Unborn Child Protection Act, which would ban abortion after 20 weeks. In January of 2015, House Republican leaders pulled the bill from consideration amidst push-back from moderates and women in the party. Republican women were par-ticularly critical of the way the rape exception clause was written in the bill, as it only exempted women if they had reported their rape to authorities. In an interview, Renee Ellmers (R-NC) made it clear that the pushback from Republican congresswomen was not in regards to the overarching goal of the legislation, but to the particular language used in the bill:

> The Republican women were the ones who went forward to our leader-ship and said . . . we love this bill, we want this bill, we believe in the 20 week Pain-Capable abortion bill. But the language basically says that if the woman is a victim of rape, she would have had to have filed a police report, [and] we know over 60 percent of rapes or sexual assaults are not reported. So we said . . . this will be harmful to what we are trying to achieve, which is changing this label and narrative that we're creating a "war on women." This is just going to play right into that . . . And it was one of those things where it was very difficult because we knew if we voted on the bill as it was, it was going to open up this Pandora's Box of ugly myths about the Republican Party and where we are with women.[78]

Indeed, Cynthia Lummis (R-WY) views this as one accomplishment of the RWPC that "stands out big time," saying that even the most anti-abortion women pushed back on the language in the bill: "We closed ranks. There are very pro-life Republican women, who came here because of the importance of social issues, and women who came here because they really wanted to emphasize fiscal issues, like me. But when it came to that issue, man, talk about closing ranks."[79] Convinced that the language in the bill was not in the best interest of the party, leaders eventually pulled the bill and replaced it with a revised version that passed in the House.

Overall, Republican congresswomen formed the RWPC as a way to gain support and recognition within their party. In many ways, they have been successful in their endeavors. Through their collective action, Republican congresswomen have created a network of social and legislative support, have worked to gender their party's messaging strategies in various ways, and have voiced their opinions on Republican legislation. Still, as I highlight in the following section, male party leaders continue to play a significant role as gatekeepers. While the RWPC has given Republican women more access to party leaders, women's collective action has also been met with challenges.

Party Leaders as Gatekeepers

Although Republican Party leadership, according to Mary Bono (R-CA), was originally dismissive of the idea of a Republican women's caucus, the political environment created incentives to eventually embrace the RWPC. Following the announcement of the caucus in May of 2012, Speaker John Boehner and Majority Leader Eric Cantor praised the group and its officers. Notably, both emphasized that the RWPC would benefit the party as a whole. Speaker Boehner said the caucus would "be an important voice for the Republican Conference," and Majority Leader Cantor said that Mary Bono's "commitment to highlight the leadership and expertise of the women in the House Republican Conference will serve as a tremendous benefit to our party . . . "[80] This vision of the RWPC as an asset to the electoral interests of the party helps to explain the relationship between Republican Party leaders and women in the conference.

As mentioned previously, one impetus for organizing collectively as Republican women was to increase their ranks within the party through formal leadership positions. Yet while the RWPC drew attention to this issue, it proved to be a tough one to address. Ileana Ros-Lehtinen, chair of the Committee on Foreign Affairs, was the only Republican woman to hold a committee chairmanship in the 112th House of Representatives (2011–2013). In the congressional sessions immediately following the creation of the RWPC, not much changed in terms of numbers. In the 113th (2013–2015) and 114th (2015–2017) Congresses, Candice Miller (R-MI), chair of the House Administration Committee, was the only woman to chair a committee in the House.

Some Republican congresswomen chalked this up simply to the fact that women lack seniority in the conference. When asked about the small number of female committee chairs, Virginia Foxx (R-NC) told a reporter in 2014, "I have not seen any discrimination in our conference. Most everything around here is done on seniority. Part of the problem we have is that we have to catch up in seniority."[81] Indeed, overcoming issues of seniority remains a challenge for Republican congresswomen, who are, on the whole, more electorally vulnerable than their male counterparts (Lawless and Pearson 2008; Lazarus and Steigerwalt 2018).[82] Still, while the House Steering Committee considers seniority as one of its criteria for recommending committee candidates to the conference, other factors—like party loyalty, relationships with other conference members, and fundraising ability—are also considered. Since 1995, House leadership in the Republican Party—and especially the Speaker, who has five votes on the Steering Committee—has had more control over committee chair assignments than in the Democratic Party, where seniority does play a larger role.

Other members of the RWPC have been more outspoken about pressuring leadership to appoint women to more prominent leadership positions. After a particularly competitive vote for chair of the Committee on Homeland Security in 2012,[83] the Steering Committee eventually voted to nominate Michael McCaul (R-TX) over Mike Rogers (R-AL) and Candice Miller (R-MI). With only two committee chairmanships (House Administration and Ethics) left to fill before the first session of the 113th Congress, Republican women lobbied Speaker Boehner to appoint women to these positions. Unlike other standing committees, the chairs of the House Administration and Ethics committees, which deal with internal congressional matters, are nominated by the Speaker of the House. Boehner selected Mike Conway of Texas for the Ethics Committee, and Candice Miller would come to chair House Administration. In the days that followed, House Republicans received media criticism for failing to elect women committee chairs; the fact that Miller chaired House Administration, which deals primarily with "housekeeping" responsibilities, also contributed to gendered critiques of the party.[84]

Speaker Boehner was well aware of the perception that the Republican Party undervalued women, and he was committed to fighting that perception and to closing the gender gap (in Chapter 5, I talk more about this and his role in encouraging Cathy McMorris Rodgers to run for Conference chair). Still, in October of 2013, the all-male Republican members of a bipartisan, bicameral budget conference committee posed for a photo-op amidst a government shutdown. The result of this photo-op was, once again, a critique that the Republican Party was not concerned with women's interests. At a meeting following this event, Renee Ellmers, chair of the RWPC at the time, told CQ Roll Call that she confronted Boehner about not having women on the conference committee. Ellmers called it a "teachable moment," saying, "[Boehner] literally got up and said, 'You know what, Renee, that was a mistake.' And I believe that it was just a very innocent mistake, and I don't think they realized how that looked. I believe it is not a mistake that will be made again."[85] Soon after, Boehner asked Diane Black (R-TN), then a member of the Budget Committee, to serve on the conference committee.

At the same time that Republican women held only one standing committee chairmanship in the House, they held a *majority* of the positions in Republican Conference leadership: Cathy McMorris Rodgers as chair; Lynn Jenkins as vice chair; Virginia Foxx as secretary; and Ann Wagner and Martha McSally as freshman representatives in the 113th and 114th Congresses, respectively. This discrepancy can be explained, in part, by the role of the Republican Conference, which is tasked with creating and disseminating the party's message. Women's consistent overrepresentation in Conference leadership and underrepresentation in committee leadership suggests Republican congresswomen are valued primarily as loyal party messengers who can work to portray the GOP as a pro-woman party.

A commitment to enhancing party loyalty and unity can also be seen in Paul Ryan's approach to leadership. In September of 2015, facing threats from the most conservative factions of the Republican Party, John Boehner resigned as Speaker. That October, the RWPC joined other caucuses, like the moderate Tuesday Group and the conservative Freedom Caucus, in officially supporting Paul Ryan (R-WI) for Speaker. Ryan, former chair of the Budget Committee and 2012 vice-presidential nominee, was at first reluctant to run. Nevertheless, he eventually committed himself to dealing with intraparty tensions as Speaker of the House. Speaker Ryan held private meetings with representatives from various party caucuses, including the RWPC, to discuss where common ground could be reached and, most importantly, to avoid public displays of infighting among congressional Republicans. Overall, while party leadership has been open to the RWPC's suggestions of putting more women in positions of power, the motivation to do so has largely stemmed from a desire to prevent an anti-woman image of the GOP, rather than any substantive belief in women's distinct interests and perspectives as policymakers.[86]

This has proven to be difficult terrain for the maintenance of the RWPC, which has attempted to elevate the voices of Republican women in the realms of messaging *and* policy. While Republican congresswomen did increase their positional power on committees in the 115th Congress,[87] at least a few women were also acutely aware that party leadership did not appreciate pushback from a collective group. One former Republican congresswoman, who wished to remain anonymous, told a reporter in 2018 that she had planned to lobby leadership to include more women in discussions of health care policy. But getting other women on board with this was difficult, as one of her female colleagues noted that "one person in leadership . . . [doesn't] like it when the women say these things."[88]

Despite a challenging 2016 election season during which the GOP continued to face claims of sexism, Republicans won the presidency and a majority in both chambers of Congress. On top of that, RWPC chair, Renee Ellmers, was targeted by conservative interest groups and lost her 2016 primary election to conservative Republican George Holding. With a unified Republican Party, no immediate need to cater to women voters, and no clear caucus leader heading into the 115th Congress, the RWPC disbanded after only three congressional terms. In a phone call, a Republican staffer told me simply that the new Speaker, Paul Ryan, no longer supported the caucus.[89] And so, while Republican congresswomen have been able to collectively mobilize their partisan-gender identity, I find that the effectiveness of that collective action is largely dependent on political opportunity structures, and in particular, perceptions by party leadership about whether or not a formal group will enhance the image and messaging strategies of the GOP.

Conclusion

This chapter traces the politics of the bipartisan CCWI and the formation of the partisan RWPC to understand how Republican congresswomen have navigated tensions between their partisan and gender identities over time. Through this analysis, I reveal the recognition and eventual institutionalization of a partisan-gender identity among Republican women in the House. More specifically, I show how increased ideological cohesion and interparty competition have resulted in incentives and political opportunities to organize formally as Republican women.

The first half of the chapter examined the evolution of CCWI membership, focusing on Republican women. I show how ideological differences, party loyalty, and institutional changes have affected Republican congresswomen's decisions to work within the bipartisan women's caucus. While Republican women have always had to negotiate tensions between their partisan and gender identities, the 104th Congress (1995–1997) marked a period of transition. The Republican Revolution brought with it the election of more conservative women, a strong Speaker of the House, and institutional changes that incentivized Republican women to begin to work explicitly as Republican women—at the intersection of their gender and partisan identities.

As I demonstrate in the second half of the chapter, this partisan-gender identity would gradually become institutionalized as the RWPC. Through an analysis of the formation of the RWPC, I show how ideological cohesion, interparty competition, and changes in the political environment have resulted in opportunities for women to organize collectively within the GOP. Importantly, while the RWPC was not a top-down product of party leadership, my analysis of its accomplishments and challenges reveals that male party leaders nevertheless play a persistent gatekeeping role. Party leaders, for instance, are supportive of Republican women working to enhance the electoral prospects of the GOP, and women are particularly embraced as party messengers.

This dynamic can also be seen in the overrepresentation of women as leaders in the Republican Conference, which functions primarily as a messaging vehicle for House Republicans. In the following chapter, I delve deeper into the experiences of women in these leadership roles to gain a better understanding of how these positions have evolved over time. Rather than focusing solely on Republican women's underrepresentation, I maintain that it is important to take a closer look at where Republican women *are* represented. Doing so can help uncover how Republican congresswomen work on behalf of women constituents and on behalf of their own representation as female legislators.

5

Amplifying a Collective Voice

Women Conference Leaders as Critical Actors

My analysis of the evolution of Republican women's representation in Congress has thus far shown how Republican congresswomen are increasingly working together as partisan women—distinguishing themselves from Democratic women and Republican men. Chapter 4 detailed how Republican women have come to recognize a distinct partisan-gender identity and how that identity was institutionalized through the creation of the Republican Women's Policy Committee (RWPC). Importantly, while the RWPC was not a top-down initiative by party leaders, I find that the success of the caucus was largely dependent on leadership's perception that promoting GOP women could enhance the image of the party and undercut claims of a Republican "war on women."

This form of "tokenism" (Kanter 1977b), in which minority group members are made disproportionately visible in comparison to dominant group members, also extends to Conference leadership positions. Notably, a House Republican woman is four times more likely than a House Democratic woman to be elected to a Conference/Caucus leadership role (Kanthak and Krause 2012, 27). Republican women have also often made up a larger proportion of their Conference leadership than Democratic women. As the main messaging vehicle of the party, the House Republican Conference is tasked with developing campaign and communication strategies. Conference leadership roles thus allow Republican women to be highly visible without the threat of more substantive proposals that can challenge the legislative power male party leaders.

Yet given changes in the way Republican congresswomen work together and organize collectively, I argue that it is important to take a closer look at the experiences of female Conference leaders. While Republican women are few in numbers, I would expect that recent Conference leaders nevertheless play important roles as critical actors (Childs and Krook 2009) by elevating women's voices within the party. In this chapter, I ask: How have the gendered

Gendering the GOP. Catherine N. Wineinger, Oxford University Press. © Oxford University Press 2022.
DOI: 10.1093/oso/9780197556542.003.0005

strategies and experiences of female House Republican Conference leaders changed over time?

To answer this question, I conducted case studies of three top female Conference leaders: Susan Molinari (R-NY), Jennifer Dunn (R-WA), and Cathy McMorris Rodgers (R-WA). Susan Molinari and Jennifer Dunn were Conference vice chairs in the 104th and 105th Congresses, respectively. Cathy McMorris Rodgers chaired the Conference in the 113th and 114th Congresses.[1] I compare each woman's pathway to leadership and experiences in carrying out gendered goals/priorities. Overall, I find that Cathy McMorris Rodgers was able to perpetuate and leverage the existence of a partisan-gender identity among Republican women in order to more easily amplify a collective, gendered party message.

Republican Congresswomen as Critical Actors

The link between women's descriptive and substantive representation in Congress is frequently used as an argument for increasing the number of women in elective office. However, these discussions are often framed in terms of critical mass (Kanter 1977a), or the theory that increasing the number of women to a certain proportion—typically 30 percent—of a legislative body will thereby increase the substantive representation of women. Rosabeth Moss Kanter (1977a) first discussed the theory of critical mass in her study of minority groups within corporations. Kanter argues that increasing the numerical composition of minority group members helps to transform them from "tokens" to "dominant members" (Kanter 1977a; 1977b). Thus, as the numerical composition of women and minorities changes, so do the dynamics within the corporation.

Building off of Kanter's study, Drude Dahlerup (1988) extends the concept of critical mass to women in the political arena, arguing that numbers matter in legislative institutions as well. Still, the impact of critical mass has at times been oversimplified;[2] the idea that merely increasing the presence of women in legislatures to an arbitrary percentage will bring about substantive changes ignores the *process* of institutional transformation (Childs and Krook 2006; 2008; 2009). Indeed, even Dahlerup pointed out that "it is not possible to conclude that these changes follow from any mixed number of women, e.g. 30 percent" (Dahlerup 1988, 287). She goes on to emphasize that there are examples of women in top positions who are able to shift perceptions about women in politics, and that "it is not the numbers that count, but the performance of a few outstanding women as role models" (Dahlerup 1988, 287).

Sarah Childs and Mona Krook (2008; 2009) have called for a shift away from analyses of critical mass to ones of critical *actors*. They argue that the focus on numerical composition overlooks the role that powerful individual actors play in shaping political institutions. Critical actors are defined as "legislators who initiate policy proposals on their own and/or embolden others to take steps to promote policies for women, regardless of the numbers of female representatives" (Childs and Krook 2009, 138). According to Childs and Krook, critical actors can enhance women's representation by reshaping political gender dynamics. Focusing on *action* rather than numbers allows us to shine light on the institutional processes that make women's representation possible.

This concept is particularly important for expanding our knowledge of Republican women's congressional representation. Examining representation through a framework of critical actors rather than critical mass presumes that the small number of Republican women in Congress does not automatically limit their impact on the institution. Indeed, as Kanthak and Krause (2012) show, the small number of Republican congresswomen has not prevented them from attaining certain leadership roles; on the contrary, it has given them direct opportunities for Conference leadership. Analyzing changes in the way Republican women use these roles to bolster their own influence within the party can provide further insight into the evolution of women's congressional representation.

Data and Methods

As discussed in Chapter 1, congressional polarization and, more significantly, party competition have resulted in a growing commitment to public relations by both congressional parties (Lee 2016; Malecha and Reagan 2012; Sellers 2010). With the goal of winning and maintaining control of Congress, political parties distinguish themselves from the opposing party by developing and disseminating cohesive messages and party brands (Harris 2013). This process has become increasingly structured in recent years (Meinke 2016), with both parties creating their own "'communications enterprises' to help them plan, coordinate, and manage their public relations efforts" (Malecha and Reagan 2012, 73).

Within the Republican Party's communications enterprise is the Republican Policy Committee, which works with party leaders to develop statements related to specific policies. Along the same lines, the National Republican Congressional Committee (NRCC) is "devoted to increasing the number of Republicans in the US House of Representatives" by recruiting/ funding competitive candidates and creating effective campaign messaging tactics.[3] Above all else, though, "the party's Conference is the core of the House Republicans' communications enterprise" (Malecha and Reagan 2012, 74). Conference leadership[4] works with the other communications arms of the party and provides staff to the Republican Theme Team[5] in order construct unified party messages and help rank-and-file members amplify those messages.

Given the significance of the House Republican Conference and the fact that women are more likely to be elected to Conference leadership roles, I conduct case studies of the three highest-ranking female Conference leaders during the periods on which this book is focused: Susan Molinari, vice chair in the 104th Congress; Jennifer Dunn, vice chair in the 105th Congress; and Cathy McMorris Rodgers, chair in the 113th and 114th Congresses. I include Jennifer Dunn in this study for two main reasons: first, there were no female Conference leaders in the 103rd Congress, and second, Dunn's ideological and personal similarities to McMorris Rodgers help pinpoint the effects of polarization and competition, as well as other institutional factors.

I once again use the elite interviews conducted by the Center for American Women and Politics (CAWP) during the 103rd, 104th, and 114th Congresses. For this chapter, I focus primarily on interviews with Republican women in Conference leadership. These include not only Molinari, Dunn, and McMorris Rodgers, but also Barbara Vucanovich (R-NV), Tillie Fowler (R-FL), and Virginia Foxx (R-NC), who served as Conference secretary in the 104th, 105th, and 113th/114th Congresses, respectively.[6] Interviews with lower-ranking female party leaders were also valuable in helping to understand the institutional dynamics at play. For instance, Sue Myrick (R-NC) was elected freshman class representative in the 104th Congress and reelected sophomore class representative in the 105th Congress. Ann Wagner (R-MO) was also elected as her class representative in the 113th and 114th Congresses (see Table 5.1 for a list of female House Republican leaders in each Congress).[7] Notably, while the earlier interviews pertained primarily to discussions about the 103rd and 104th Congresses, some interviews were conducted during the 105th Congress, between October 1997 and July

Table 5.1   Women in House Republican Leadership Positions, Highest to Lowest Rank

104th Congress	105th Congress	113th Congress	114th Congress
Susan Molinari (Conference Vice Chair)	Jennifer Dunn (Conference Vice Chair)	Cathy McMorris Rodgers (Conference Chair)	Cathy McMorris Rodgers (Conference Chair)
Barbara Vucanovich (Conference Secretary)	Tillie Fowler (Conference Secretary)	Lynn Jenkins (Conference Vice Chair)	Lynn Jenkins (Conference Vice Chair)
Sue Myrick (Freshman Representative)	Sue Myrick (Sophomore Representative)	Virginia Foxx (Conference Secretary)	Virginia Foxx (Conference Secretary)
		Ann Wagner (Freshman Representative)	Ann Wagner (Sophomore Representative)
			Mimi Walters (Freshman Representative)

1998.[8] Thus, while Dunn, Fowler, and Myrick recalled their time in the 104th Congress (1995–1997), they also spoke about their experiences in leadership during the 105th Congress (1997–1999).

I use these interviews to compare the experiences of female Conference leaders; to shine light on any institutional differences; and to better understand the relationships between Conference leaders, other women in the party, and male party leaders. This interview data was again supplemented with primary and secondary sources from the Library of Congress, the National Archives, C-SPAN oral history interviews, news articles, and memoirs written by members of Congress. These sources offered further insight into the political climate and provided additional context for the claims made by interviewees.

Susan Molinari: Conference Vice Chair, 104th Congress (1995–1997)

Susan Molinari was elected to the House of Representatives in a special election in March 1990 following the resignation of her father, Congressman Guy Molinari.[9] Prior to her congressional career, Molinari worked as a finance assistant for the Republican Governor's Association and was elected to the city council of New York, where she served as the only Republican member.[10] Originally assigned to work on the Small Business and Public Works and Transportation Committees, she served on the Budget Committee in the 104th Congress (1995–1997) and was elected vice chair of the Conference following the 1994 midterms.[11]

Molinari was a moderate Republican and explicitly feminist in her many of her policy stances. She was pro-choice, was eager to join the Congressional Caucus for Women's Issues (CCWI; Gertzog 2004), and "believed more women's issues should [have been] included [in the Contract with America]" (Molinari 1998, 179). During her tenure as vice chair of the Republican Conference, however, Molinari consistently toed the party line and even campaigned for pro-life Republican men. The gender gap was very much on the minds of Republican leaders at this time, and Molinari did see herself as role model for women and young girls. Nevertheless, she did not develop specific outreach campaigns for women and viewed her leadership role as a way to bring the party together.

Pathway to Leadership: Paved with IOUs

In response to Democratic success in the 1992 "Year of the Woman," Republican Party leaders made efforts to mobilize women voters and elect women candidates. Representative Newt Gingrich (R-GA), who had openly discussed his efforts to close the gender gap, "created a 'buddy system'" prior to the 1994 election, "linking female Republican members of Congress and female congressional candidates around the country."[12] As discussed in Chapter 4, after being elected Speaker of the House in 1995, Gingrich worked to bring House Republican women together by scheduling biweekly meetings and appointing women to leadership positions.

Yet while women's visibility in the party was important to many party leaders,[13] Molinari said that she was not explicitly recruited to run for Conference vice chair. She claimed there were colleagues who told her, "I think you should do this. We need a woman, someone who is comfortable speaking [and] disagreeing."[14] But her decision to run was a result of her "own personal ambition" and a "feeling that there needed to be a woman in leadership."[15] As a moderate Republican deeply concerned with women's issues, Molinari viewed herself as an important dissenting voice in party leadership who could share her opinions with Speaker Gingrich and John Boehner, then-chair of the Republican Conference. "I think it's good for the party," she said, "It's great to have additional voices and dissent."[16]

In her 2012 interview with the Office of the Historian, Molinari suggests this was actually one of the reasons she *was* elected vice chair: "I think one of the reasons that I did win was that there was a recognition that they needed women in leadership and a moderate. So, I did enter this institution at a time when diversity was not present but was recognized as a necessity and a good political thing to have, and I benefited from that as opposed to being hampered by it."[17] Of course, this is not to say that Molinari did not face challenges. She spoke specifically about the gendered hurdles she faced while running for vice chair, arguing that she had to work harder to build personal relationships with men in the party:

> I was running against a great guy from Florida named Cliff Stearns, and I had people who would come up to me and say . . . "I'd love to vote for you, but Cliff and I . . . have become such good friends at the gym." Hm, the gym I'm not allowed into? Back in the day, we had our separate gyms . . . I don't necessarily need to work out with a bunch of sweaty men, but that was another one of those occasions where you interacted not as Members of Congress . . . I wasn't allowed to be in the House Gym, and I had to overcome that from a relationship standpoint.[18]

One way Molinari was able to overcome this gendered obstacle was to support and campaign for her Republican colleagues. "The road to victory," she wrote in her memoir, "was paved with the IOUs I could collect by helping Republican candidates all over the country" (Molinari 1998, 160). Molinari also did this with the help of her husband, fellow Republican member of the House and chair of the NRCC, Bill Paxon (R-NY). She notes that her husband was "very helpful" in building support from her Republican colleagues: "I surround myself with strong political people. One happened to be my father; one happened to be my husband."[19] She and Paxon campaigned for Republican candidates across the country—in 84 House districts and 36 states[20]—and across the ideological spectrum (Gertzog 2004, 42). Through this display of party loyalty, Molinari built important relationships and eventually defeated Stearns. She became the highest-ranking Republican woman, the second woman ever elected to Conference leadership, and the first CCWI member to be elected to party leadership (Gertzog 2004, 42).

Priorities and Strategies: A Big Tent Party

Molinari, described in the *Washington Post* as "a gum-snapping feminist" and the first woman to ever wear pants on the House floor,[21] believed her position in leadership could help her promote some of the more feminist policies discussed in the CCWI (Gertzog 2004). She viewed her role as one in which she could disagree with party leadership and work to bring moderate and conservative Republicans together. She told CAWP in an interview, "In terms of getting [women] to the points of power and influence, the 104th [Congress], from a Republican perspective anyway, has seen 180-degree change. So we are able to affect the policies that we care about maybe a little bit easier."[22]

But as vice chair of the Conference, Molinari was first and foremost a messenger for the Republican Party—and a good one at that. A spokesman for Majority Leader Dick Armey told a reporter in 1995, "We instantly recognized that while Susan Molinari may not agree with the majority of [the conference], she's very politically astute . . . She's also good with media, she has a sense of what matters in the Northeast, and better than anyone at the table she understands women voters."[23] Bill Paxon made a similar statement: "Susan is very knowledgeable in communications strategy, which is an area quite frankly not many in our leadership have a strong hand in."[24] Indeed, even Molinari understood that she was meant to be a loyal voice for the party—particularly for the Contract with America—and she viewed it as an opportunity for many Republican women: "[Party leadership] wanted you out there espousing and speaking and doing talk shows and getting on [TV], particularly CNN, and doing whatever you needed to do to get the message out there, to be a messenger for the Republican Party. Women did a lot of that."[25]

Molinari was an effective communicator who often refrained from speaking about her more moderate positions in order to contribute to the perception of a unified Republican Party. In 1996, GOP presidential nominee, Bob Dole, asked Molinari to be a keynote speaker at the Republican National Convention. The decision was immediately reported as an effort to reach out to women voters and help close the gender gap.[26] But while Molinari was inherently a different messenger, her messages did note deviate from the party's messages and, notably, were not specific to her gender. Unlike Jennifer Dunn and Cathy McMorris Rodgers, as I demonstrate in the following sections, Molinari did not have explicitly gendered messaging goals. She publicly echoed the conservative policy stances with which she agreed, and she attempted to work behind the scenes to push congressional leaders on those which she did not.

Overall, though, Molinari was largely unsuccessful in her attempts at moderating her party's policies. She would later write in her memoir:

> I'd become Vice Chair of the Republican Conference . . . but that was as far as a moderate female from the northeast could go in the Republican con-ference. While my input was accepted and sometimes even acted upon, I could never feel like a real player. I was a member of the leadership, but I was not, for example, a member of Newt's inner circle, the Speaker's ad-visory group, which is where ninety-nine percent of the decisions that are supposed to be made in leadership meetings are actually formulated. (Molinari 1998, 260)

One Democratic congressman told a reporter, "The Republicans don't be-come any more pro-choice by having her in the room . . . She's the apotheosis of style over substance. She doesn't change a thing."[27] Molinari's persistent and public support of the Contract with America also earned her the "femi-Newtie" label—what Pat Schroeder (D-CO) called Republican women who did not openly challenge their party's conservative stances (Molinari 1998, 186).

At the same time, Barbara Vucanovich (R-NV), as Conference secre-tary, was passionate about another gendered issue: getting more Republican women elected to office. While they had become friends during their time in Congress, Vucanovich supported anti-abortion policies and was significantly more conservative than Molinari.[28] In her interview with CAWP, Vucanovich complained about the Speaker's frequent meetings with Republican women, finding them to be unproductive when it came to discussing issues on which there were clear disagreements between the women.[29] Nevertheless, she said Speaker Gingrich was supportive of Republican women working on their own gender-related projects. In May of 1996, Vucanovich partnered with po-litical consultants and the Republican Network to Elect Women (RENEW), a Washington-based Republican women's organization, to host the first Women Leaders Summit.

A two-day conference of Republican women leaders from various indus-tries across the country, the Women Leaders Summit functioned as a way to empower Republican women and to demonstrate the GOP's commitment to women. Unlike Molinari, Vucanovich's goal was less about moderating the party and more about highlighting how women's experiences and interests were in line with the Republican Party's principles. Vucanovich wrote in her memoir, "I felt at the time, and still do, that Republicans were not getting their message out to women in America that there was room in the Republican Party for women from all walks of life and with varying philosophies. The summit was an opportunity to showcase Republican women and our ideals" (Vucanovich and Cafferata 2005, 197).

The two women in Conference leadership positions in the 104th Congress, Susan Molinari and Barbara Vucanovich, both viewed their gender as an important part of their identity, albeit in different ways. Due in part to ideological differences, though, there was little concerted effort between them to promote a unified, gendered party message. In the following sections, I show how Jennifer Dunn's communications efforts as vice chair were more explicitly gendered, and how Cathy McMorris Rodgers has been more easily able to amplify a collective voice.

Jennifer Dunn: Conference Vice Chair, 105th Congress (1997–1999)

Jennifer Dunn was one of only three new Republican women elected to the House of Representatives during the "Year of the Woman" in 1992. Prior to running for Congress, she was chair of the Washington State Republican Party from 1981–1992 and a delegate to the United Nations Commission on the Status of Women in 1984 and 1990.[30] Though she lacked prior legislative experience, Dunn was elected secretary and then vice chair of the House Republican Conference in her second term with the help of Speaker Newt Gingrich.

Succeeding Molinari as Conference vice chair, Dunn focused primarily on narrowing the gender gap and reaching out to women. In many ways, Dunn was the perfect spokesperson for the role. Her life experiences—the fact that she had been, at different points in her life, a wife, a stay-at-home mom, and a working single mother—allowed her to connect with women from various walks of life. Some also noted that Dunn's femininity distinguished her from other party leaders. Hanna Rosin, in a 1997 *New York Magazine* article, wrote:

In the U.S. House of Representatives' popularity contest, this year's Northwestern Glamour Girl is Jennifer Dunn, the fetching blonde congresswoman from the Nordstrom suburbs of Seattle . . . With her lemon-meringue suits and curlered hair, Dunn offers everything the rest of her party does not: poignancy, poise, smoothness, a lush bit of femininity. "If you watch her for ten minutes, it becomes apparent why she is a rising star," says one proud Republican consultant. "You have Newt Gingrich with his bulging waistline and Dick Armey with his bulging neckline, and then you have Jennifer Dunn—smart, beautiful, cleans up well. The total package."[31]

This "Glamour Girl" depiction of Dunn, in some ways, functioned as a double-edged sword. On the one hand, members of her own party viewed her femininity as an asset, hoping she would soften perceptions of a hyper-masculine, anti-woman Republican Party. On the other hand, as I discuss later in this chapter, it worked to tokenize her and made climbing the leadership ladder more challenging.

Nevertheless, Jennifer Dunn was a trailblazer for women in the institution, becoming the highest-ranking Republican woman the 105th Congress and the first woman of either party to run for House majority leader. With the help of male party leaders, Dunn quickly navigated her way onto the Ways and Means Committee and into Conference leadership. In her time as vice chair of the House Republican Conference, she worked primarily to change the messaging strategy of the party. Her work unquestionably inspired future Republican women leaders, including Cathy McMorris Rodgers.

Pathway to Leadership: Gingrich Protégé

Following the 1994 Republican Revolution, Jennifer Dunn "became a protégé of Newt Gingrich," working closely with him to implement the Contract with America (Heffernan 2012, 45). While pro-choice on abortion, Dunn was more ideologically conservative than Susan Molinari, and according to her brother, "100 percent a Reagan Republican" (Heffernan 2012, 17).[32] As a second-term member and with the help of the newly-elected Speaker of the House, Dunn became the fifth woman to land a seat on the powerful Ways and Means committee. In the following Congress, she decided to run for Conference secretary. Dunn knew she wanted to be in leadership since the moment she entered Congress. But while she had "laid the groundwork" from the beginning, she said in a C-SPAN interview:

> I decided that I'd wait for a while because there were so many top-level people in the Republican side of the House that it wasn't the right thing for me to do at the beginning. But later on I thought, "I could do this." And now that we're in the majority it would be great fun because we were making history . . . When you have confidence that you're going to work hard, that you're going to be open and fair and have integrity and represent the people you're leading, then that's a good time to move into leadership. I did that after I'd been here for four years.[33]

Running unopposed, Dunn won her seat as secretary, joining Conference chair John Boehner and Conference vice chair Susan Molinari, who had won her re-election.

In May of 1997, Molinari unexpectedly announced her retirement from Congress,[34] and Dunn gave up her seat as secretary to run in the special election for vice chair. This time, Dunn would run against a colleague from the Ways and Means Committee, Representative Jim Nussle of Iowa. "With a strong endorsement from Gingrich" (Heffernan 2012, 47), Dunn "won big," defeating Nussle by a two-to-one margin.[35] At the same time, Tillie Fowler (R-FL) also won the race for Conference secretary. Dunn viewed their victories as an important step forward for the image of the party, saying that it "shows a real validation of the fact Republicans want women to be not just in the ranks but in the highest levels of leadership" (Heffernan 2012, 48).

Priorities and Strategies: Toward a Softer Conservative Message

President Bill Clinton won his 1996 re-election with what was, at the time, the largest voting gender gap in history.[36] Jennifer Dunn was dedicated to closing this gap, telling CAWP researchers that it "should be a political motivating and energizing impetus" and that "it's obviously very important" to her.[37] As Conference vice chair, Dunn worked to create what she called "a softer edge to the conservative message" (Heffernan 2012, 49) by speaking on conservative issues—"on tax, on welfare, on crime, on education, on health care, on anything you want to talk about"[38]—in a way that resonated with women. In her CAWP interview, she elaborated: "I think we can make a difference if we begin to focus our message and interpret and translate the policies that we are behind and help generate." Conference chair John Boehner agreed with Dunn's assessment, saying, "Clearly, our message hasn't been articulated as well to women in America as it could be" (Heffernan 2012, 48).

In 1998, Dunn founded The Permanent Majority Project, which focused on reaching out to women voters and inspiring women's interest in the party. With women on board, she argued, Republicans could retain a permanent majority in Congress. Dunn also hosted that year's Republican Women Leaders Forum, focusing on empowering and energizing women in the party. Her strategy as Conference vice chair involved giving "women a much greater responsibility in being a messenger of the Republican message"[39] and educating male members on how best to speak about Republican policies. She placed particular emphasis on what she called "finishing the sentence." "Don't just say a big blend of things," Dunn would tell her Republican colleagues, "Finish the sentence. Tell them we want tax relief, but why. That can be money in your pocket that you can choose to spend on child care, and that sort of thing."[40] Doing this, Dunn maintained, could help women understand how conservative policies would benefit their lives and the lives of their families.

Despite conducting research "to identify what women expect from their federal leaders" (Heffernan 2012, 49), Dunn worked more often to bring a palatable Republican message to women rather than bringing women's policy concerns to Republican leaders. In fact, at times, Dunn was so focused on messaging over actual policy details that it could be frustrating to her colleagues. In an interview with *New York Magazine*, one Republican staffer recalled a meeting of Republican women in which Representative Nancy Johnson (R-CT) attempted to discuss specific amendments to a bill she believed the women should consider supporting. The staffer noted that, much to the dismay of Susan Molinari, Dunn (Conference secretary at the time) repeatedly cut Johnson off, emphasizing the importance of messaging strategy rather than the minutia of legislation.[41]

Of course, this is not to say that Jennifer Dunn did not care about policy. It is clear from interviews with Dunn that she believed the perspectives of Republican women could help to advance the interests of the party. Dunn used her platform as vice chair to speak about a variety of issues and the way those issues—from education to taxes—affected the lives of women. Moreover, her gendered life experiences often informed her policy positions in addition to her messaging strategy. In a 1997 C-SPAN interview, for example, Dunn said,

> I like to involve a lot of stories in my speeches. I like to personalize things a lot. For example, I'm talking to a group on welfare reform. I like to tell them why the Republicans put together the package the way that we did . . . And I use my own experiences. Why child care is so important to finance as we move welfare parents off welfare into the workforce because I remember what it was like when I was having to work and get good child care for my children. I was always concerned about it.[42]

As discussed in Chapters 2 and 3, welfare reform, or the Personal Responsibility and Work Opportunity Reconciliation Act of 1996 (PRWORA), included an amendment that increased funding for childcare. According to Dunn, "it was the Republican women who put that amendment together."[43]

Indeed, while Dunn's main strategy as vice chair was to reframe the conservative message, she also viewed the role of Republican women Conference leaders as important for shaping legislation in the first place. Dunn spoke about herself and Tillie Fowler (R-FL), who was Conference Secretary at the time, as policy resources for men in the party:

> Out of the seven members of leadership who were elected, two of us are women and we're very practical. We're both women who have juggled many, many life experiences, and I've been a single mother for 20 years, since my kids were six and eight. So there are issues I understand and can interpret for my male colleagues. I have become a resource that they turn to on certain votes to say, "Is this really something we want to do or something we don't want to do?" Now that we control the majority, that kind of thinking starts much earlier because we generate the legislation now. So I think when we're in the room, and with the general training that we've begun to do with our male colleagues, I think we've begun to have quite an impact.[44]

It was not an easy feat to be at the leadership table attempting to convince male Republican leaders that women's perspectives matter, although Dunn was certainly committed to doing so. In one particularly heated moment, "Dunn interrupted a tax-cutting diatribe by Majority Leader Richard Armey, urging him to consider the impact of tax cuts on the programs many women were finding indispensable" (Gertzog 2004, 140).

One challenge that Dunn faced as vice chair was that she was "unable to establish a thoroughly trustful working relationship with Conference chair John Boehner" (Gertzog 2004, 140). While Boehner agreed with Dunn's general approach to messaging, he was reluctant to hand over too much power to the women in the Conference. In fact, when Dunn asked to be given more control over the Conference's communication strategies and finances, Boehner said he was unsure "whether he had the authority to delegate more power" to her (Gertzog 2004, 140). As Conference vice chair in the 107th Congress (2001–2003), Deborah Pryce (R-OH) noted a similarly difficult relationship with Boehner (Gertzog 2004, 140).

Another challenge was that the Republican women in the 104th and 105th Congresses were far less ideologically cohesive than they are today. According to Barbara Vucanovich (R-NV), even when Republican women gathered together for informal dinners, there were intense discussions among them regarding policy. "Marge Roukema and Nancy Johnson . . . would get into almost knock-down, drag-out battles!" Vucanovich said, "Whoa! And I couldn't believe how strongly they felt on certain issues . . . Nobody saw it exactly the same way, and they were all Republican women!"[45] Even on welfare reform, where Republican women were perceived to work together, "It was not monolithic," Vucanovich said, "And I think that a lot of people just plunk every woman together. They're all pro-life or . . . they all think the same way. Well, they don't."[46]

Despite these challenges, Speaker Gingrich remained supportive of Republican women's outreach efforts. As Tillie Fowler saw it, Gingrich worked hard to listen to the concerns of everyone in the party: "His mantra is 'Listen, Learn, and Lead.' He is very good . . . about . . . finding out where the problems are and . . . work[ing] them out."[47] Dunn agreed with that sentiment, saying that the Speaker was open to letting women in the party take the reins on the gender gap issue:

When I'm [meeting with Speaker Gingrich about] my gender gap project . . . I say, 'This is what we want to do. Are you with me on this? I'm going to bring this to the leadership table.' . . . And he'll say, 'Yes, yes.' He'll come and speak when we have our gender gap sessions . . . and he'll come to my vice chairman's advisory board of all the women lobbyists . . . because they know the issue, and know what we've done to take credit for, and what we haven't done that we need to write into legislation. It's just a different form of his supporting what we're trying to do.[48]

Barbara Vucanovich further noted that meetings with Gingrich, while challenging because there were many ideological disagreements among the women, also gave women an opportunity to pursue gendered initiatives. She said in her 1997 CAWP interview, "[Speaker Gingrich] did allow us all to go off and do these various things. And I think Deborah Pryce is still meeting with women lobbyists and different groups."[49]

Indeed, Deborah Pryce (R-OH), who would go on to be elected the first female Conference chair in 2002, helped launch a political action committee in 1997. Value in Electing Women PAC (VIEW PAC) is, still to this day, dedicated to electing Republican women to Congress. Pryce told a reporter in 1997, "If American women voters see more women Members and realize that [the Republican Party is] not an all-white-male party, they will look more closely at us and give us their ear more readily."[50] According to VIEW PAC, incumbent members of Congress "have no official operational role," but they do often attend events and can serve as honorary board members—which Cathy McMorris Rodgers would later go on to do.[51]

Overall, Jennifer Dunn's priority as Conference vice chair was to narrow the gender gap by creating and disseminating a party message that would appeal to women voters. While ultimately unsuccessful in closing that gap (the 2000 presidential election resulted in a 10-point gender gap),[52] Dunn did develop explicitly gendered frames for her messages in a way that Molinari did not. In her 1999 State of the Union Response, for instance, Dunn used her experience as a single mother to discuss conservative economic policies:

> I've been a single mother since my boys were little—six and eight. My life in those days was taken up trying to make ends meet . . . I know how that knot in the pit of your stomach feels. I've been there. I'm still a practical person. You heard the president make a lot of promises to a lot of people tonight, but I'd like to talk to you about two very practical Republican priorities: tax relief and Social Security reform. (Heffernan 2012)

Dunn also had the help of other women in the party like Deborah Pryce and Tillie Fowler, who were particularly interested in creating opportunities for women to run as Republican candidates.

Still, Jennifer Dunn faced institutional and ideological challenges that made it difficult to promote a more unified message. First, ideological disagreements among Republican women during this era prevented them from speaking collectively from a gendered perspective. While Republican women were placed in public messaging roles on television and in Conference leadership, my analyses of partisan woman-invoked rhetoric in Chapters 2 and 3 suggest there was comparatively little concerted effort among women in the party to engage in explicitly gendered messaging tactics. Second, as vice chair, Dunn did not have the authority that John Boehner had as Conference chair. While it is unclear whether Boehner's reluctance to give Dunn more control over Conference finances and messaging strategies had any tangible effect, it was nevertheless one barrier that Dunn faced during her time in leadership. In the following section, I show that Cathy McMorris Rodgers and Jennifer Dunn had nearly identical gendered priorities and messaging strategies; their leadership experiences differed mainly in that McMorris Rodgers was able to leverage institutional and political opportunities that had not been available to Dunn.

Cathy McMorris Rodgers: Conference Chair, 113th and 114th Congresses (2013–2017)

The impact that Jennifer Dunn had on her colleagues and on future Republican women leaders is clear. Speaking about Dunn, Cathy McMorris Rodgers (R-WA), chair of the House Republican Conference from 2013 to 2019, remarked, "Wow. What a foundation that she laid. Today it is common for us to refer back to the work that Jennifer Dunn did. We certainly recognize that we're standing on her shoulders" (Heffernan 2012, 51). McMorris Rodgers was no stranger to politics or leadership when she was elected to the House in 2004. She became a member of the Washington State House at age 24, where she served for ten years—two of which were spent as minority leader.

Like Susan Molinari and Jennifer Dunn, McMorris Rodgers entered Conference leadership at a time when her party recognized the necessity of attracting women voters. Barack Obama won the 2008 presidential election with a 7-point gender gap,[53] and that November, McMorris Rodgers was elected Conference vice chair. Following President Obama's reelection and another large, 10-point gender gap in 2012,[54] McMorris Rodgers was elected Conference chair with the backing of Speaker John Boehner (R-OH).

The influence of Jennifer Dunn is evident in the gendered communication strategies of McMorris Rodgers. "I find myself today saying many of the things that I heard Jennifer say when I heard her from afar," said McMorris Rodgers, "I do think conservative women bring an important voice to the debate and the Republican Party" (Heffernan 2012, 51). As Conference chair, McMorris Rodgers used her position to advance the interests of the GOP and to amplify the voices of women within the party. In many ways, her pathway to leadership and her messaging efforts are similar to Dunn's, though in important ways they are also unique. In what follows, I illustrate how McMorris Rodgers took advantage of changes in the institutional and political landscapes in an effort to give Republican women a louder and more unified voice in Republican Party politics.

Pathway to Leadership: Encouragement from Boehner

Although Cathy McMorris Rodgers had leadership experience during her time in the state legislature, she did not come to Congress with the intention of becoming a party leader. She said in her interview with CAWP,

> For me, it is never about a title or a position. It's really about wanting to be effective. John Boehner encouraged me to run for leadership, which is interesting to note. I didn't get to Congress and say, "This is what I want to do." It was John Boehner who called me up and encouraged me to seek a leadership position.[55]

Following the 2008 presidential election, then-Minority Leader Boehner tapped McMorris Rodgers for the position of Conference vice chair. Boehner's spokesman at the time, Michael Steel, said, "She impressed him as being energetic, sincere, hardworking, a team player, and someone people kind of relate to very well."[56] McMorris Rodgers ran unopposed, becoming the highest-ranking woman in Republican leadership.

In 2011, McMorris Rodgers called Boehner, who had recently been elected Speaker of the House, and told him that she intended to run for Conference chair the following year. McMorris Rodgers ran against Representative Tom Price of Georgia, who at the time chaired the Republican Policy Committee.

Price received the endorsements of more conservative members—including 2012 vice presidential nominee Paul Ryan (R-WI) and then-chair of the Conference Jeb Hensarling (R-TX). Nevertheless, with Speaker Boehner's endorsement, McMorris Rodgers won her race, becoming the fourth-ranking Republican in the House and only the second woman in history to hold the position.[57]

Boehner's endorsement of McMorris Rodgers and her subsequent victory were criticized by some as an empty symbolic gesture. Many believed her gender—and her ability to speak as a woman against "war on women" rhetoric—was the primary reason behind her rise to Conference chair.[58] McMorris Rodgers rejected that sentiment. "I think it's an easy shot for people to make, to say that it's just because I was a woman," she said, "There was a lot taken into consideration, and it was the leadership that I had shown in the past."[59] Yet while the tokenization of McMorris Rodgers is debatable, her emphasis on women's mobilization, recruitment, and promotion is not.

Priorities and Strategies: Amplifying a Collective Voice

Cathy McMorris Rodgers underscored in her CAWP interview that, as a Conference leader, she was "responsible for communications" and was passionate about making sure House Republicans could effectively communicate issues not only as individual members, "but also as a body."[60] Following the 2008 election, Cathy McMorris Rodgers worked to modernize the Republican Party and improve the online influence of GOP members. As Conference vice chair, she initiated campaigns that incentivized the creative use of social media, and she enhanced the online presence of party leaders through blogs and videos.[61] This boom in social media and online engagement coincided with her efforts to promote a more woman-friendly image of the Republican Party.

Like Dunn, McMorris Rodgers used her Conference leadership positions to soften the message of the GOP, attempting to make it more appealing to women and families. In 2014, while serving as Conference chair, McMorris Rodgers became the fifth woman[62] to the deliver the Republican Response to the State of the Union address. In line with Jennifer Dunn's messaging style, McMorris Rodgers took time to speak about her personal experiences as a mother and how those experiences align with the principles and policies of the Republican Party:

I was single when I was elected—but it wasn't long before I met Brian, a retired Navy commander, and now we have three beautiful children, one who was born just eight weeks ago. Like all parents, we have high hopes and dreams for our children, but we also know what it's like to face challenges. Three days after we gave birth to our son, Cole, we got news no parent expects. Cole was diagnosed with Down syndrome. The doctors told us he could have endless complications, heart defects, even early Alzheimer's. They told us all the problems. But when we looked at our son, we saw only possibilities. We saw a gift from God . . . The President talks a lot about income inequality. But the real gap we face today is one of opportunity inequality. And with this Administration's policies, that gap has become far too wide. . . . Republicans have plans to close the gap. Plans that focus on jobs first without more spending, government bailouts, and red tape. Every day, we're working to expand our economy, one manufacturing job, nursing degree and small business at a time. We have plans to improve our education and training systems so you have the choice to determine where your kids go to school, so college is affordable, and skills training is modernized. And yes, it's time to honor our history of legal immigration.[63]

McMorris Rodgers believed that she could build support for a myriad of conservative policies by discussing her individual experiences of motherhood, thereby connecting with voters on a more personal level. But more than that, McMorris Rodgers focused on giving women a visible platform in the party. To her, the messenger was just as important as the message itself. She told CAWP, "People are going to listen to what [women] have to say in a different way than perhaps they've heard from their male counterparts."[64] Changing the messenger, McMorris Rodgers believed, would be an effective tool for reaching a broader audience.

To accomplish this, Cathy McMorris Rodgers took advantage of various political and institutional opportunities that were not available to Jennifer Dunn. First, as described in Chapter 4, the broader political landscape encouraged national and state party leaders to prioritize women's outreach and candidate recruitment. Following a loss in the 2012 election during which claims of a Republican "war on women" were used to discredit GOP candidates, the Republican National Committee (RNC) released an autopsy report in 2013 that prescribed recommendations for reaching out to women and minority voters.[65] That same year in the House, the NRCC launched Project Growing Republican Opportunities for Women (Project

GROW), an initiative dedicated to recruiting and electing more Republican women candidates.[66] And later that month, women from six Republican committees—the RNC, NRCC, National Republican Senatorial Committee, Republican Governors Association, Republican State Leadership Committee, and College Republican National Committee—announced the launch of Women on the Right UNITE, which focused "on various sectors including recruitment, messaging, polling, training for candidates, localized field events, fundraising, strong digital presence and harnessing the power of data to increase female voter participation" (Burrell 2018, 106). That Republicans were already united in these gendered efforts created a welcoming environment for McMorris Rodgers's priorities as Conference chair.

A second advantage was McMorris Rodgers's institutional rank and the gender composition of Conference leadership. Whereas Jennifer Dunn was often at the whim of John Boehner's decisions, McMorris Rodgers, as chair, had more control over the Conference's finances and messaging strategies. In addition, two other women, Lynn Jenkins of Kansas and Virginia Foxx of North Carolina, were Conference vice chair and secretary, respectively. At the leadership table more broadly were Ann Wagner (R-MO) and Mimi Walters (R-CA), who were their respective class representatives (see Table 5.1).

These women were sympathetic to McMorris Rodgers's communications efforts and, in the case of Wagner and Foxx, were also in valuable institutional positions. Ann Wagner, for instance, was involved with the NRCC in helping to recruit women candidates. As I sat with her in her Capitol Hill office, Wagner told me in her interview, "Probably the [biggest] role that I have played specifically for women within our conference is . . . across the street at the NRCC. I have worked on, very aggressively, along with Congresswoman Diane Black and others that are supportive, women's recruitment."[67] As a member of the Rules Committee and someone who had a good working relationship with Speaker Boehner,[68] Virginia Foxx also encouraged Republican women to speak out on a broad range of issues. In her CAWP interview, McMorris Rodgers pointed to this specifically, saying, "Virginia Foxx, as the secretary of the Conference, has really worked to get women involved in the debate. She's also on the Rules Committee, so she's on the floor a lot, no matter what the legislation may be. [She] wants to have women engaged in the debate no matter what the issue."[69] An institutional environment in which congresswomen were not only passionate about Republican women's representation, but were also in other formal communications roles, provided

McMorris Rodgers with a messaging network that was not available to previous female Conference leaders.

Third, the institutionalization of a *partisan-gender identity* gave House Republican women the ability to meet and discuss issues collectively. When I asked Virginia Foxx whether the election of more conservative women to Congress had strengthened the comradery among Republican women, she replied, "I do think we have good comradery . . . When we need to, we get together as a women's group."[70] That comradery, as described in Chapter 4, manifested in 2012 as the RWPC, the first Republican women's caucus in Congress. While serving as chair of the RWPC, Renee Ellmers told a reporter, "I think the culture that has existed within our own party has been led by men, by and large. Women have not necessarily been putting themselves out there for recognition. . . . Now we have a group of women empowering each other, whereas in the past women were more independent agents."[71]

Indeed, this collective empowerment also gave Republican women the opportunity to promote more unified, gendered party messages. In her interview with CAWP, Cathy McMorris Rodgers told us that the RWPC "absolutely" makes women's leadership more visible and that, as RWPC chair, Ellmers would "organize special orders on the House floor where we can go down and talk about a particular issue."[72] According to McMorris Rodgers, getting women to be messengers on every issue was important, and "the Republican Women's Policy Committee [was] . . . kind of the gathering of all that."[73]

Finally, aside from the more substantive benefits of women in leadership roles, entering Congress with women in party leadership and an established caucus for Republican women seems to have given newer Republican congresswomen a stronger sense of partisan-gender identity. Making a direct comparison to Democratic women, Elise Stefanik (R-NY), who was elected in 2014, told CAWP, "Half of our [elected Republican] leadership is women. And that is a higher percentage than on the Democratic side."[74] Elected to the 113th Congress in 2012, Susan Brooks (R-IN) pointed to the women in leadership as a sign of the opportunities available for Republican women:

> Ann Wagner was chosen to be the representative of our class, . . . [and] she's still there . . . at the leadership table. Interestingly, this class of the 114th Congress . . . chose a woman also, Mimi Walters, so she's at the leadership table. And then when I got here, all of our Conference positions, Cathy McMorris Rogers, Virginia Fox, and Lynn Jenkins were elected and

defeated men for their spots in the Conference leadership. So I've been really pleased at the opportunities presented to the women and there just aren't enough of us.[75]

Indeed, Ann Wagner, also first elected in 2012, was immediately motivated to run for leadership and to work her way onto important committees:

When I won my election in November the very first time, we celebrated that night and then I told everybody, "Alright, 9:00 a.m., back at the campaign office. You can wear your fuzzy slippers, but we have another campaign to run." And that was to sit at the leadership table. I wanted to be elected by my classmates that were entering Congress . . . because I wanted to have a female voice there and be a part of shaping the agenda and messaging and communicating that agenda.[76]

Wagner went on, referencing the importance of women's descriptive representation at the leadership table: "My goodness, between Cathy McMorris Rodgers, Virginia Foxx, Lynn Jenkins, myself, Mimi Walters . . . there are at least five women that sit at that leadership table in the Republican [conference]. That's why I also thought it was important to . . . [get] on a top committee . . . that a lot of women just shy away from"[77] Wagner was elected class representative, earned positions on the Financial Services Committee and Foreign Affairs Committee, and has been vice ranking member on each in the 116th and 117th Congresses. "You have to work hard," she told me, "You have to prove yourself, and you have to step out of comfort zone and step up and go after these positions if you're going to make a difference."[78]

Much of this motivation among newer Republican congresswomen to seek leadership and actively mentor other Republican women can be attributed to the leadership style of Cathy McMorris Rodgers. Several women members talked about McMorris Rodgers as someone who would take them under her wing—both as candidates and as newly elected representatives. Elise Stefanik (R-NY), at the time the youngest woman ever elected to Congress, has been outspoken about the mentoring she received from McMorris Rodgers.[79] Mimi Walters (R-CA) and Susan Brooks (R-IN) have also discussed the importance of mentoring women candidates as a result of the support they received from McMorris Rodgers. Walters, first elected in 2014, said, "As a Member of Congress, I feel it is my duty to help mentor younger women. When I was running, Cathy was wonderful to us."[80] Susan Brooks noted that *collective* mentoring efforts for female candidates really began after the 2012 election:

> We [Republican congresswomen] are very much about mentoring women who are thinking about running and it has happened since I've been here. It didn't happen for me to get here, really, except for Cathy McMorris Rogers, [who] did mentor me a bit. But nobody else really did, and then . . . a number of us . . . said, hey, this has to be more formalized for women who are running.[81]

Indeed, as honorary chair of VIEW PAC, McMorris Rodgers has been passionate about recruiting and mentoring Republican women candidates—even at the primary level.[82] Brooks went on to say that Republican women in the 114th Congress were "making sure that we are helping new members and that we are really supporting each other as our female members are trying to strive to get more leadership positions."[83]

As Conference chair, Cathy McMorris Rodgers also sought to amplify a unified and explicitly gendered party message. While both Dunn and McMorris Rodgers were committed to communicating a softer conservative message, McMorris Rodgers's experiences differed due to various institutional and political factors that allowed her to work more easily with an ideologically cohesive group of female colleagues. Notably, McMorris Rodgers worked to simultaneously leverage and strengthen a partisan-gender identity among House Republican women, elevating Republican women as party messengers and emphasizing the importance of mentorship and comradery. One result of this can be seen in the increasing use of partisan woman-invoked rhetoric on the House floor (see Chapters 2 and 3). But while female Conference leaders have the ability to function as critical actors for Republican women's representation, the gatekeeping role of male party leaders and the continued valuation of women as tokens still presents challenges for reaching higher levels of leadership within the party.

Climbing the Ladder: Beyond Conference Leadership?

While women in recent years have been consistently represented in Republican Conference leadership, they have yet to rise beyond that. At the time of this writing, Conference chair is the highest position a Republican woman has ever held in the House of Representatives. In this section, I delve deeper into the experiences of Jennifer Dunn and Cathy McMorris Rodgers. Dunn's historic run for House majority leader and McMorris Rodgers's decision *not* to seek the majority leader post highlight the fact that the perception of Republican women as tokens may prevent them from climbing higher up the ladder of congressional leadership.

As described earlier, Jennifer Dunn and Cathy McMorris Rodgers were actively encouraged and supported by the Speaker of House. In both cases, this support, while helpful in their races for Conference leadership, also created subsequent challenges. After serving one term as Conference vice chair, Dunn made history in 1998 as the first woman to run for House majority leader. Challenging incumbent House Majority Leader Dick Armey (R-TX), Dunn was in a three-way race that also included Steve Largent, a conservative Republican from Oklahoma.

Jennifer Dunn had the support of many in her party—especially those who believed in the importance of messaging and diversifying the image of the GOP. One Republican colleague, Rick White of Washington, said Dunn was "very persuasive and very captivating . . . She speaks in ways people can understand more intuitively. She persuades you logically but also, you know, tugs at their heartstrings a little bit."[84] White added that Dunn "functions particularly well in a male environment."[85] In describing the reason for her support of Dunn, Tillie Fowler (R-FL), who had served as secretary of the Conference, said, "I'm looking for diversity. When you look at the whole leadership, you've got to have better diversity. We've got a great opportunity right now."[86]

Still, Dunn faced significant challenges in her race for majority leader. Compared to those of her conservative opponents, Dunn's more moderate policy stances—in particular, her views on abortion—were problematic for some of her Republican colleagues. While Armey and Largent were adamantly anti-abortion, Dunn leaned libertarian and believed "each individual should be under as little regulation as possible, and should therefore have the right to make that decision herself" (Heffernan 2012, 28). Dunn ran her leadership campaign with an understanding that her identity as a woman was important and that her position on abortion was controversial. Abortion "will never be my key issue," she said, "I don't think there's any 'women's issues' anymore. By the year 2000, women will be running over 50 percent of the world's businesses . . . Women care about issues in the marketplace."[87]

Aside from some ideological tensions between her partisan and gender identities, Dunn's connection to Gingrich and her rapid rise in party politics did not sit well with all members. One colleague, critical of Dunn and skeptical of her ability to lead, told *The Washington Post*: "She's good in managed settings but not when she's going to get off the [cue] cards . . . She moved up the line in the House because she was the speaker's person and she was a symbol."[88] The perception that Dunn was handpicked by Gingrich simply as a symbolic token for the party was a distinctly gendered obstacle that she had to overcome. Indeed, Dunn ended up losing her race for majority leader, coming in third behind Armey and Largent, respectively. Dunn's brother, John Blackburn, said in an interview, "When she ran for a top House position, she was beaten out by a person who had less ability but was a 'good ole boy' from Texas" (Heffernan 2012, 52). Following her loss, Dunn said her historic run would make it possible for future women to earn a position at the highest levels of Republican leadership: "I'm not really disappointed. I was cracking that glass ceiling. No woman has ever run for a leadership position like this. I felt it was worth it just for that."[89]

That glass ceiling in the House has yet to be shattered by a Republican woman. Much like the connection Dunn had to Speaker Gingrich, the relationship McMorris Rodgers had with Speaker Boehner was simultaneously a benefit and an obstacle on her pathway to congressional leadership. On September 25, 2015, Boehner announced that he would resign from the speakership. His term was wrought with battles with conservative Republicans who expected the Speaker to take hardline positions on legislation. Shortly after his announcement, it was rumored that this may open the door for Republican women's leadership. Cathy McMorris Rodgers, who was the highest-ranking Republican woman at the time, was expected to run either for speaker or majority leader. "I had looked at the majority leader position as a position where I could even be more effective in helping lead the party's vision and agenda as well as communications effort," she said in her CAWP interview, "And so there was a time, when John Boehner had first announced his retirement, where I spent some days talking to some other members about the possibility of seeking the majority leader's position."[90] Ultimately, though, she decided against running.

When asked about this decision, McMorris Rodgers noted her similarities with Dunn. "I found myself wanting to talk to Jennifer Dunn," she told CAWP, "I was thinking, oh, Jennifer, [I would] really like to be able to talk to you about this question."[91] After speaking with her colleagues about a potential run for majority leader, McMorris Rodgers said she needed some time to distinguish herself from the former Speaker:

At the end of several days of talking to the members, I concluded that at this time it was smarter and more effective for me to stay in my current position. And part of it was for people to be able to see me separate from John Boehner. You know, he invited me on the leadership team . . . And although I'm very proud of the work that I have done, and was excited about the vision, and I'd put together a whole strategic plan for being majority leader, I found that . . . people need to see me separate from John Boehner, at least my colleagues do for a while.[92]

Often viewed as a token,[93] McMorris Rodgers has had to work to overcome the taint of her connection to an unpopular Speaker and the notion that she was pushed into leadership simply as an effort to showcase diversity.

The challenges for House Republican women are clear. While they are often valued by male party leaders for Conference leadership and messaging roles, that valuation fails to extend to the highest levels of leadership. Ileana Ros-Lehtinen (R-FL), who was a member of Congress for 30 years before retiring in 2019, told a reporter, "You think it would be helpful to be a female, but it's sort of a detraction. I can't believe I would say that, but it shows. Some of these guys, they just see themselves in those [top leadership] positions and they want it for themselves. And they think if it goes to a woman they will never be able to grab it again."[94] In a similar vein, a top Republican staffer said, "You won't see a woman in a leadership spot besides Conference chair for many years. The House GOP isn't built for it . . . I don't think there is a concerted effort to keep women out of leadership, but given a choice, this conference will always go the other way."[95]

Conclusion

Martha McSally (R-AZ), first elected in 2014, talked to CAWP about the importance of attaining a critical mass of Republican women in Congress:

We certainly need more [Republican women]. From my experiences in the military, generally speaking, you are treated as an exception and a token sociologically until you have about 25%, right? I mean that's when it's a

game-changer and you actually become . . . part of what defines the organization and is helping to lead the organization. So on the Republican side
we've got a long way to go to get to that 25%.[96]

At their peak, House Republican women have made up only 14.7 percent
of their conference.[97] Yet despite their small numbers, they have been consistently represented in Conference leadership positions. In this chapter,
my comparative analysis of the experiences of Susan Molinari, Jennifer
Dunn, and Cathy McMorris Rodgers shows that female House Republican
Conference leaders have operated as "critical actors" (Childs and Krook
2009) for women's representation within their party. That is, they have
attempted to use their positions of power to draw attention to Republican
women's institutional interests and priorities, despite their small numbers.

This chapter further demonstrates how personal, political, and institutional factors gave Cathy McMorris Rodgers a larger role in advancing the
voices of women members. Most significantly, McMorris Rodgers was able
to both leverage and perpetuate the existence of a partisan-gender identity
among Republican women. Republican congresswomen's ideological cohesion and dedication to women's political representation, for example, made it
easier for McMorris Rodgers to elevate women's voices and amplify a collective, gendered party message in ways that previous Conference leaders could
not. Indeed, at the same time that she called for a critical mass of Republican
women, McSally also emphasized the significance of the women already sitting at the leadership table: "It's not just, 'Oh, we need a woman token.' These
women were elected. I think that shows that we are hopefully potent even
though we're small." "Since I've been here," McSally said, "we've had to force
our way in to say [to male party leaders], 'Do not do that stupid thing that
you are about to do,' and all 23 of us [women] are in agreement. We've been
able to be a strong voice."[98]

Despite this strong voice, my analysis nevertheless paints a more complex
picture of Republican women's congressional representation. First, in an increasingly competitive and gendered political environment, it is the small
number of women in the party that has given them the opportunity to sit in
top Conference leadership positions. Women are often encouraged by male
party leaders to seek these positions as a way to help combat an anti-woman
image of the GOP. I show throughout this book that Republican women
are promoted and valued, first and foremost, as loyal party messengers.
In analyzing the effects of polarization, I have also found that the relative

ideological cohesion among Republican congresswomen today has given female Conference leaders a greater ability to increase the visibility of Republican women in Congress.

At the same time, however, this analysis of intraparty gender dynamics helps to explain Republican congresswomen's continued substantive under-representation and begins to shed light on the limitations of critical actors. Rather than attaining more legitimacy within the party, Republican women's visibility and promotion to party messaging roles can present another gen-dered hurdle to overcome. In particular, I show how the women best posi-tioned to climb the GOP leadership ladder struggle to rise above Conference leadership, in part because they are viewed by their male colleagues as tokens for the party. In my final chapter, I discuss the potential implications of these findings for the future of women's congressional representation.

6

Conclusion

Gendering the GOP

The election of President Donald J. Trump in 2016 sparked intense backlash from women across the country. Trump defeated his Democratic opponent, Hillary Rodham Clinton, who was the first woman to ever secure a major political party's presidential nomination. Marching in pink knitted "pussy hats," millions of women took to the streets on January 21, 2017 in the largest single-day demonstration in American history.[1] In the months following the election, record numbers of Democratic women also registered for campaign training programs and ran for political office.[2] And it paid off.

The 2018 midterm elections resulted in a Democratic takeover of the House of Representatives and a record number of women members of Congress.[3] In the House, Democrats flipped a total of 41 seats for a net gain of 39 seats—the largest victory for the Democratic Party since the 1974 elections following President Richard M. Nixon's resignation.[4] These results widened the partisan gap between Democratic and Republican women in the House: while Democratic women gained 28 seats, bringing their total to 89,[5] Republican women lost 10 seats, dropping them to 13.[6] As illustrated in Figure 6.1, Republican women comprised only 6.5 percent of all House Republicans in the 116th Congress—their smallest proportion in 25 years.

In the aftermath of the 2018 midterms, Republican congresswomen once again demanded that their party's leadership prioritize the election of Republican women and reach out to women voters. "Fifty-two Republican women ran for Congress . . . And only 13 of us made it across the finish line," said Susan Brooks (R-IN), who had recently succeeded Elise Stefanik (R-NY) as recruitment chair of the National Republican Congressional Committee (NRCC).[7] Brooks told *Roll Call*: "It's important that we, as a conference, do a better job of looking like America, and better representing the very diverse country that we have."[8] In a closed-door conference meeting, Stefanik confronted party leaders about the need to advocate for Republican women's representation. She later told a reporter, "I am going to keep pointing out to

Gendering the GOP. Catherine N. Wineinger, Oxford University Press. © Oxford University Press 2022.
DOI: 10.1093/oso/9780197556542.003.0006

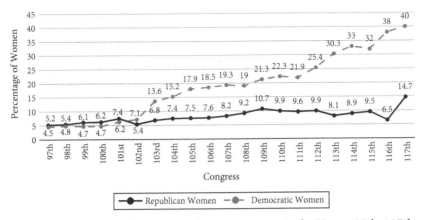

Figure 6.1 Women as a Percentage of Party Caucuses in the House, 97th–117th Congresses (1981–2023)

Data source: Center for American Women and Politics

my colleagues that we are at a crisis level for GOP women . . . This election should be a wake-up call to Republicans that we need to do better . . . We need to be elevating women's voices, not suppressing them."[9]

And yet, while male party leaders have generally supported this sentiment, they have also been hesitant to empower women or make substantive changes beyond optics. For instance, despite encouragement from Republican congresswomen and support from other colleagues, Ann Wagner (R-MO) decided against running for chair of the NRCC after a phone call with Majority Leader Kevin McCarthy. "The leader had a different plan," Wagner told reporters.[10] Leadership was also reluctant to back Stefanik's effort to address the gender diversity issue in the party. Frustrated with her inability to support women in primary elections as NRCC recruitment chair, Stefanik stepped down from her position in December 2018 and focused instead on using her leadership political action committee, now called Elevate PAC (E-PAC), to elect more Republican congresswomen. "I want to play in primaries, and I want to play big in primaries," Stefanik told *Roll Call*.[11] But NRCC Chair Tom Emmer was weary of the decision, saying, "If that's what Elise wants to do, then that's her call, her right, but I think that's a mistake . . . It shouldn't be just based on looking for a specific set of ingredients—gender, race, religion—and then we're going to play in the primary."[12] Stefanik responded to Emmer's comment in a Twitter thread. With flashing red sirens, she wrote:

I will continue speaking out [about] the crisis level of GOP women in Congress & will try to lead and change that by supporting strong GOP women candidates through my leadership PAC . . . But 📖📖 NEWSFLASH 📖📖 I wasn't asking for permission.[13]

Displayed prominently on E-PAC's website, "I wasn't asking for permission" has become somewhat of a rallying cry for Republican women candidates.[14]

In what has come to be called the "Year of the Republican Woman," 2020 resulted in unexpected gains for House Republicans, bringing in a record number of GOP women. While still a significantly smaller proportion of their conference than their Democratic colleagues, women more than doubled their ranks in the House GOP (see Figure 6.1). The electoral success of women in 2020 can be attributed, in part, to Republican women's engagement of and mobilization around their partisan-gender identity. New groups like E-PAC and Winning for Women—along with existing groups like VIEW PAC— have taken advantage of a competitive, gendered political landscape and have focused on recruiting and supporting Republican women candidates. *Democratic* women's increased prominence and political power also inspired women's participation on the other side of the aisle. "Conservative women said, 'Hey, wait a minute, not every woman is a Democrat,'" noted Stephanie Bice (R-OK), who went on to defeat Democratic incumbent Kendra Horn.[15]

Although Tom Emmer and other male party leaders eventually endorsed Stefanik's initiative, it is clear that GOP leaders are still reluctant to fully support Republican women or embrace the fact that women bring unique and important gendered perspectives to the party. Speaking with *NPR* in a post-election interview, Emmer praised Republicans for their victories and argued that the party had both the best candidates and the best messaging that year. But not once in that interview did Emmer specifically mention the record number of women—or the fact that it was *women* who won most of the seats flipped[16] by Republican candidates.[17] When pressed in another interview about the record diversity in the House GOP, Emmer emphasized, "These people are not going to be great representatives just because of their gender, their race. . . we wanted the best candidates."[18]

My analysis of intraparty politics helps to explain these dynamics and complicates traditional understandings of the relationship between descriptive and substantive representation. I have shown how party polarization and competition affect Republican congresswomen's collective efforts to push for women's increased representation within their party, as well as male leadership's conditional support for women in positions of power. This book looks beyond legislative behavior, shining light on the ongoing challenges Republican women face, the intricate gender dynamics they must learn to navigate in their party, and potential opportunities for change. In this final chapter, I discuss my findings in terms of their implications for gender politics research as well as the potential consequences for the future of Republican women's representation in Congress.

Rethinking the Difference Republican Women Make: The Politics of Party Messengers

I began this project with a broad, overarching question: How has Republican women's congressional representation evolved time? Recent research on the gendered effects of polarization has shown that women in Congress are less likely than in previous decades to work across the aisle on legislation and are no longer more bipartisan than their male counterparts (Lawless, Theriault, and Guthrie 2018). Yet legislative activity may not be the only place—or, indeed, the most relevant place—acts of representation can be found. My findings in this book reveal that Republican congresswomen today work to represent women not by moderating their party's policies, but by working as partisans in gendered ways.

Kathryn Pearson's (2015b) work on "gendered partisanship" in the House of Representatives lends further evidence to the idea that partisanship is not gender neutral. On the contrary, Pearson finds that, beginning in the mid-1990s, women on both sides of the aisle have expressed party loyalty more frequently than their male colleagues. Republican women, in particular, are more likely to deliver partisan speeches than Republican men (Pearson 2015b). Moving beyond an analysis of roll call votes and co-sponsorships allows us to uncover the intensifying partisanship of congresswomen, as well as how that partisanship is gendered. Focusing on intraparty politics, in particular, allows for a deeper understanding of "the difference women make" (Swers 2002) not simply in the realm of policy, but also in shaping and advancing the gendered strategies of their parties.

Admittedly, because congresswomen do value their partisan identities and understand that public infighting can be damaging to themselves and their party, it may be increasingly difficult to measure the substantive impact of women in this era of congressional polarization. Nevertheless, I show that through in-depth, qualitative analyses, scholars can begin to reveal the representational efforts of partisan women as well as their successes and continued challenges.

I find that strengthening partisanship, ideological cohesion, and interparty competition have shaped congresswomen's role in Republican Party politics by affecting the way they interact with each other and with male party leaders. In particular, Republican congresswomen increasingly speak as and on behalf of women in ways that align with GOP principles. Yet while they embrace their role as Republican Party messengers, they also recognize and collectively advocate for their gendered interests as women within their party. I therefore maintain that continuing to study the *process* of women's substantive representation—how women acquire influential leadership positions and use those positions to represent women in various ways—remains an important endeavor (see also Childs and Krook 2006).

The Emergence of Partisan Woman-Invoked Rhetoric

In Chapters 2 and 3, I used a multi-method approach to analyze changes in the floor speeches of House Republican women over time. Through a combination of content analyses and elite interviews, I found that Republican congresswomen are more likely than they had been in the past to engage in *partisan woman-invoked rhetoric*. That is, they speak collectively as and on behalf of women in ways that align with the GOP's policy platform, messaging strategies, and party culture. Notably, this rhetoric genders ideologically conservative ideals without actively challenging those ideals.

This emergence of partisan woman-invoked rhetoric tells us that Republican congresswomen are more aligned with their party's principles than they had been in previous decades. More significantly, though, it can also begin to shed light on the relationship between party culture, ideology, and gender. While previous literature on representative claims-making (Saward 2006; 2010) has shown that ideology can shape the gendered claims of political elites (Celis et al. 2008; Celis and Childs 2012; 2018; Erzeel and Celis 2016), my work advances this scholarship in two main ways.

First, my inclusion of *identity claims*—claims in which women speak *as* women—in addition to representative claims provides a more nuanced interpretation of the way conservative women represent women. If one were to look only at the representative claims of Republican congresswomen—in which they speak *on behalf* of women—one would find a gradual decline in such claims (see Chapter 3). But by including the use identity claims, I show that women's representation can occur in subtler ways. In the case of Republican congresswomen, invoking their own gender identity rather than speaking overtly on behalf of a social group allows them to fall in line with their party's conservative notions of "family values" and rejection of group "identity politics." By speaking as women—and, in particular, as mothers, wives, and conservative women—Republican congresswomen can simultaneously represent a specific subset of women and credential themselves as ideologically aligned with their party's base.

Second, by examining the evolution of Republican congresswomen's woman-invoked rhetoric over time, rather than during one legislative session, I am able to show how individual ideology and various institutional factors shape the types of claims that are made. In particular, I help to reveal the process by which congressional polarization has created a collective voice among Republican women and has amplified gendered claims-making within GOP politics. In the following sections, I detail this process and the broader implications for Republican women's representation.

Messenger Politics and Women's Collective Action in the GOP

In addition to revealing rhetorical shifts over time, this book investigates changes in partisan and gender dynamics in Congress, focusing on the experiences of Republican women. In doing so, I deepen our understanding of women's collective action in the House and the Republican Party's use of gender as a political tool. Through several case studies in Chapters 4 and 5, I show that partisan woman-invoked rhetoric is not simply a top-down messaging strategy; rather, the development and institutionalization of a *partisan-gender identity* among Republican congresswomen has helped shape women's roles as messengers in the party.

The increased ideological cohesion among Republican women in Congress has strengthened their commitment to working together not simply as women or as Republicans, but as Republican women. Taking advantage of a competitive political environment that made women's visibility seemingly important for the electoral prospects of the GOP, Republican congresswomen formed the RWPC in 2012. Coming together as a group gave

House Republican women opportunities to mentor one another, shape the messaging strategies of the party, and advocate for their own institutional power. Importantly, though, their success has been largely dependent on party leadership's perception of how women can benefit the party. As a result, Republican women have been limited primarily to messaging roles or symbolic placements. While Republican women have undoubtedly embraced their role as party messengers, gaining and maintaining more substantive positions of power remains a challenge within the current GOP.[19]

These findings have helped unveil some of the previously overlooked effects of ideological polarization and party competition. Indeed, the implications of polarization on the legislative process have been well-documented (Binder 2003; 2016; Lee 2009; 2016; Pearson 2015). Scholars have also noted the growing emphasis on congressional communications (Lee 2016; Malecha and Reagan 2012; Meinke 2016; Sellers 2010) and have found that members' rhetoric has become increasingly partisan (Lipinksi 2004; Russell 2018). My gender analysis of rhetoric adds to this discussion by expanding our understanding of how partisan rhetoric is developed and disseminated.

In line with congressional communications literature, I find that individual members are committed to participating in party messaging because it simultaneously benefits their own electoral interests and those of their party. What I further demonstrate, however, is how shifts in the political landscape can shape party leaders' perceptions of who is an effective party messenger. By focusing on gender, I paint a more complex picture of party communications, showing how the symbolism of *messengers*—not only messages—plays a significant role in party messaging strategies.

More than that, my analysis of the formation of the RWPC highlights the complexities of organizing within the GOP's top-down party structure (Freeman 1986, 339). Despite claims that party loyalty and deference to leadership may be waning following the existence of a "confrontational" Tea Party faction in Congress (Grossmann and Hopkins 2016, 104), my study shows that Republican women were able to successfully organize only insofar as they were able to "plead . . . [their] case to the leadership as furthering the basic values of the party" (Freeman 1986, 339). Indeed, this book illustrates how a combination of partisanship, ideological cohesion, and party competition has created an environment in which women have been able to successfully appeal to party leadership on some gendered demands while remaining unsuccessful in others.

Implications: A Paradox for Republican Women's Representation?

In what the *New York Times* called "an intraparty battle of the sexes," Dr. Joan Perry and Dr. Greg Murphy faced off in a special election Republican primary in the summer of 2019.[20] The death of Congressman Walter B. Jones earlier that year created an open seat in North Carolina's 3rd congressional district—a solidly Republican district. This was the first election following the 2018 wave of newly-elected Democratic women, and gender was an important consideration for those who wanted to address the GOP's diversity problem. Dr. Perry was endorsed by the all 13 Republican women in the House and was further supported by Winning for Women, a super PAC founded in 2017 that is dedicated to electing Republican women. Despite this, Dr. Perry lost to her male opponent by a 19-point margin.

"Women tend to get labeled as a moderate based on gender," noted Rebecca Schuller, executive director of Winning for Women. "Women have to prove themselves differently, and that's exactly why we exist."[21] Indeed, Dr. Perry was a candidate whose conservative ideology aligned with the voters in her district and who, as a pediatrician, emphasized her anti-abortion views throughout her campaign. Her loss to Dr. Murphy, a state assembly member and former physician with similar ideological values, is not an uncommon experience for GOP women.

Existing research on the electoral barriers for Republican women candidates highlights the relationship between gender, ideology, and representation. One result of polarization is that women on the right often perceive themselves to be ideologically distant from their party and choose not to run for office (de Geus and Shorrocks 2020; Thomsen 2017). If they do run, Republican women—as Schuller rightly noted—must overcome gender stereotypes in order to prove their ideological credentials to a conservative primary base (King and Matland 2003; Schneider and Bos 2016).[22] Identity-based groups for Republicans, like Winning for Women, are also generally less effective than Democratic women's groups, as they are not adequately supported by Republican donors, who tend to be more conservative and ideologically opposed to "identity politics" (Crowder-Meyer and Cooperman 2018; Kitchens and Swers 2016). These challenges help to explain the descriptive underrepresentation of Republican women in Congress—that is, why Republican congresswomen are so few in number (see also Elder 2021).

The practical implications of this book, I argue, are important to consider in terms of multiple dimensions of Republican women's congressional representation. Questions of women's political representation tend to center primarily on the link between descriptive and substantive representation (Pitkin 1967): Do women represent women? But by delving deeper into the question of *how* women represent women (see: Childs and Krook 2006) in this era of polarization, I complicate current understandings of Republican women's underrepresentation in Congress.

Attempts to explain the lack of Republican women in elective office have mainly focused on barriers at the point of candidate emergence (Thomsen 2015; 2017; Elder 2018; Erler 2018) or within political campaigns (Crowder-Meyer and Cooperman 2018; Dittmar 2015; Shames 2018; Wineinger 2021). But my findings also point to the ways elected officials may be inadvertently contributing to a hostile political environment for potential Republican women candidates. In particular, my analysis of intraparty politics begins to uncover a multidimensional paradox in which Republican women's overrepresentation as party messengers is cyclically related to their descriptive underrepresentation in Congress (see Figure 6.2).

First, as Kanthak and Krause (2012) have pointed out, Republican congresswomen have had access to Conference leadership opportunities not *in spite* of their small numbers, but *because* of them. Indeed, since the 1990s, party leaders like Speaker Gingrich have often tokenized and increased the visibility of Republican women in attempts to improve the image of the GOP. As detailed in Chapters 4 and 5, my analysis further shows how

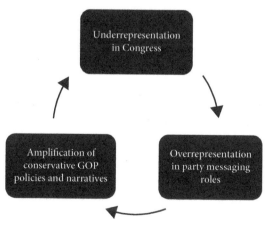

Figure 6.2 A Paradox for Republican Women's Congressional Representation

institutional and political changes in recent years have strengthened the role of female Conference leaders as critical actors by making it easier to elevate the voices of rank-and-file Republican congresswomen and promote them as party messengers. Once again, this increased representation of Republican women in party messaging roles is paradoxically a result of the descriptive *under*representation of women in the party: to combat images of the GOP as anti-woman, party leaders often encourage women's visibility and embrace the idea of women as party spokespeople.

The overrepresentation of women as Republican Party messengers, while empowering in some ways, may also potentially uphold electoral barriers for GOP women candidates. First, increased visibility of Republican congresswomen can give Republican voters the impression that women are not, in fact, underrepresented in their party. One goal of placing women in party messaging roles, after all, is to create the appearance that women already have a place in GOP politics. Yet by doing so, party elites may be perpetuating the belief that Republican women's political underrepresentation is simply not an issue that needs to be addressed. In her research on public support for women in elected office, Kira Sanbonmatsu (2021) finds that people who overestimate the level of women's representation in Congress are less interested in electing more women. And in fact, a 2018 Pew Research study found that only 33 percent of GOP voters believe "there are too few women in high political offices" compared to 79 percent of Democratic voters.[23] Rebecca Schuller, of Winning for Women, noted this discrepancy, saying, "Republican leaders have a job to do in simply convincing voters that there is a problem."[24]

Second, as I find in Chapters 2 and 3, Republican congresswomen's current use of woman-invoked rhetoric neither challenges their party's conservative policies nor disrupts its cultural values. On the contrary, Republican women are collectively maintaining the raced-gendered norms that have been shown to prevent women and people of color from identifying and successfully running as Republicans. This becomes particularly important when considering that the claims made by political elites have the potential to shape public interests and perceptions (Celis et al. 2008; Saward 2006; Harris 2013; Winter 2006). Indeed, Sellers (2010) shows that legislators can gain media attention through consistent, unified messaging. In the context of a polarized media environment, Harris (2013) contends, "members of Congress, especially high-profile elected party leaders ... produce and model party rhetoric likely to be echoed by party activists and other attentive elements of the public in ways that propel further party polarization" (110).

In short, the messages put forth by Republican congresswomen can have tangible effects on the political landscape. By collectively producing gendered messages that align with the GOP's conservative policy platform, messaging strategies, and culture, Republican congresswomen are potentially perpetuating, rather than challenging, the ideological barriers that prevent female Republican candidates from running for and winning congressional seats. Future research should examine the extent to which this type of partisan woman-invoked rhetoric may affect women's decisions to identify and/or run as Republicans.

Breaking the Cycle: The Potential Power of a Partisan-Gender Identity

This multidimensional paradox, in which Republican women's descriptive and substantive *under*representation is linked in various ways to their *over*representation as party messengers, may seem like an endless cycle. Yet this book also highlights the potentially transformative power of a *partisan-gender identity* among Republican congresswomen. As Conference chair, Cathy McMorris Rodgers not only leveraged the Republican Women's Policy Committee to amplify women's voices; she also helped strengthen the recognition of a partisan-gender identity through her mentorship. As a result, and as I show in Chapter 5, women like Elise Stefanik and Susan Brooks entered the institution motivated to work as and on behalf of Republican women. A recognition that their experiences differ from those of Democratic women and Republican men, and a willingness to challenge male party leaders in order to advance their interests, may hold the key to breaking the cycle of Republican women's underrepresentation in Congress—especially in a post-Trump era.

GOP at a Crossroads

On January 6th, 2021, President Donald Trump spoke at the "Save America" rally hosted by Women for America First, a pro-Trump political action committee founded in 2019 by former Tea Party Express chair Amy Kremer.

Although Joe Biden was declared President-elect on November 7, 2020, Trump and his supporters, including QAnon conspiracy theorists, refused to accept the results of the 2020 presidential election. At the rally, Trump encouraged his supporters to "stop the steal," telling them, "We're going walk down to the Capitol, and we're going to cheer on our brave senators and congressmen and women. We're probably not going to be cheering so much for some of them because you'll never take back our country with weakness. You have to show strength, and you have to be strong."[25] Soon after, pro-Trump insurrectionists stormed the United States Capitol building in a violent attempt to stop the certification of the 2020 election.

Following this now infamous attack on the US Capitol, members of the House of Representatives voted to impeach Donald Trump (a second time) on January 13, 2021. Votes were cast largely along party lines, with the exception of 10 Republicans—including two women, Reps. Liz Cheney (R-WY) and Jaime Herrera Beutler (R-WA)—who voted in favor of impeachment.[26] The House also voted in February 2021 to remove Rep. Marjorie Taylor Greene (R-GA) from her committee assignments as a result of her vocal support of QAnon conspiracy theories. Eleven Republicans—including three Republican women of color, Reps. Young Kim (R-CA), Nicole Malliotakis (R-NY), and Maria Elvira Salazar (R-FL)—joined House Democrats in support of the resolution.[27]

Cheney, who had been serving as House Republican Conference Chair since 2017, faced immediate backlash for her impeachment vote. Believing that her opposition to Trump put them in a vulnerable electoral position, several Republican members called for her to be removed as Conference chair. While Cheney survived the first conference vote in February, she was eventually ousted from her position in May 2021 and replaced by another woman: Rep. Elise Stefanik.

This move highlights the crossroads the modern GOP is currently facing, in terms of both party strategy and gender politics. One thing I emphasize in this book is the significance of increased ideological cohesion among House Republican women. But in the case of the 117th Congress (2021–2023), it is clear there are stark ideological divisions within the House Republican conference—including among the women. The biggest divide exists regarding the role Donald Trump will play in the future of the party. Whereas Cheney has continually said that Trump "does not have a role as a leader of our party going forward,"[28] other women, like Greene, have insisted, "The party is his. It doesn't belong to anyone else."[29] The path the GOP chooses to take in this era could have significant consequences for women in the party.

Challenges and Opportunities for Republican Women

In her cross-national study of women's political representation, Melody Valdini (2019) argues that male party elites are "neither angels nor devils" (19). On the left and the right, men function instead as rational opportunists who advocate for women's representation when it benefits their own political interests. The fight for women's representation, Valdini writes, must take into consideration "men's strategic decisions about women's representation" (Valdini 2019, 147). In other words, if women want their parties to actively support women in positions of political power, they will first need to convince male party leaders that women's representation is a cause worth pursuing. In the current political climate, and as this book shows, this can be a particularly daunting task for Republican women, who must work within a party culture that is more hierarchical (Freeman 1986, 339) and denounces what it perceives to be "identity politics."

In some ways, convincing Republican voters and party leaders to prioritize women's representation became even more challenging in the wake of the 2016 presidential election. Despite Donald Trump's explicit sexism on the campaign trail and his turn away from the suggestions of the RNC's 2013 autopsy report, he nevertheless won the support of a majority of white women voters (Jaffe 2018). That a lack of women in power did not prevent the Republican Party from gaining control of the presidency and both chambers of Congress in 2016 may make the case for championing women's representation a tricky one to present to party leaders. At the same time, the success of Republican women in 2020 (including their ability to flip 11 House seats) strengthens the argument Stefanik has been making to party leaders for years: "Republican women are majority makers."[30]

Still, Republican women's strategic attempts to convince leaders that women are electorally valuable to the party have often fallen short (see also Wineinger and Nugent 2020). As I demonstrate in this book, even when Republican congresswomen have been able to organize and gain some power within their party, that power has been predominantly limited to messaging roles (like Conference Chair) as opposed to more substantive policymaking roles. Breaking this cycle of underrepresentation will likely require a significant shift in party culture to one that values the unique contributions and broad ideological perspectives women can bring to the party and to elected office more broadly.

The relative racial and ideological diversity of House Republican women in the 117th Congress compared to previous years presents a unique opportunity. In this highly polarized and competitive political environment, both parties are developing strategies to gain and maintain control of government (Lee 2016). While disagreements between Republican women can make it difficult to organize, the continued ideological distance between Republican and Democratic women may still be enough to incentivize Republican women to work together as partisan women. Republican women, for example, have campaigned together against the four prominent Democratic women known as "The Squad": Representatives Alexandria Ocasio-Cortez (D-NY), Rashida Tlaib (D-MI), Ayanna Pressley (D-MA), and Ilhan Omar (D-MN). During orientation for the freshman class of the 117th Congress, Maria Elvira Salazar tweeted a photo with her colleagues, Victoria Spartz (R-IN) and Nancy Mace (R-SC), with the caption: "We are the New Faces of the @GOP . . . We're all working moms & we're a true FORCE to be reckoned with."[31] The photo of the "Force" mirrored the original "Squad" photos posted by Ocasio-Cortez and Tlaib at freshman orientation two years prior.[32]

The overarching lesson of this book is that Republican women can and should organize around a partisan-gender identity. Importantly, though, this collective action should be used to advocate for structural change within the party, rather than maintaining the barriers that keep women out. If Republican congresswomen can come together, despite their differences, to convince party leaders that a more ideologically diverse and inclusive party is the key to winning and maintaining a governing majority, then we may begin to see a shift in party culture—and new opportunities for Republican women.

Gendering the GOP

Survey data has shown that Republican women voters are significantly more moderate than their Republican male counterparts (Barnes and Cassese 2017). But in Congress, this ideological gender gap is no longer evident (Frederick 2009). Normatively speaking, if we care about the quality of political representation, then we should be advocating for the representation of the full ideological spectrum of Republican women. Instead, what I find is that Republican congresswomen are not only increasingly conservative, but also increasingly partisan and thus tend to amplify gendered messages that perpetuate ideological and cultural hurdles for Republican women.

Throughout this book, I make the case that studying Republican women's representational behavior is an important endeavor if we are to truly understand the evolving dynamics of women's congressional representation. Republican congresswomen recognize the value of their presence in the institution; they believe in the importance of reaching out to women voters and recruiting women candidates; and perhaps most significantly, they have sought ways to mentor one another and organize collectively around their partisan-gender identity. Yet in their attempts to the elevate women's voices within GOP, they have been relegated primarily to party messenger roles. Whether and how Republican congresswomen will gain enough institutional power and choose to use that power to break down existing barriers for Republican women remains to be seen.

APPENDIX A
List of Republican Congresswomen Interviewees

103rd/104th Congresses	114th Congress
Helen Bentley	Diane Black
Jennifer Dunn	Marsha Blackburn
Tillie Fowler	Susan Brooks
Nancy Johnson	Renee Ellmers
Sue Kelly	Virginia Foxx
Jan Meyers	Kay Granger
Susan Molinari	Vicky Hartzler
Constance Morella	Cynthia Lummis
Sue Myrick	Cathy McMorris Rodgers
Deborah Pryce	Martha McSally
Ileana Ros-Lehtinen	Kristi Noem
Marge Roukema	Martha Roby
Olympia Snowe	Ileana Ros-Lehtinen
Barbara Vucanovich	Elise Stefanik
	Ann Wagner
	Jackie Walorski

APPENDIX B

Complete List of Issues in Woman-Invoked Speeches

Complete List of Issues in Woman-Invoked Speeches: 103rd/104th Congresses

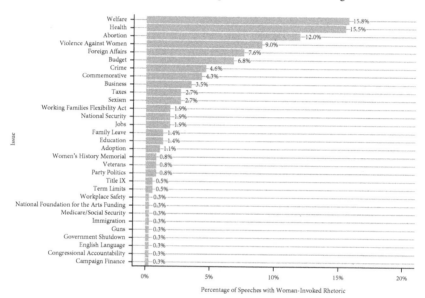

Complete List of Issues in Woman-Invoked Speeches: 113th/114th Congresses

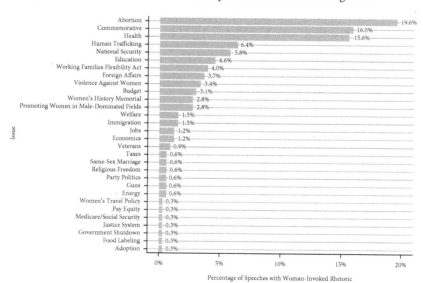

Complete List of Unconventional Women's Issues: 103rd/104th Congresses

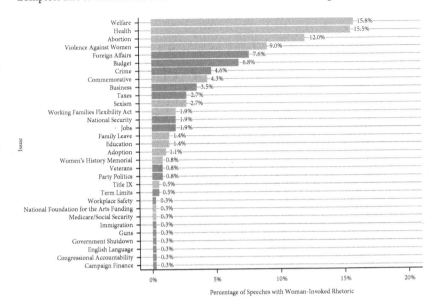

Percentage of Speeches with Woman-Invoked Rhetoric

Complete List of Unconventional Women's Issues: 113th/114th Congresses

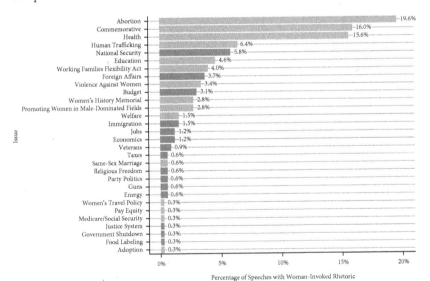

Percentage of Speeches with Woman-Invoked Rhetoric

Notes

Chapter 1

1. "Democratic Women Senators on 2011 Budget," *C-SPAN Video Library*, April 8, 2011, <https://www.c-span.org/video/?298931-1/democratic-women-senators-2011-budget&start=12>

2. Rep. Cathy McMorris Rodgers (R-WA) served as vice chair of the House Republican Conference from 2009 to 2013. She then served as chair from 2013 to 2019, after which she was succeeded by Rep. Liz Cheney (R-WI). In May 2021, Cheney was ousted from her position and replaced by another woman, Rep. Elise Stefanik of New York.

3. In her opening remarks, McMorris Rodgers said, "I'm joined today by my fellow women Republicans from the House and they're all going to share a little perspective with you." See "House Republican Women on 2011 Budget."

4. "McMorris Rodgers Gives Birth to Baby Girl," *Press release*, December 1, 2010. Congresswoman Cathy McMorris Rodgers, <https://mcmorris.house.gov/mcmorris_rodgers_gives_birth_to_baby_girl/>

5. "House Republican Women on 2011 Budget," *C-SPAN Video Library*, April 8, 2011, <https://www.c-span.org/video/?298940-1/house-republican-women-2011-budget>.

6. Ibid.

7. Graph: "Women as a Percentage of Party Caucuses US House and Senate, 1917–2013," Footnotes, Center for American Women and Politics, <https://cawp.rutgers.edu/footnotes/life-party-women%E2%80%99s-representation-congressional-party-caucuses>

8. This was the total number of House Democratic women at the beginning of the first session of the 116th Congress. The number includes Congresswoman Katie Hill (D-CA), who later resigned in October 2019. "History of Women in the U.S. Congress," Center for American Women and Politics at the Eagleton Institute of Politics at Rutgers University, Retrieved November 1, 2021. https://cawp.rutgers.edu/history-women-us-congress.

9. "Speaker John Boehner on 2011 Budget," *C-SPAN Video Library*, April 8, 2011, <https://www.c-span.org/video/?298928-1/speaker-john-boehner-2011-budget>

10. For example, see Jeff Lewis, "Why Are Ocasio-Cortez, Omar, Pressley, and Tlaib Estimated to Be Moderates by NOMINATE?", *VoteView*, August 5, 2019, <https://voteview.com/articles/Ocasio-Cortez_Omar_Pressley_Tlaib>

11. House Democrats held the majority in the 110th, 111th, 116th, and 117th Congresses. House Republicans held the majority in the 112th, 113th, 114th, and 115th Congresses.

12. This number does not include Delegates to the House of Representatives. For the number of women in Congress over time, see "History of Women in the U.S. Congress," Center for American Women and Politics at the Eagleton Institute of Politics at Rutgers University, Retrieved November 1, 2021 https://cawp.rutgers.edu/history-women-us-congress.

13. Ibid.

14. Ibid.

15. Susan Carroll, for example, argues that women in political leadership must learn to strike a balance between femininity and masculinity in a way that men do not. She writes, "Margaret Thatcher, for example, struck this balance, in part, by always dressing stylishly, carrying a handbag, and wearing her signature pearls. She consciously adopted a very feminine appearance to complement her very masculine political behavior." Susan J. Carroll, "Reflections on Gender and Hillary Clinton's Presidential Campaign: The Good, the Bad, and the Misogynic," *Politics & Gender* 5, no. 1 (2009): 1–20.

16. Also see CAWP analysis: Kelly Dittmar, "Primary Problems: Women Candidates in US House Primaries." (Center for American Women and Politics at Rutgers University, 2013), <http://www.cawp.rutgers.edu/sites/default/files/resources/primary-problems-10-1-13.pdf.

17. Although 2020 was a record-breaking year for Republican women of color, they are still drastically underrepresented compared to Democratic women of color. Five Republican women of color serve in the 117th Congress (breaking their previous record of three), compared to 44 women of color on the Democratic side of the aisle. See "Election 2020 Results Tracker," Center for American Women and Politics, <https://cawp.rutgers.edu/election2020-results-tracker>.

18. Bill Clinton and Barack Obama served as President during the 103rd/104th and 113th/114th Congresses, respectively.

19. Among other issues, Anita Hill's testimony during the 1991 congressional hearing of Supreme Court nominee, Clarence Thomas, brought issues of sexual assault to the forefront during the 1992 election. The 103rd Congress was the result of the "Year of the Woman," in which a record number of Democratic women were elected to Congress. President Clinton won his 1992 election with a 4-point gender gap and his 1996 election with an 11-point gender gap. Well aware of the need to reach out to women voters, Newt Gingrich, Speaker of the House in the 104th Congress, actively sought out women as candidates and spokespeople for the party. Gendered issues played a similar role two decades later. Throughout this time, the Republican Party was accused of fighting a "war on women," and President Obama's gender gap widened from 7 points in 2008 to 10 points in 2012. The Republican National Committee addressed this in a 2013 "autopsy" report titled the "Growth and Opportunity Project," which outlined recommendations for reaching out to women and minority voters through messaging tactics and candidate recruitment. The National Republican Congressional Committee also founded Project GROW, which was devoted to recruiting and training Republican women candidates across the country.

20. Unlike in the Senate, "rules in the House of Representatives typically limit the time allowed for floor speeches and require debate to be germane to pending business" (Judy Schneider, "Special Order Speeches and Other Forms of Non-Legislative Debate in the House," Congressional Research Service, November 26, 2012 <https://sgp.fas.org/crs/misc/RS21174.pdf>.

21. Number of Republican women by Congress and chamber: 103rd: 2 senators, 12 representatives; 104th: 4 senators, 17 representatives; 113th: 4 senators, 19 representatives; 114th: 6 senators, 22 representatives. Source: "History of Women in the U.S. Congress," Center for American Women and Politics, Eagleton Institute of Politics, Rutgers University, <https://cawp.rutgers.edu/history-women-us-congress>.

22. This study was made possible with funding from the Charles H. Revson Foundation and the Ford Foundation.

23. The study was made possible with funding from the Political Parity Project at the Hunt Alternatives Fund.

24. CAWP's public report can be found here: Kelly Dittmar, Kira Sanbonmatsu, Susan J. Carroll, Debbie Walsh, and Catherine Wineinger, *Representation Matters: Women in the U.S. Congress* (New Brunswick, NJ: Center for American Women and Politics, Eagleton Institute of Politics, Rutgers, The State University of New Jersey, 2017), <https://www.cawp.rutgers.edu/sites/default/files/resources/representationmatters.pdf.

   Also see Kelly Dittmar, Kira Sanbonmatsu, and Susan J. Carroll, *A Seat at the Table: Congresswomen's Perspectives on Why Their Presence Matters* (New York, NY: Oxford University Press, 2018).

25. Legislative debates in the House are subject to restrictions that are recommended by the Rules Committee. Unlike in the Senate, no member can hold the floor for more than one hour. Most bills and resolutions are considered for a maximum of 40 minutes on the House floor. One-minute and special order speeches are forms of non-legislative debate in the House. One-minute speeches are no longer than one minute in length and are typically given at the beginning of the legislative day. Special order speeches by individual members can be up to five minutes or 60 minutes in length, and are typically given at the end of the legislative day and reserved in advance through party leadership. For more information, see Judy Schneider, Judy. "Special Order Speeches and Other Forms of Non-Legislative Debate in the House," Congressional Research Service, November 26, 2012, https://fas.org/sgp/crs/misc/RS21174.pdf; and Christopher M. Davis, "The Legislative Process on the House Floor: An Introduction," Congressional Research Service, December 13, 2018, < https://crsreports.congress.gov/product/pdf/RL/95-563 >.

26. One of the most recent examples of this is Alexandria Ocasio-Cortez's (D-NY) first congressional floor speech. In January 2019, Ocasio-Cortez tweeted a C-SPAN video of her speech, which garnered 1.16 million views within the first 12 hours. Mahita Gajanan, "Alexandria Ocasio-Cortez's First House Speech Broke a C-SPAN Record: Here's What She Said," *Time Magazine*, January 18, 2019.

27. Hinojosa, Carle, and Woodall (2018) call this "descriptive presentation." Magda Hinojosa, Jill Carle, and Gina Serignese Woodall, "Speaking as a Woman: Descriptive

Presentation and Representation in Costa Rica's Legislative Assembly," *Journal of Women, Politics & Policy* 39, no. 4 (2018): 407–429.

28. In the 1980s and early 1990s, the CCWI played an important role in legislation such as the Child Support Enforcement Act, the Violence Against Women Act, and the Family and Medical Leave Act. More recently, while the caucus has been active on issues of human trafficking in the 114th Congress, a lot of its activity has been more symbolic and uncontroversial in nature, such as advocating for a women's history museum.

Chapter 2

1. Representative Ellmers (NC), "Imminent Threats to Our National Security," *Congressional Record* 161, no. 109 (July 14, 2015): H5153.
2. Ibid.
3. Judy Schneider, "Special Order Speeches: Current House Practices." *Congressional Research Service*, April 1, 2008. <https://archives-democrats-rules.house.gov/CRS_Rpt/rl30136.pdf>.
4. As discussed in Chapter 1, conventional women's issues are those which scholars have typically identified as (1) advancing women's equity in society (equal pay, family leave, etc.), (2) addressing women or women's particular needs, even from a neutral or anti-feminist standpoint (abortion, domestic violence, recognizing women's achievements, etc.), or (3) being associated with women's traditional roles as caregivers (education, health care, welfare, etc.).
5. See Chapter 1 for detailed descriptions of interview data and Appendix A for the complete list of Republican women interviewed in each Congress.
6. Nancy Johnson, Center for American Women and Politics Interview, August 7, 1995.
7. Ann Wagner, Center for American Women and Politics Interview, April 28, 2016.
8. Rosa DeLauro, Center for American Women and Politics Interview, June 30, 1995.
9. Karen Thurman, Center for American Women and Politics Interview, June 30, 1995.
10. Kay Granger, Center for American Women and Politics Interview, January 7, 2016.
11. Helen Delich Bentley, Center for American Women and Politics Interview, August 2, 1995.
12. Tillie Fowler, Center for American Women and Politics Interview, August 3, 1995.
13. Sue Myrick, Center for American Women and Politics Interview, February 25, 1998.
14. Martha Roby, Center for American Women and Politics Interview, February 2, 2016.
15. The correlations in the 103rd and 104th Congresses are statistically significant at the .05 and .10 levels, respectively. In both Congresses, Connie Morella (R-MD) was an outlier, giving the most woman-invoked speeches. If I remove her from the analysis, the results are no longer statistically significant. That said, the point of this analysis is not to determine how individual ideology drives the use of woman-invoked rhetoric; rather, it is to better understand the collective messages about women that are being put forth in each Congress. This is also why I chose to analyze the total number of

woman-invoked speeches instead of the percentage of said speeches for each member. In doing so, I show that Republican women's messages about women in the 1990s were coming most frequently from moderate voices.

16. For a full list of unconventional women's issues, see Appendix B.

17. The Contract with America, discussed further in Chapter 4, was a pledge led by Newt Gingrich and signed by Republican congressional candidates during the 1994 election that said they would work to enact ten conservative policies within their first 100 days of office, if Republicans gained control of the House. Welfare reform was a central component of the Contract with America. The ten policies in the pledge were: the Fiscal Responsibility Act, the Taking Back Our Streets Act, the Personal Responsibility Act, the Family Reinforcement Act, the American Dream Restoration Act, the National Security Restoration Act, the Senior Citizens Fairness Act, the Job Creation and Wage Enhancement Act, the Common Sense Legal Reform Act, and the Citizen Legislature Act.

18. Only domestic policies were coded as "abortion" issues. Abortion issues related to populations outside of the United States were coded as "foreign affairs."

19. Henry Barbour, Sally Bradshaw, Ari Fleischer, Zori Fonalledas, and Glenn McCall, "Growth and Opportunity Project," Republican National Committee, 2013.

20. Ibid.

21. Ibid.

22. Representative Lummis (WY), "Women's History Month," *Congressional Record* 162, no. 42 (March 16, 2016): H1404.

23. Barbara Vucanovich, Center for American Women and Politics Interview, July 20, 1995.

24. Representative Roukema (NJ), "Freedom of Access to Clinic Entrances Act of 1993," *Congressional Record* 140 (November 18, 1993): H10090.

25. Representative Morella (MD), "Pass the Freedom of Access to Clinic Entrances Act," *Congressional Record* 140 (March 11, 1993): H1175.

26. Many feminist activists believe the terms "anti-abortion" or "anti-choice" more accurately describe those who oppose abortion rights than "pro-life." In this book, I use the terms "pro-abortion rights" and "anti-abortion rights," given the controversy over "pro-life" and "pro-choice" labels. See also Alicia C. Shepard, "In the Abortion Debate, Words Matter," NPR, March 18, 2010. <https://www.npr.org/sections/publiceditor/2010/03/18/114576700/in-the-abortion-debate-words-matter>

27. Representative Morella (MD), "Pass the Freedom of Access to Clinic Entrances Act," *Congressional Record* 140 (March 11, 1993): H1175.

28. Helen Delich Bentley, Center for American Women and Politics Interview, August 2, 1995.

29. Barbara Vucanovich, Center for American Women and Politics Interview, November 18, 1997.

30. Sue Myrick, Center for American Women and Politics Interview, February 25, 1998.

31. "The Vision Shared: The Republican Platform, Uniting Our Family, Our Country, Our World," The American Presidency Project: Political Party Platforms, University of California, Santa Barbara, August 17, 1992.

32. Representative Smith (WA), "Senate Amendments to H.R. 1833, Partial-Birth Abortion Ban Act," *Congressional Record* 142, no. 44 (March 27, 1996): H2927.

33. Representative Seastrand (CA), "Discharging the Committee on the Judiciary from Further Consideration of the President's Veto of H.R. 1833, Partial-Birth Abortion Ban Act of 1995," *Congressional Record* 142, no. 130 (September 9, 1996): H10612.

34. R. Seth Williams, "In the Court of Common Pleas First Judicial District of Pennsylvania Criminal Trial Division in Re: Misc. No. 0009901-2008 County Investigating: Grand Jury XXIII," Pennsylvania Grand Jury Report, January 14, 2011.

35. Representative Bachmann (MN), "Pain-Capable Unborn Child Protection Act," *Congressional Record* 159, no. 87 (June 18, 2013): H3732.

36. For an analysis of how this type of framing is being used in regulatory abortion legislation at the state level, see Amanda Roberti, *"Women Deserve Better": Pro-Woman Issue Framing of Regulatory Abortion Policy in the States*. Dissertation, New Brunswick: Rutgers, the State University of New Jersey, 2017.

37. Representative Hartzler (MO), "Forty Years of Victims' Legacy of Abortion," *Congressional Record* 159, no. 7 (January 22, 2013): H211.

38. Representative Wagner (MO), "Defund Planned Parenthood Act of 2015," *Congressional Record* 161, no. 135 (July 21, 2015): H6163.

39. Martha Roby, Center for American Women and Politics Interview, February 12, 2016.

40. Representative Roby (AL), "The Pro-Life Caucus," *Congressional Record* 160, no. 9 (January 15, 2014): H454.

41. "We Believe in America: 2012 Republican Platform," The American Presidency Project: Political Party Platforms. University of California, Santa Barbara, August 27, 2012.

42. Cathy McMorris Rodgers, Center for American Women and Politics Interview, December 4, 2015.

43. Renee Ellmers, Center for American Women and Politics Interview, December 2, 2015.

44. Representative Johnson (CT), "Health Care Reform," *Congressional Record* 140 (June 16, 1994): H4651.

45. Representative Meyers (KS), "Employer Mandate Would Harm Women-Owned Businesses," *Congressional Record* 140 (June 21, 1994): H4730.

46. Barbour, Henry, Sally Bradshaw, Ari Fleischer, Zori Fonalledas, and Glenn McCall, "Growth and Opportunity Project," Republican National Committee, 2013.

47. Representative Black (TN), "Save American Workers Act of 2014," *Congressional Record* 160, no. 54 (April 3, 2014): H2866.

48. Representative Blackburn (TN), "Save American Workers Act of 2014," *Congressional Record* 160, no. 54 (April 3, 2014): H2868.

49. Deborah Pryce, Center for American Women and Politics Interview, September 28, 1995.

50. Representative Johnson (CT), "Health Care Debate," *Congressional Record* 140 (March 16, 1994): H1423

51. Elise Stefanik, Center for American Women and Politics Interview, October 20, 2015.

52. Representative Ellmers (NC), "ObamaCare," *Congressional Record* 159, no. 170 (December 3, 2013): H7437.

53. "We Believe in America: 2012 Republican Platform," The American Presidency Project: Political Party Platforms. University of California, Santa Barbara, August 27, 2012.

54. Representative Snowe (ME), "Minority Health Improvement Act of 1994," *Congressional Record* 140 (May 23, 1994): H3826.

55. Representative Morella (MD), "Women and AIDS," *Congressional Record* 140 (June 10, 1993): H3439.

56. This is consistent with Christina Xydias's findings that Republican women in the 113th Congress tended to stick to the "party script" in legislative debates. Xydias, Christina. 2018. "Republican Female Lawmakers' Contributions to Leglsiative Debates in the 113th U.S. Congress." In *The Right Women: Republican Party Activists, Candidates, and Legislators*, edited by Malliga Och and Shauna Shames. Colorado: Praeger/ABC-Clio Press, 247–258.

57. Representative Meyers (KS), "State Department, USIA, and Related Agencies Authorization Act, Fiscal Years 1994–1995," *Congressional Record* 140 (June 16, 1993): H3675.

58. Representative Seastrand (CA), "American Overseas Interests Act of 1995," *Congressional Record* 141, no. 87 (May 24, 1995): H5498.

59. Representative Ros-Lehtinen (FL), "Ladies in White and President Obama's Trip to Cuba," *Congressional Record* 162, no. 44 (March 21, 2016): H1467.

60. Representative Foxx (NC), "The Hypocrisy of the United Nations," *Congressional Record* 161, no. 48 (March 23, 2015): H1810.

61. Representative Love (UT), "Imminent Threats to Our National Security," *Congressional Record* 161, no. 109 (July 14, 2015): H5155.

62. Representative Fowler (FL), "Conference Report on H.R. 2401, National Defense Authorization Act for Fiscal Year 1994," *Congressional Record* 140 (November 15, 1993): H9647.

63. Representative Chenoweth (ID), "Bosnia and the Budget," *Congressional Record* 141, no. 194 (December 7, 1995): H14234.

64. Representative Blackburn (TN), "Imminent Threats to Our National Security," *Congressional Record* 161, no. 109 (July 14, 2015): H5156.

65. Kristi Noem, Center for American Women and Politics Interview, November 17, 2015.

66. The Republican women who participated in the July 2015 special order on national security were Diane Black, Marsha Blackburn, Vicky Hartzler, Mia Love, Cynthia Lummis, Martha McSally, and Ann Wagner.

Chapter 3

1. "Palin's Speech at the Republican National Convention." Transcript. *New York Times*, September 3, 2008.

2. Ibid.

3. Amy Gardner, "Sarah Palin Issues a Call to Action to 'Mama Grizzlies,'" *Washington Post*, May 14, 2010.

4. Ibid.

5. See Chapter 1 for detailed descriptions of interview data and Appendix A for the complete list of Republican women interviewed in each Congress.

6. Eva Clayton, Center for American Women and Politics Interview, September 15, 1995.

7. Lois Frankel, Center for American Women and Politics Interview, December 2, 2015.

8. Jennifer Dunn, Center for American Women and Politics Interview, June 15, 1998.

9. Kay Granger, Center for American Women and Politics Interview, January 7, 2016.

10. Vicky Hartzler, Center for American Women and Politics Interview, December 1, 2016.

11. Cheri Bustos, Center for American Women and Politics Interview, December 1, 2016.

12. Grace Meng, Center for American Women and Politics Interview, October 21, 2015.

13. Cathy McMorris Rodgers, Center for American Women and Politics, December 4, 2015.

14. Ibid.

15. Kristi Noem, Center for American Women and Politics Interview, November 17, 2015.

16. Alma Adams, Center for American Women and Politics Interview, October 22, 2015.

17. Marsha Blackburn, Center for American Women and Politics Interview, November 17, 2015. .

18. Ibid.

19. One of the narratives during the welfare reform debate centered on "welfare mothers" or "welfare queens"—women and mothers who took advantage of the welfare system. In my analysis, I only included speeches in which members either (1) claimed to represent women or mothers or (2) identified as women or mothers. I did not include speeches that demonized or blamed women or mothers on welfare.

20. Representative Dunn (WA), "Personal Responsibility Act of 1995," *Congressional Record* 141, no. 52 (March 21, 1995): H3361.

21. Representative Molinari (NY), "Welfare Reform," *Congressional Record* 140 (May 4, 1994): H3046.

22. Representative Vucanovich (NV), "Welfare and Medicaid Reform Act of 1996," *Congressional Record* 142, no. 106 (July 18, 1996): H7818.

23. Dorothy Gilliam, "Ugly Ways on the Hill," *Washington Post*, March 25, 1995, B1.

24. Representative Roukema (NJ), "Strict Enforcement of Child Support Orders Vital to Welfare Reform," *Congressional Record* 140 (May 19, 1994): H3695.

25. Representative Morella (MD), "Welfare and Medicaid Reform Act of 1996," *Congressional Record* 142, no. 106 (July 18, 1996): H7986.

26. Representative Fowler (FL), "Welfare and Medicaid Reform Act of 1996," *Congressional Record* 142, no. 105 (July 17, 1996): H7754.

27. Representative Chenoweth (ID), "War on Poverty," *Congressional Record* 141, no. 54 (March 23, 1995): H3720.

28. Representative Kelly (NY), "Welfare Reform: Real Change versus False Hope," *Congressional Record* 141, no. 40 (March 3, 1995): H2589.

29. As Casey and Carroll (2001) describe the role moderate Republican women played in tempering the effects of welfare reform. Women like Nancy Johnson (R-CT) and Jennifer Dunn (R-WA) were particularly vocal in their support of childcare provisions. Connie Morella (R-MD) also used her role as co-chair of the CCWI to garner bipartisan support for a less conservative alternative welfare reform bill called the Castle-Tanner Bipartisan Welfare Reform Act of 1996 (Casey and Carroll 2001, 125).

30. Representative Roukema (NJ), "Family and Medical Leave Act of 1993," *Congressional Record* 140 (February 3, 1993): H405.

31. Representative Morella (MD), "Appointments of Conferees on H.R. 3666, Departments of Veterans Affairs and Housing and Urban Development, and Independent Agencies Appropriations Act, 1997," *Congressional Record* 142, no. 124 (September 11, 1996): H10186.

32. Representative Bachmann (MN), "Immigration," *Congressional Record* 159, no. 96 (July 8, 2013): H4205–H4206.

33. Representative Brooks (IN), "ObamaCare and Choices," *Congressional Record* 159 no. 170 (December 3, 2013): H7404.

34. Representative Smith (WA), "Adoption Promotion and Stability Act of 1996," *Congressional Record* 142, no. 65 (May 10, 1996): H4820.

35. Representative Fowler (FL), "Working Families Flexibility Act of 1996," *Congressional Record* 142, no. 114 (July 30, 1996): H8782.

36. Representative Seastrand (CA), "Providing Consideration of House Joint Resolution 159, Constitutional Amendment Relating to Taxes," *Congressional Record* 142, no. 47 (April 15, 1996): H3281.

37. Representative Myrick (NC), "The 7-Year Balanced Budget Reconciliation Act of 1995," *Congressional Record* 141, no. 166 (October 25, 1995): H10789.

38. The eight issue areas in the 103rd/104th Congresses were abortion, adoption, budget, family leave, health, national security, taxes, and welfare. The 16 issue areas in the 113th/114th Congresses were abortion, budget, commemorative, education, energy, guns, health, human trafficking, immigration, national security, promoting women in male-dominated fields, veterans, violence against women, welfare, TSA regulations, and family leave.

39. Representative Foxx (NC), "Providing Consideration of H.R. 5, Student Success Act," *Congressional Record* 159, no. 103 (July 18, 2013): H4617.

40. Representative Blackburn (TN), "Clear Law Enforcement for Criminal Alien Removal Act," *Congressional Record* 161, no. 110 (July 15, 2015): H5180.

41. Representative Noem (SD), "Second Amendment Rights," *Congressional Record* 159, no. 58 (April 25, 2013): H2338.

42. Representative Myrick (SD), "Seven-Year Balanced Budget Reconciliation Act of 1995," *Congressional Record* 141, no. 167 (October 26, 1995): H11350.

43. Representative Seastrand (CA), "Women's History Month," *Congressional Record* 142, no. 40 (March 21, 1996): H2656.

44. Representative Smith (WA), "Providing for Consideration of House Joint Resolution 159, Constitutional Amendment Relating to Taxes," *Congressional Record* 142, no. 47 (April 15, 1996): H3302.

45. Representative Roby (AL), "Solutions for Our Country," *Congressional Record* 159, no. 105 (July 22, 2013): H4845.

46. Representative Blackburn (TN), "Concurrent Resolution on the Budget for Fiscal Year 2015," *Congressional Record* 160, no. 58 (April 9, 2014): H3076.

47. Representative Love (UT), "Student Success Act," *Congressional Record* 161, no. 105 (July 8, 2015): H4924.

48. Representative Foxx (NC), "Providing Consideration of H.R. 1732, Regulatory Integrity Protection Act of 2015; Providing For Consideration of Conference Report on S. Con. Res. 11, Concurrent Resolution on the Budget," *Congressional Record* 161, no. 64 (April 30, 2015): H2673.

49. Representative Hartzler (MO), "Second Amendment Rights," *Congressional Record* 159, no. 58 (April 25, 2013): H2343.

50. Representative Foxx (NC), "An American Budget, A Family Budget," *Congressional Record* 161, no. 48 (March 23, 2015): H1834.

51. Representative Black (NC), "Concurrent Resolution on the Budget for Fiscal Year 2016," *Congressional Record* 161 no. 50 (March 25, 2015): H1942.

52. For example, if a woman gave 13 woman-invoked speeches and 4 of them contained only identity claims, her Woman Identity Score would be .308.

53. Representative Bentley (MD), "Richard Milhous Nixon: His Strength and Flaws Were the Stuff of Shakespeare," *Congressional Record* 140 (April 28, 1994): H2848.

54. Representative Bachmann (MD), "America: Land of Liberty," *Congressional Record* 160, no. 149 (December 9, 2014): H8923.

55. Representative Granger (TX), "Remembering the Hon. C.W. Bill Young," *Congressional Record* 159, no. 151 (October 23, 2013): H6815.

56. Representative Ros-Lehtinen (FL), "Honoring Representative Michael Garver 'Mike' Oxley," *Congressional Record* 162, no. 25 (February 11, 2016): H756.

57. Representative Snowe (ME), "Congressional Accountability Act," *Congressional Record* 140 (August 10, 1994): H7342.

58. Representative Morella (MD), "Unfunded Mandate Reform Act of 1995," *Congressional Record* 141, no. 17 (January 27, 1995): H830.

59. Representative Foxx (NC), "Their Way or the Highway," *Congressional Record* 159, no. 140 (October 9, 2013): H6425.

60. Representative Black (NC), "Imminent Threats to Our National Security," *Congressional Record* 161, no. 109 (July 14, 2015): H5156.

61. Representative McSally (AZ), "Imminent Threats to Our National Security," *Congressional Record* 161, no. 109 (July 14, 2015): H5158.

62. Representative Bachmann (MN), "America: Land of Liberty," *Congressional Record* 160, no. 149 (December 9, 2014): H8924.

63. Representative Walters (CA), "Honoring the Service of Corporal Fred Whitaker, Sr.," *Congressional Record* 161, no. 79 (May 21, 2015): H3510.

64. Representative Black (NC), "Hire More Heroes Act of 2015," *Congressional Record* 161, no. 1 (September 9, 2014): H31.

65. Representative Ros-Lehtinen (FL), "Vietnam Human Rights Act of 2013," *Congressional Record* 159, no. 112 (July 31, 2013): H5253.

66. Kristi Noem, Center for American Women and Politics Interview, November 17, 2015.

67. Ibid.

68. Martha Roby, Center for American Women and Politics Interview, February 12, 2016.

69. Ibid.

70. Henry Barbour, Sally Bradshaw, Ari Fleischer, Zori Fonalledas, and Glenn McCall, "Growth and Opportunity Project" (Republican National Committee, 2013), 120.

Chapter 4

1. Bedard, Paul. "Mary Bono Mack: GOP Clueless in Talking to Women," *Washington Examiner*, October 4, 2012.

2. My analysis of Republican women's congressional behavior is informed by the concept of intersectionality (see Crenshaw 1989; Collins 1990) in that I acknowledge how multiple intersecting identities (in this case, partisanship and gender) can influence group experiences and actions. However, I do not claim to be engaging in an intersectional analysis, which is more explicitly concerned with the liberation of systemically marginalized groups. While some scholars argue that intersectionality can be applied to marginalized and privileged identities alike (McCall 2005; Carbado 2013), some Black feminist theorists have emphasized the importance of centering the experiences of women of color. As argued by Nikol Alexander-Floyd (2012), a lack of focus on women of color serves to "colonize intersectionality and redeploy it in ways that deplete its radical potential." (18). See Leslie McCall, "The Complexity of Intersectionality," *Signs* 30, no. 3 (2005): 1771–1800; Devon W. Carbado, "Colorblind Intersectionality," *Signs* 38, no. 4 (2013): 811–845; Nikol G. Alexander-Floyd, "Framing Condi(licious): Condoleezza Rice and the Storyline of 'Closeness' in U.S. National Community Formation," *Politics & Gender* 4, no. 3 (2012): 427–449.

3. At the state level, Holman and Mahoney (2018) further show that women's caucuses facilitate legislative collaboration—even in polarized environments—within Democratic-controlled legislatures and as the number of women increase. Mirya R. Holman and Anna Mahoney, "Stop, Collaborate, and Listen: Women's Collaboration in US State Legislatures," *Legislative Studies Quarterly* 43, no. 2 (2018):179–206.

4. The six types of congressional caucuses identified by Hammond (1998) are (1) personal-interest caucuses, whose members tend to be bipartisan and focus on one particular issue; (2) regional caucuses, whose members come from a particular region and focus on issues related to that region; (3) state/district caucuses, which focus on the interests of a specific state or district (4) industry caucuses, which focus on issues related to a particular industry, (5) intraparty caucuses, whose members come from the same party and share similar ideologies; and (6) national constituency

caucuses, whose members are bipartisan and work on a range of issues pertaining to a specific constituency.

5. The Democratic Women's Working Group was originally created in the 113th Congress. In March 2019, the group changed its name to the Democratic Women's Caucus, and it has formally registered as a CMO. Susan Webb Hammond, *Congressional Caucuses in National Policymaking* (Baltimore: Johns Hopkins University Press, Hammond).

6. See Appendix A for a detailed description of interview data and Appendix B for a list of Republican women interviewees.

7. Mildred Amer, "Women in the United States Congress: 1917–2008," Congressional Research Service, July 23, 2008.

8. "Women in Congress, 1917–2017," prepared under the direction of the Committee on House Administration of the US House of Representatives, Gregg Harper, chairman, Robert A. Brady, ranking minority member, by the Office of the Historian and Office of the Clerk, US House of Representatives (Washington, DC: US Government Publishing Office, 2017).

9. Ibid.

10. Ibid.

11. Four moderate Republican women were elected to Congress in 1980: Bobbi Fiedler (CA), Lynn Martin (IL), Marge Roukema (NJ), and Claudine Schneider (RI).

12. Steven V. Roberts, "Congress Stages a Preemptive Strike on the Gender Gap," *New York Times* (May 6, 1984): 227.

13. Ibid.

14. Remarks at a Fundraiser for Republican Women Candidates on the Occasion of Susan B. Anthony's Birthday, February 15, 1984. The Ronald Reagan Presidential Library. <https://www.reaganlibrary.gov/archives/speech/remarks-fundraiser-republican-women-candidates-occasion-susan-b-anthonys-birthday>.

15. As described by authors like Jo Freeman (2000) and Catherine Rymph (2006), the Republican Party, even more than the Democratic Party, values women as party loyalists. Republican women's organizations, in fact, are often auxiliary groups working to advance the party's policies rather than attempting to challenge or reform them. Jo Freeman, *A Room at a Time: How Women Entered Party Politics* (Lanham, MD: Rowman & Littlefield, 2000); Catherine E. Rymph, *Republican Women: Feminism and Conservatism from Suffrage through the Rise of the New Right* (University of North Carolina Press, 2006).

16. For a historical analysis of the gender gap and why it matters in American politics, see Susan J. Carroll, "Voting Choices: How and Why the Gender Gap Matters," in *Gender and Elections: Shaping the Future of American Politics, Third Edition*, edited by Susan J. Carroll and Richard Fox (New York: Cambridge University Press, 2014).

17. Ibid.

18. Susan Molinari, Center for American Women and Politics Interview, June 27, 1995.

19. Connie Morella, Center for American Women and Politics Interview, June 22, 1995.

20. The six women supporting the Hyde Amendment were Lindy Boggs (D-LA), Mary Rose Oakar (D-OH), Marilyn Lloyd (D-TN), Marjorie Holt (R-MD), Margaret Heckler (R-MA), and Virginia Smith (R-NE).

21. Martin Tolchin, "House Bars Medicaid Abortions and Funds for Enforcing Quotas," *The New York Times*, June 18, 1977.

22. For an in-depth historical analysis of this partisan transformation and the politics behind the explicit adoption of abortion language in the parties' national platforms, see Jo Freeman, *We Will Be Heard: Women's Struggles for Political Power in the United States* (Lanham, MD: Rowman & Littlefield, 2008).

23. This number includes Eleanor Holmes Norton, a non-voting delegate representing Washington, D.C.

24. "Year of the Woman, 1992," *History, Arts, and Archives. United States House of Representatives*, < https://history.house.gov/Exhibitions-and-Publications/WIC/His torical-Essays/Assembling-Amplifying-Ascending/Women-Decade/>.

25. "History of Women in the US Congress," *The Center for American Women and Politics at the Eagleton Institute of Politics at Rutgers University*, < https://cawp.rutgers.edu/history-women-us-congress>.

26. Ileana Ros-Lehtinen, Center for American Women and Politics Interview, October 9, 1997.

27. Ibid.

28. Barbra Vucanovich, Center for American Women and Politics Interview, July 20, 1995.

29. Tillie Fowler, Center for American Women and Politics Interview, August 3, 1995.

30. Jennifer Dunn, Center for American Women and Politics Interview, June 15, 1998.

31. "History of Women in the US Congress," *The Center for American Women and Politics at the Eagleton Institute of Politics at Rutgers University*, < https://cawp.rutgers.edu/history-women-us-congress>.

32. Michael Ross, "GOP Plans to Cut Funds for Black Caucus, Others," *The Los Angeles Times*, December 7, 1994..

33. Nancy Johnson, Center for American Women and Politics Interview, December 3, 1997.

34. Jan Meyers, Center for American Women and Politics Interview, November 18, 1997.

35. Tillie Fowler, Center for American Women and Politics Interview, August 3, 1995.

36. Marge Roukema, Center for American Women and Politics Interview, September 22, 1997.

37. Jennifer Dunn, Center for American Women and Politics Interview, June 15, 1997.

38. Barbara Vucanovich, Center for American Women and Politics Interview, November 18, 1997.

39. Catherine Wineinger, "War against Women," in *Women in the American Political System: An Encyclopedia of Women as Voters, Candidates, and Office Holders*, edited by Dianne Bystrom and Barbara Burrell. Vol. 2: ABC-Clio.

40. "History of Women in the US Congress," *The Center for American Women and Politics at the Eagleton Institute of Politics at Rutgers University*, < https://cawp.rutgers.edu/history-women-us-congress>.

41. TMP TV, "Republican Women Defend Sarah Palin," *YouTube*, September 3, 2008.

42. House Republicans, "House Republican Women Speak on the Pelosi Health Care Bill," *YouTube*, November 3, 2009.

43. Ibid.

44. David Weigel, "The War on Women Is Over," *Slate Magazine*, April 12, 2012.

45. In the months leading up to the 2012 election, two male Republican Senate candidates made controversial claims while defending their anti-abortion policy stances. Missouri Senate candidate Todd Akin argued against rape exceptions for anti-abortion laws, saying, "If it's a legitimate rape, the female body has ways to try to shut that whole thing down" (see John Eligon and Michael Schwirtz, "Senate Candidate Provokes Ire with 'Legitimate Rape' Comment," *The New York Times*, August 19, 2012). Two months later, Indiana Senate candidate, Richard Mourdock, made a similar comment: "Even when life begins in that horrible situation of rape, that is something that God intended to happen" (see Jonathan Weisman, "Indiana Senate Candidate Draws Fire for Rape Comments," *The New York Times*, October 23, 2012).

46. House Republicans, "4/18/11 Republican Women's Press Conference on the Budget and Keeping the Government Open." *YouTube*, April 8, 2011.

47. "113th Congress Congressional Member Organizations (CMOs)," Committee on House Administration, updated October 10, 2014, < https://cha.house.gov/sites/democrats.cha.house.gov/files/documents/cmo_cso_docs/113th%20Congress%20Congressional%20Member%20Organizations%20Updated%2010-10-14.pdf>.

48. Jada F. Smith, "Forming a Caucus, Republican Women Send a Message," *The New York Times*, May 22, 2012.

49. Virginia Foxx, Center for American Women and Politics Interview, March 18, 2015.

50. Marsha Blackburn, Center for American Women and Politics Interview, November 28, 2015.

51. Ibid.

52. Ibid.

53. Cynthia Lummis, Center for American Women and Politics Interview, February 29, 2016.

54. Ileana Ros-Lehtinen, Center for American Women and Politics Interview, March 1, 2016.

55. Kay Granger, Center for American Women and Politics Interview, January 7, 2016.

56. Virginia Foxx, Center for American Women and Politics Interview, March 18, 2015.

57. "CMO/CSO Registration Form," Committee on House Administration, <https://cha.house.gov/member-services/congressional-member-and-staff-organizations/cmocso-registration-form>.

58. For more information about Congressional Member Organizations, see <https://fas.org/sgp/crs/misc/R40683.pdf>.

59. Lucy Madison, "Republicans Push 'New Perspective' on Women," *CBS News*, May 22, 2012, <https://www.cbsnews.com/news/republicans-push-new-perspective-on-women/>.

60. Kristi Noem, Center for American Women and Politics Interview, November 17, 2015.

61. Marsha Blackburn, Center for American Women and Politics Interview, November 17, 2015.

62. Lucy Madison, "Republicans Push 'New Perspective' on Women," *CBS News*, May 22, 2012, <https://www.cbsnews.com/news/republicans-push-new-perspective-on-women/>.

63. Renee Ellmers, Center for American Women and Politics Interview, December 2, 2015.

64. Ibid.

65. Ibid.

66. Diane Black, Center for American Women and Politics Interview, October 28, 2015.

67. Ann Wagner, Center for American Women and Politics Interview, April 28, 2016.

68. Elise Stefanik, Center for American Women and Politics Interview, October 28, 2015.

69. Republican congresswomen are much more ideologically aligned with one another and with their party's policy positions. Some former Republican congresswomen have spoken out against the increasing conservatism of the GOP and of women in the party. Speaking specifically about the RWPC, former Republican Representative Claudine Schneider, who served in the House during 1981–1991, said she would not feel welcome in the caucus. She argued that today's Republican congresswomen do not adequately address issues of women's health and safety "because they are afraid of losing in the primaries. They have drunk the Kool-Aid that makes them think it is more important to win, than to do what is right by ending discrimination" (Josh Israel, "Former GOP Congresswoman Blasts New GOP Women's Caucus: 'They're Not Voting in Best Interest of All Women,'" *Think Progress*, May 25, 2012).

70. Lauren Fox, "Republican Women Wonder When They'll Get a Female Speaker of the House," *CNN*, April 24, 2018, <https://www.cnn.com/2018/04/24/politics/women-house-speaker-nominee-republicans/index.html>.

71. Renee Ellmers, Center for American Women and Politics Interview, December 2, 2015.

72. Cathy McMorris Rodgers, Center for American Women and Politics Interview, December 4, 2015.

73. Kristi Noem, Center for American Women and Politics Interview, November 17, 2015.

74. Cathy McMorris Rodgers, Center for American Women and Politics Interview, December 4, 2015.

75. Kristi Noem, Center for American Women and Politics Interview, November 17, 2015.

76. Diane Black, American Women and Politics Interview, October 28, 2015.

77. Ileana Ros-Lehtinen, Center for American Women and Politics Interview, March 1, 2016.

78. Renee Ellmers, Center for American Women and Politics Interview, December 2, 2015.

79. Cynthia Lummis, Center for American Women and Politics Interview, February 29, 2016.

80. Mary Bono Mack, "Republicans Launch Women's Policy Committee in House; New Caucus Gives Voice to Key Group on Important Issues," Press Release, *Vote Smart*, May 21, 2012.

81. Daniel Newhauser, Sarah Mimms, and National Journal, "In a Republican Congress, Few Gavels for Women," *The Atlantic*, October 6, 2014.

82. At the time of this writing, the most senior Republican women in the 117th House of Representatives (2021–2023) are Kay Granger, who entered Congress in 1997, followed by Virginia Foxx and Cathy McMorris Rodgers, whose first term began in 2005. The remaining House Republican women entered Congress in 2011 or later. By contrast, the five most senior Republican men entered Congress in 1973, 1981, 1987, and 1993, respectively.

83. The 2012 vote by the Steering Committee to nominate the chair of the Committee on Homeland Security was especially close. The first three rounds of votes resulted in a three-way tie between McCaul, Rogers, and Miller. Miller was eliminated in the fourth round, but it took another five rounds to break the tie between McCaul and Rogers. "I've been here 22 years, and I've never seen anything like this before," said Speaker Boehner. Daniel Newhauser, "Vote for Homeland Gavel Was Closest in Memory for Some Lawmakers," *Roll Call*, November 28, 2012.

84. One anonymous Democratic official told a *Talking Points Memo* reporter, "I'm not sure which was worse: House Republicans refusing to have any women chair a legislative committee or only appointing a woman to chair the Congressional Housekeeping Committee" (Evan McMorris-Santoro, "Dems, Progressives Snicker as House GOP Finally Appoints Female Committee Chair," *Talking Points Memo*, November 30, 2012). Several news headlines highlighted the lack of Republican women as committee chairs (e.g., Jennifer Bendery, "House GOP Committee Chairs Will All Be White Men in Next Congress," *HuffPost Politics*, November 27, 2012; Dashiell Bennett, "House Republicans Pick Only White Men to Be Committee Chairmen," *The Atlantic*, November 28, 2012; Morgan Whitaker, "House Republicans Choose All-White, All-Male Committee Chairs," MSNBC, November 28, 2012).

85. Emma Dumain, "Boehner Finds the Woman for the Job," *CQ Roll Call*, October 22, 2013.

86. Paul Ryan, in particular, has been vocal in his denunciation of "identity politics," calling it his "biggest concern of politics these days." Following the announcement of his retirement, Ryan said in 2018, "If you can deny the oxygen of identity politics, the best way to do that is to have a faster-growing economy, more upward mobility, higher wages, getting people from poverty into the workforce." (Tara Golshan, "The Reason Republican Women Are on the Decline in the House," *Vox*, December 4, 2018.)

87. In the 115th (2017–2019) House of Representatives, Diane Black chaired the Budget Committee, Virginia Foxx chaired the Committee on Education and the Workforce, and Susan Brooks chaired the Ethics Committee. These positions were short-lived, however, as Diane Black announced her resignation of the chairmanship in December 2017 to run for governor of Tennessee and Susan Brooks announced her retirement in 2019.

88. Lauren Fox, "Republican Women Wonder When They'll Get a Female Speaker of the House," *CNN*, April 24, 2018.

89. Phone call with a Republican staffer in 2017.

Chapter 5

1. McMorris Rodgers was also chair of the House Republican Conference in the 115th Congress, before being succeeded by Liz Cheney (R-WY) in the 116th Congress.
2. For a more in-depth discussion of the concept and utility of critical mass in gender politics scholarship, see "Do Women Represent Women? Rethinking the 'Critical Mass' Debate," Critical Perspectives on Gender and Politics, *Politics & Gender*, 2, no. 4 (2006): 491–530.
3. "About," National Republican Congressional Committee, <https://www.nrcc.org/about/>.
4. Conference leadership's main function was not always party communications. The Republican Party was the first to focus on external communications in the 1980s, as it attempted to increase efforts to win the majority in the House. One of the first "vigorous public counteroffensive[s]" was led by Rep. Richard Armey (R-TX) as Conference Chair in 1992 in legislative opposition to President Clinton. Gary Lee Malecha and Daniel J. Reagan, *The Public Congress: Congressional Deliberation in a New Media Age* (New York: Taylor & Francis, 2012), 74.
5. The Republican Theme Team is a group of 50 to 90 Republican House members that helps organize non-legislative debate speeches (one-minute and special order) in order to deliver a collective party message on the House floor. On the other side of the aisle, the Democratic Message Board (DMB) provides the same function. Douglas Harris, "Orchestrating Party Talk: A Party-Based View of One-Minute Speeches in the House of Representatives," *Legislative Studies Quarterly*, 30, no. 1 (2012): 127–141; Gary Lee Malecha and Daniel J. Reagan, *The Public Congress: Congressional Deliberation in a New Media Age* (New York: Taylor & Francis, 2012).
6. Interviews were not conducted with Lynn Jenkins (R-KS), vice chair of the Conference in the 113th and 114th Congresses; nor Mimi Walters (R-CA), freshman representative in the 114th Congress.
7. Eight Republican leadership positions in the House are elected directly by conference members: (1) the Speaker; (2) the Republican Leader; (3) the Republican Whip; (4) the Chair of the Republican Conference; (5) the Chair of the National Republican Congressional Committee; (6) the Chair of the Committee on Policy; (7) the Vice-Chair of the Republican Conference; and (8) the Secretary of the Republican Conference. There are also six designated leadership positions, which are recommended to the conference by the Republican Steering Committee: (1) the Chair of the House Committee on Rules; (2) the Chair of the House Committee on Ways and Means; (3) the Chair of the House Committee on Appropriations; (4) the Chair of the House Committee on the Budget; (5) the Chair of the House Committee on Energy and Commerce; (6) the Chief Deputy Whip. The final two designated leadership positions are elected directly by the sophomore and freshman classes, respectively: (7) the sophomore representative; and (8) the freshman representative.
8. See Chapter 1 for complete description of interview data.
9. Guy Molinari (R-NY) served in the House from 1981 to 1990, when he resigned to become Borough President of Staten Island.

10. Susan Molinari, "History, Art, & Archives. United States House of Representatives," <https://history.house.gov/People/Detail/18389>.

11. Ibid.

12. Elinor Burkett, "In the Land of Conservative Women," *The Atlantic*, September 1996.

13. Another example of this comes from Helen Bentley's (R-MD) experience on the Appropriations Committee's Labor, Health, and Human Services Subcommittee. She said in a 1995 CAWP interview, "I was the only [woman] on the Republican side, and Joe McDade [vice chairman of the Appropriations Committee] wanted me on there, particularly because there were four Democratic women on the other side. He said, 'We've got to have at least one woman.'" "Otherwise it looks bad?" the CAWP interviewer asked. "Yeah," Bentley replied. Helen Bentley, Center for American Women and Politics Interview, August 2, 1995.

14. "The Honorable Susan Molinari Oral History Interview," Office of the Historian, US House of Representatives, May 25, 2012.

15. Ibid.

16. Ibid.

17. Ibid.

18. Ibid.

19. Ibid.

20. Laura Blumenfeld, "The Life of the Party," *The Washington Post*, August 13, 1996.

21. Ibid.

22. Susan Molinari, Center for American Women and Politics Interview, June 27, 1995.

23. Geraldine Baum, "A Rising Voice in the Revolution: Politics; As she ascends the Republican ranks, outspoken moderate Rep. Susan Molinari may be just what the GOP needs to stay in the majority," *Los Angeles Times*, March 6, 1995.

24. Ibid.

25. "The Honorable Susan Molinari Oral History Interview," Office of the Historian, US House of Representatives, May 25, 2012.

26. For example, see Laura Ingraham, "Convention Preview: How the Gender Gap Is Driving the Dole Girl Crazy," *The Washington Post*, August 4, 1996.

27. Geraldine Baum, "A Rising Voice in the Revolution: Politics; As she ascends the Republican ranks, outspoken moderate Rep. Susan Molinari may be just what the GOP needs to stay in the majority." *Los Angeles Times*, March 6, 1995.

28. Susan Molinari and Barbara Vucanovich have DW-NOMINATE scores of .256 and .441, respectively.

29. As a member of the leadership team, Vucanovich had vowed not to let the issue of abortion divide Republicans. When asked in a CAWP interview if she thought she had succeeded in this goal, she said, "No . . . I don't think you change anyone's minds by what you get up and say. People feel the way they feel." She went on to say that the Speaker's biweekly meetings with Republican women were largely ineffective: "Time after time, before we knew it, we were into the abortion issue again. You know, Republicans don't agree on that issue! We would sit in Newt's office, and finally I would just think, 'Oh, the hell with this, I've been here before. Just let me go home.'"

Barbara Vucanovich, Center for American Women and Politics Interview, November 18, 1997.

30. Jennifer Blackburn Dunn, "History, Art, & Archives. United States House of Representatives," <https://history.house.gov/People/Listing/D/DUNN,-Jennifer-Blackburn-(D000549)/>.

31. Hanna Rosin, "Pretty on the Outside," *New York Magazine*, April 28, 1997, 20–23.

32. Dunn admired Ronald Reagan so much that she named her second-born son after him. Reagan Dunn, notably, was named not after President Reagan but after *Governor Reagan*—"nearly 10 years ahead of the Reagan Revolution" (Heffernan 2012, 18). "Now, as fate will have it," Reagan Dunn said, "he turned out to be a pretty darn good president . . . He wasn't, you know, Nixon. If my name were Nixon Dunn, it would be different. Maybe there is a little luck" (Heffernan 2012, 19). See Trova Heffernan, *A Woman First: The Impact of Jennifer Dunn* (Washington State Legacy Project, Office of the Secretary of State, Centralia, WA: Gorham Printing, 2012), 18, 19.

33. Life and Career of Jennifer Dunn, "American Profile Interview," *C-SPAN*, December 18, 1997.

34. Susan Molinari," "History, Art, & Archives, United States House of Representatives," <https://history.house.gov/People/Detail/18389>.

35. Life and Career of Jennifer Dunn, "American Profile Interview," *C-SPAN*, December 18, 1997.

36. The gender gap in 1996 was 11 points. There was also an 11-point and 12-point gender gap in the 2016 and 2020 presidential elections, respectively. "The Gender Gap: Voting Choices in Presidential Elections," Fact Sheet. Center for American Women and Politics, Eagleton Institute of Politics at Rutgers University, <https://cawp.rutgers.edu/sites/default/files/resources/ggpresvote.pdf>

37. Jennifer Dunn, Center for American Women and Politics Interview, June 15, 1998.

38. Ibid.

39. Ibid.

40. Ibid.

41. Hanna Rosin, "Pretty on the Outside," *New York Magazine*, April 28, 1997, 20–23.

42. Life and Career of Jennifer Dunn, "American Profile Interview," *C-SPAN*, December 18, 1997.

43. Jennifer Dunn, Center for American Women and Politics Interview, June 15, 1998.

44. Ibid.

45. Barbara Vucanovich, Center for American Women and Politics Interview, November 18, 1997.

46. Ibid.

47. Tillie Fowler, Center for American Women and Politics Interview, November 6, 1997.

48. Jennifer Dunn, Center for American Women and Politics Interview, June 15, 1998.

49. Barbara Vucanovich, Center for American Women and Politics Interview, November 18, 1997.

50. Eliza Newlin Carney, "And There's the House's Gender Gap," *The National Journal*, October 18, 1997.

51. "About," Value in Electing Women Political Action Committee, Retrieved November 1, 2021. <https://viewpac.org/about/>.

52. "The Gender Gap: Voting Choices in Presidential Elections," Fact Sheet. Center for American Women and Politics, Eagleton Institute of Politics at Rutgers University, January 2017 <https://cawp.rutgers.edu/sites/default/files/resources/ggpresvote.pdf>

53. Ibid.

54. Ibid.

55. Cathy McMorris Rodgers, Center for American Women and Politics Interview, December 4, 2015.

56. Sarah Mimms, "Is Cathy McMorris Rodgers More than a Token?" *The Atlantic*, September 19, 2011.

57. Deborah Pryce (R-OH) was the first woman to chair the House Republican conference. She was elected in the 108th Congress and served two terms as chair.

58. Sarah Mimms, "Is Cathy McMorris Rodgers More than a Token?" *The Atlantic*, September 19, 2011.

59. Ibid.

60. Cathy McMorris Rodgers, Center for American Women and Politics Interview, December 4, 2015.

61. "Vice Chair Accomplishments," Congresswoman Cathy McMorris Rodgers, March 3, 2011, <https://mcmorris.house.gov/vice_chair_accomplishments/>.

62. Four women gave the Republican Response to the State of the Union address prior to Cathy McMorris Rodgers: Charlotte Reid in 1968, Christine Todd Whitman in 1995, Jennifer Dunn in 1999, and Susan Collins in 2000. Ileana Ros-Lehtinen delivered a Republican Response in Spanish in 2014 following McMorris Rodgers' response. Joni Ernst delivered the response in 2015, and Nikki Haley did so in 2016.

63. "State of the Union GOP Response: Cathy McMorris Rodgers," Transcript, *Politico*, January 28, 2014.

64. Cathy McMorris Rodgers, Center for American Women and Politics Interview, December 4, 2015.

65. Henry Barbour, Sally Bradshaw, Ari Fleischer, Zori Fonalledas, and Glenn McCall, "Growth and Opportunity Project," Republican National Committee, 2013.

66. "NRCC Announces New Women's Initiative: Project GROW," National Republican Congressional Committee, June 28, 2013. <https://www.nrcc.org/2013/06/28/nrcc-announces-new-womens-initiative-project-grow/>.

67. Ann Wagner, Center for American Women and Politics Interview, April 28, 2016.

68. In her interview with CAWP, Foxx told us that she has a strong working relationship with Speaker John Boehner "as a result of having served on his committee" (the House Education Committee).

69. Cathy McMorris Rodgers, Center for American Women and Politics Interview, December 4, 2015.

70. Virginia Foxx, Center for American Women and Politics Interview, September 18, 2015.

71. Emma Dumain, "GOP Women Seek Broader Influence with Committee." *Roll Call*, June 21, 2013.

72. Cathy McMorris Rodgers, Center for American Women and Politics Interview, December 4, 2015.

73. Ibid.

74. Elise Stefanik, Center for American Women and Politics Interview, October 20, 2015.

75. Susan Brooks, Center for American Women and Politics Interview, October 27, 2015.

76. Ann Wagner, Center for American Women and Politics Interview, April 28, 2015.

77. Ibid.

78. Ibid.

79. At a breakfast I attended honoring Cathy McMorris Rodgers on December 4, 2015, hosted by the American Dream Project, Elise Stefanik told the audience that McMorris Rodgers took her under her wing and mentored her as a freshman congresswoman.

80. "Every Issue Affects Women," The Ripon Society, October 13, 2015, <https://www.riponsociety.org/2015/10/every-issue-affects-women/>.

81. Susan Brooks, Center for American Women and Politics Interview, October 27, 2015.

82. Cathy McMorris Rodgers, Center for American Women and Politics Interview, December 4, 2015.

83. Susan Brooks, Center for American Women and Politics Interview, October 27, 2015.

84. Libby Ingrid Copeland, "Dunn, GOP's Smooth Referee, Aims for the No. 2 Spot," *The Washington Post*, November 16, 1998.

85. Ibid.

86. Ibid.

87. Ibid.

88. Ibid.

89. Ralph Thomas, "Jennifer Dunn, Who Inspired Face of Today's State GOP, Dies at 66," *The Seattle Times*, September 6, 2007.

90. Cathy McMorris Rodgers, Center for American Women and Politics Interview, December 4, 2015.

91. Ibid.

92. Ibid.

93. "When she was selected to respond to President Obama's State of the Union address earlier this year, McMorris Rodgers was seen as a diversity pick, not the best person for the job. Some Republicans and pundits hinted at tokenism, but Democrats came right out and said it, with Rep. Steny Hoyer calling her selection nothing more than a 'transparent' ploy by the GOP to appeal to female voters" Sarah Mimms, "Is Cathy McMorris Rodgers More than a Token?" *The Atlantic*, September 19, 2011.

94. Scott Wong, "Female Lawmakers Flee for Higher Office, Retirement," *The Hill*, May 17, 2017.

95. Ibid.

96. Martha McSally, Center for American Women and Politics Interview, March 16, 2016.

97. "History of Women in the US Congress," Center for American Women and Politics, Eagleton Institute of Politics at Rutgers University, <https://cawp.rutgers.edu/history-women-us-congress>.

98. Martha McSally, Center for American Women and Politics Interview, March 16, 2016.

Chapter 6

1. Sarah Frostenson, "The Women's Marches May Have Been the Largest Demonstration in US History," *Vox*, January 31, 2017.
2. Danielle Kurtzleben, "More than Twice as Many Women Are Running for Congress in 2018 Compared with 2016," *NPR*, February 20, 2018.
3. For a gender analysis of the 2018 midterm election results, see Kelly Dittmar, *Unfinished Business: Women Running in 2018 and Beyond*. Center for American Women and Politics, Eagleton Institute of Politics (New Brunswick, NJ: Rutgers University, 2019). <https://womenrun.rutgers.edu/2018-report/>.
4. Domenico Montanaro, "It Was a Big, Blue Wave: Democrats Pick up Most House Seats in a Generation," *NPR*, November 14, 2018.
5. This is the total number of House Democratic women at the beginning of the first session of the 116th Congress. The number includes Congresswoman Katie Hill (D-CA), who later resigned in October 2019.
6. Press Release, "Results: Women Candidates in the 2018 Elections," Center for American Women and Politics, Eagleton Institute of Politics at Rutgers University, November 29, 2018.
7. Maureen Groppe, "Brooks Says House GOP Women Looking for Answers as Their Ranks Shrink to Lowest Levels in 25 Years," *Indianapolis Star*, December 13, 2018.
8. Bowman, Bridget Bowman, "House Recruiter to GOP: 'Do a Better Job of Looking like America,'" *Roll Call*, April 10, 2019.
9. Rachael Bade and Sarah Ferris, "'I Wasn't Asking for Permission': GOP Women Put Leaders on Notice," *Politico*, December 11, 2018.
10. Ibid.
11. Simone Pathe, "Elise Stefanik Wants to Play in Primaries to Help Republican Women," *Roll Call*, December 4, 2018.
12. Ibid.
13. Elise Stefanik, @EliseStefanik *Twitter*. December 4, 2018, 9:43 A.M., <https://twitter.com/elisestefanik/status/1069950316483874816>
14. "About," Elevate PAC, <https://elevate-pac.com/about/>.
15. Caroline Kitchener, "More Women Are Running for House Seats than Ever. Even 2018," *The Lily*, May 13, 2020, <https://www.thelily.com/more-women-are-running-for-house-seats-than-ever-even-2018/>.
16. Women won 11 of the 15 House seats flipped by Republicans in the 2020 cycle.
17. Ari Shapiro, "Minnesota Rep. Tom Emmer on How the GOP Whittled Away at Democrats' House Majority," *NPR*, November 10, 2020, <https://www.npr.org/sections/live-updates-2020-election-results/2020/11/10/933548695/nrcc-chair-on-how-gop-won-some-new-congressional-seats-and-held-onto-most-old-on>.

18. Danielle Kurtzleben, "How a Record Number of Republican Women Got Elected to Congress," *NPR*, November 13, 2020, <https://www.npr.org/2020/11/13/934249216/how-a-record-number-of-republican-women-got-elected-to-congress>.

19. While House Republican women were able to increase their ranks in the 115th (2017–2019) Congress, those positions have not been maintained. Republican women held three committee chairmanships in the 115th Congress: Diane Black chaired the Budget Committee, Virginia Foxx chaired Education and Labor, and Susan Brooks chaired the Ethics Committee. Black vacated her seat in 2018 to run for governor—a race she lost in the primary to Bill Lee. Brooks stepped down from Ethics to become recruitment chair of the NRCC before announcing her decision to retire in 2019. In the 117th (2019–2020) House, Kay Granger, the second most-senior Republican woman in the House, was elected ranking member of Appropriations, Cathy McMorris Rodgers was elected ranking member of Energy and Commerce, and Virginia Foxx will serve as ranking member of Education and Labor. The current total number of Republican women ranking committee members to three. By comparison, Democratic women will chair six committees in the 117th House.

20. Julie Hirschfeld Davis, "Joan Perry's Defeat in G.O.P Primary Points up Party's Gender Woes," *The New York Times*, July 10, 2019.

21. Paul Kane, "North Carolina runoff a test of women's standing in the Republican Party," *The Washington Post*, July 8, 2019.

22. Also see CAWP analysis: Kelly Dittmar, "Primary Problems: Women Candidates in US House Primaries," A Closer Look. *Center for American Women and Politics at Rutgers University*, 2013, <http://www.cawp.rutgers.edu/sites/default/files/resources/primary-problems-10-1-13.pdf>.

23. Juliana Menasce Horowitz, Ruth Igielnik, and Kim Parker, "Women and Leadership 2018: Wide Gender and Party Gaps in Views about the State of Female Leadership and the Obstacles Women Face," *Pew Research Center*, July 20, 2018

24. Rebecca Schuller, "Yes, the GOP Has a Woman Problem—Yes, It Can Be Solved," *The Hill*, July 26, 2019.

25. "Donald Trump Speech 'Save America' Rally," Transcript, January 6, 2021, <https://www.rev.com/blog/transcripts/donald-trump-speech-save-america-rally-transcript-january-6>.

26. The other eight Republicans who voted in favor of impeachment were Reps. Tom Rice (R-SC), Dan Newhouse (R-WA), Adam Kinzinger (R-IL), Anthony Gonzalez (R-OH), Fred Upton (R-MI), Peter Meijer (R-MI), John Katko (R-NY), and David Valadao (R-CA).

27. The other eight Republicans who voted to remove Greene from her committees were Reps. Mario Diaz-Balart (R-FL), Brian Fitzpatrick (R-PA), Carlos Gimenez (R-FL), Chris Jacobs (R-NY), John Katko (R-NY), Adam Kinzinger (R-IL), Chris Smith (R-NJ), and Fred Upton (R-MI).

28. Amy B. Wang, "GOP Rep. Liz Cheney Says Trump 'Does Not Have a Role as a Leader of Our Party Going Forward,'" *The Washington Post*, February 7, 2021. <https://www.washingtonpost.com/politics/2021/02/06/wyoming-gop-censures-rep-liz-cheney-voting-impeach-trump/>.

29. Mariam Khan, "Marjorie Taylor Greene Declares She Is 'Freed' after Being Booted from House Committees," *ABC News*, February 5, 2021, <https://abcnews.go.com/Politics/greene-declares-freed-booted-house-committees/story?id=75706246>.

30. Melanie Zanona and Ally Mutnick, "Recruitment Push Fuels Record Number of Women in the House GOP," *Politico*, November 4, 2020, <https://www.politico.com/news/2020/11/04/house-gop-republican-recruitment-women-434107>.

31. @MaElviraSalazar (María Elvira Salazar), *Twitter*, December 2, 2020, 4:46 P.M. <https://twitter.com/MaElviraSalazar/status/1334297991654612992>.

32. Antonia Blumberg, "Rashida Tlaib, Alexandria Ocasio-Cortez Post 'Squad' Pics of Diverse New Members of Congress," *Huffpost*, November 12, 2018, <https://www.huffpost.com/entry/rashida-tlaib-alexandria-ocasio-cortez-post-squad-pics-of-diverse-new-members-of-congress_n_5bea1284e4b044bbb1a798a1>.

Bibliography

Abramovitz, Mimi. 2006. "Welfare Reform in the United States: Gender, Race, and Class Matter." *Critical Social Policy* 26 (2): 336–364.

Adams, Alma. 2015. Center for American Women and Politics Interview, October 22.

Aldrich, John H., and David W. Rohde. 1997. "The Transition to Republican Rule in the House: Implications for Theories of Congressional Politics." *Political Science Quarterly* 112 (4): 541–567.

Aldrich, John H., and David W. Rohde. 2000. "The Consequences of Party Organization in the House: The Role of the Majority and Minority Parties in Conditional Party Government." In *Polarized Politics: Congress and the President in a Partisan Era*, edited by Jon R. Bond and Richard Fleisher, 31–72. Washington, D.C.: CQ Press.

Aldrich, John, and David W. Rohde. 2010. "Consequences of Electoral and Institutional Change: The Evolution of Conditional Party Government in the U.S. House of Representatives." In *New Directions in American Political Parties*, edited by Jeffrey M. Stonecash, 234–250. New York: Routledge.

Alexander-Floyd, Nikol G. 2008. "Framing Condi(licious): Condoleezza Rice and the Storyline of 'Closeness' in U.S. National Community Formation." *Politics & Gender* 4 (3): 427–449.

Alexander-Floyd, Nikol G. 2012. "Disappearing Acts: Reclaiming Intersectionality in the Social Sciences in a Post-Black Feminist Era." *Feminist Formations* 24 (1): 1–25.

Alphonso, Gwendoline M. 2018. *Polarized Families, Polarized Parties: Contesting Values and Economics in American Politics*. Philadelphia, PA: University of Pennsylvania Press.

Amer, Mildred. 2008. "Women in the United States Congress: 1917–2008," Congressional Research Service, July 23.

Angevine, Sara. 2017. "Representing All Women: An Analysis of Congress, Foreign Policy, and the Boundaries of Women's Surrogate Representation." *Political Research Quarterly* 70 (1): 98–110.

Anzia, Sarah F., and Christopher R. Berry. 2011. "The Jackie (and Jill) Robinson Effect: Why Do Congresswomen Outperform Congressmen?" *American Journal of Political Science* 55 (3): 478–493.

Atkinson, Mary Layton, and Jason Harold Windett. 2018. "Gender Stereotypes and the Policy Priorities of Women in Congress." *Political Behavior* 41: 769–789.

Bade, Rachael, and Sarah Ferris. 2018. " 'I Wasn't Asking for Permission': GOP Women Put Leaders on Notice," *Politico*, December 11.

Barbour, Henry, Sally Bradshaw, Ari Fleischer, Zori Fonalledas, and Glenn McCall. 2013. "Growth and Opportunity Project," Republican National Committee.

Barnes, Tiffany D., and Erin C. Cassese. 2017. "American Party Women: A Look at the Gender Gap within Parties." *Political Research Quarterly* 70 (1): 127–141.

Barot, Sneha, and Susan A. Cohen. 2015. "The Global Gag Rule and Fights over Funding UNFPA: The Issues That Won't Go Away." *Guttmacher Policy Review* 18 (2): 27–33.

Baum, Geraldine. 1995. "A Rising Voice in the Revolution: Politics; As she ascends the Republican ranks, outspoken moderate Rep. Susan Molinari may be just what the GOP needs to stay in the majority." *Los Angeles Times*, March 6.

Beail, Linda, and Rhonda Kinney Longworth. 2013. *Framing Sarah Palin: Pit Bulls, Puritans, and Politics*. New York: Routledge Press.

Beckwith, Karen. 2014. "Plotting the Path from One to the Other: Women's Interests and Political Representation." In *Representation: The Case of Women*, edited by Michelle Taylor Robinson and Maria Escobar-Lemmon, 19–40. New York: Oxford University Press.

Bedard, Paul. 2012. "Mary Bono Mack: GOP Clueless in Talking to Women." *Washington Examiner*, October 4.

Bejarano, Christina E. 2013. *The Latina Advantage: Gender, Race, and Political Success*. Austin: The University of Texas Press.

Bentley, Helen Delich. 1995. Center for American Women and Politics Interview, August 2.

Binder, Sarah A. 2003. *Stalemate: Causes and Consequences of Legislative Gridlock*. Washington, D.C.: Brookings Institution Press.

Binder, Sarah A. 2016. "Polarized We Govern?" In *Governing in A Polarized Age: Elections, Parties, and Political Representation in America*, edited byAlan Gerber and Eric Shickler, 223–242. Cambridge University Press.

Black, Diane. 2015. Center for American Women and Politics Interview, October 28.

Blackburn, Marsha. 2015. Center for American Women and Politics Interview, November 17.

Blum, Rachel M. 2020. *How the Tea Party Captured the GOP: Insurgent Factions in American Politics*. Chicago: The University of Chicago Press.

Blumberg, Antonia. 2018. "Rashida Tlaib, Alexandria Ocasio-Cortez Post 'Squad' Pics of Diverse New Members of Congress." *Huffpost*, November 12.

Blumenfeld, Laura. 1996. "The Life of the Party." *The Washington Post*, August 13.

Bono Mack, Mary. 2012. "Republicans Launch Women's Policy Committee in House; New Caucus Gives Voice to Key Group on Important Issues." Press Release, *Vote Smart*, May 21.

Bowman, Bridget. 2019. "House Recruiter to GOP: 'Do a Better Job of Looking like America.'" *Roll Call*, April 10.

Bratton, Kathleen, and Kerry Haynie. 1999. "Agenda Setting and Legislative Success in State Legislatures: The Effects of Race and Gender." *The Journal of Politics* 61 (3): 658–679.

Brooks, Susan. 2015. Center for American Women and Politics Interview, October 27.

Brown, Nadia. 2014. *Sisters in the Statehouse: Black Women & Legislative Decision Making*. New York: Oxford University Press.

Bryant, Lisa A., and Julia Hellwege. 2019. Working Mothers Represent: How Children Affect the Legislative Agenda of Women in Congress. *American Politics Research* 47 (3): 447–470.

Burden, Barry C., Gregory A. Caldeira, and Tim Groseclose. 2000. "Measuring the Ideologies of U.S. Senators: The Song Remains the Same." *Legislative Studies Quarterly* 25 (2): 237 258.

Burkett, Elinor. 1996. "In the Land of Conservative Women." *The Atlantic*, September.

Burrell, Barbara C. 1994. *A Woman's Place Is in the House: Campaigning for Congress in the Feminist Era*. Ann Arbor: University of Michigan Press.

Burrell, Barbara. 2018. *Women and Politics: A Quest for Political Equality in an Age of Economic Inequality*. New York: Taylor & Francis.

Bustos, Cheri. 2016. Center for American Women and Politics Interview, December 1.

Campbell, Rosie. 2016. "Representing Women Voters: The Role of the Gender Gap and the Response of Political Parties." *Party Politics* 22 (5): 587–597.

Carbado, Devon W. 2013. "Colorblind Intersectionality." *Signs* 38 (4): 811–845.

Carew, Jessica D. 2016. "How Do You See Me? Stereotyping of Black Women and How It Affects Them in an Electoral Context." In *Distinct Identities: Minority Women in U.S. Politics*, edited by Nadia Brown and Sarah Allen Gershon, 95–115. New York: Routledge.

Casey, Kathleen J., and Susan J. Carroll. 2001. "Welfare Reform in the 104th Congress: Institutional Position and the Role of Women." In *Women and Welfare: Theory and Practice in the United States and Europe*, edited by Nancy Hirschmann and Ulrike Liebert, 111–132. New Brunswick, NJ: Rutgers University Press.

Carney, Eliza Newlin. 1997. "And There's the House's Gender Gap." *The National Journal*, October 18.

Carroll, Susan J., ed. 2001. *The Impact of Women in Public Office*. Bloomington, IN: Indiana University Press.

Carroll, Susan J. 2002. "Representing Women: Congresswomen's Perceptions of Their Representational Roles." In *Women Transforming Congress*, edited by Cindy Simon Rosenthal, 50–68. Norman, OK: University of Oklahoma Press.

Carroll, Susan J. 2008. "Security Moms and Presidential Politics: Women Voters in the 2004 Election." In *Voting the Gender Gap*, edited by Lois Duke Whitaker, 75–90. Urbana and Chicago, IL: University of Illinois Press.

Carroll, Susan J. 2009. "Reflections on Gender and Hillary Clinton's Presidential Campaign: The Good, the Bad, and the Misogynic." *Politics & Gender* 5 (1): 1–20.

Carroll, Susan J. 2014. "Voting Choices: How and Why the Gender Gap Matters." In *Gender and Elections: Shaping the Future of American Politics*, 3rd ed., edited by Susan J. Carroll and Richard Fox, 119–145. New York: Cambridge University Press.

Carroll, Susan J., and Debra J. Liebowitz. 2003. "New Challenges, New Questions, New Directions." In *Women and American Politics*, edited by Susan J. Carroll, 1–32. New York: Oxford University Press.

Carroll, Susan J., and Ronnee Schreiber. 1997. "Media Coverage of Women in the 103rd Congress." In *Women, Media, and Politics*, edited by Pippa Norris, 131–148. New York: Oxford University Press.

Celis, Karen, Sarah Childs, Johanna Kantola, and Mona Lena Krook. 2008. "Rethinking Women's Substantive Representation." *Representation* 44 (2): 99–110.

Celis, Karen, and Sarah Childs. 2012. "The Substantive Representation of Women: What to Do with Conservative Claims?" *Political Studies* 60 (1): 213–225.

Celis, Karen, and Sarah Childs. 2018. "Conservatism and Women's Political Representation." *Politics & Gender* 14: 5–26.

Childs, Sarah and Mona Krook. 2006. "Should Feminists Give Up on Critical Mass? A Contingent Yes." *Politics and Gender* 4: 522–530.

Childs, Sarah, and Mona Krook. 2008. "Critical Mass Theory and Women's Political Representation." *Political Studies* 56: 725–736.

Childs, Sarah, and Mona Krook. 2009. "Analyzing Women's Substantive Representation: From Critical Mass to Critical Actors." *Government and Opposition* 44 (2): 125–145.

Childs, Sarah, and Paul Webb. 2012. *Sex, Gender, and the Conservative Party: From Iron Lady to Kitten Heels.* New York: Palgrave Macmillan.

Clayton, Eva. 1995. Center for American Women and Politics Interview, September 15.

Collins, Patricia Hill. 1990. *Black Feminist Thought: Knowledge, Consciousness, and the Politics of Empowerment.* New York: Routledge.

Combahee River Collective. [1977] 1995. "A Black Feminist Statement." In *Words of Fire: An Anthology of African American Feminist Thought*, edited by Beverly Guy-Sheftall, 232–240. New York: New Press.

Connelly, William F., and John J. Pitney. 1994. *Congress' Permanent Minority? Republicans in the U.S. House.* Rowman and Littlefield Publishers.

Cooper, Melinda. 2017. *Family Values: Between Neoliberalism and the New Social Conservatism.* Cambridge, MA: MIT Press.

Copeland, Libby Ingrid. 1998. "Dunn, GOP's Smooth Referee, Aims for the No. 2 Spot." *The Washington Post*, November 16.

Cox, Gary W., and Mathew D. McCubbins. 1993. *Legislative Leviathan: Party Government in the House.* Berkeley: University of California Press.

Cox, Gary, and Mathew McCubbins. 2005. *Setting the Agenda: Responsible Party Government in the U.S. House of Representatives.* New York: Cambridge University Press.

Crenshaw, Kimberle. 1989. "Demarginalizing the Intersection of Race and Sex: A Black Feminist Critique of Antidiscrimination Doctrine, Feminist Theory and Antiracist Politics." *University of Chicago Legal Forum* 1989 (1): 139–167.

Crowder-Meyer, Melody, and Rosalyn Cooperman. 2018. "Can't Buy Them Love: How Party Culture among Donors Contributes to the Party Gap in Women's Representation." *The Journal of Politics* 80 (4): 1211–1224.

Dahlerup, Drude. 1988. "From a Small to a Large Minority: Women in Scandinavian Politics." *Scandinavian Political Studies* 11 (4): 275–297.

Darcy, R., Susan Welch, and Janet Clark. 1994. *Women, Elections, and Representation.* Lincoln, NE: University of Nebraska Press.

Davis, Julie Hirschfeld. 2019. "Joan Perry's Defeat in G.O.P Primary Points up Party's Gender Woes." *The New York Times*, July 10.

de Geus, Roosmarjin, and Rosalind Shorrocks. 2020. "Where Do Female Conservatives Stand? A Cross-National Analysis of the Issue Positions and Ideological Placement of Female Right-Wing Candidates." *Journal of Women, Politics & Policy* 41 (1): 7–35.

Deckman, Melissa. 2016. *Tea Party Women: Mama Grizzlies, Grassroots Leaders, and the Changing Face of the American Right.* New York: New York University Press.

DeLauro, Rosa. 1995. Center for American Women and Politics Interview, June 30.

Delegard, Kristen. 2012. "It Takes Women to Fight Women: Woman Suffrage and the Genesis of Female Conservatism in the United States." In *Women of the Right: Comparisons and Interplay across Borders*, edited by Kathleen M. Blee and Sandra McGee Duetsch, 211–225. Penn State University Press.

De Wilde, Pieter. 2013. "Representative Claims Analysis: Theory Meets Method." *Journal of European Public Policy* 20 (2): 278–294.

Dittmar, Kelly. 2013. "Primary Problems: Women Candidates in US House Primaries." Center for American Women and Politics at Rutgers University. <http://www.cawp.rutgers.edu/sites/default/files/resources/primary-problems-10-1-13.pdf

Dittmar, Kelly. 2015. *Navigating Gendered Terrain: Stereotypes and Strategy in Political Campaigns.* Philadelphia, PA: Temple University Press.

Dittmar, Kelly. 2019. *Unfinished Business: Women Running in 2018 and Beyond*. Center for American Women and Politics, Eagleton Institute of Politics. New Brunswick, NJ: Rutgers University. <https://womenrun.rutgers.edu/2018-report/>.

Dittmar, Kelly. 2021. "Invisible Forces: Gender, Race, and Congressional Staff." In *Politics, Groups, and Identities, Ahead-of-Print*, 1–17. New York: Routledge. DOI: 10.1080/21565503.2021.1908370.

Dittmar, Kelly, Kira Sanbonmatsu, Susan J. Carroll, Debbie Walsh, and Catherine Wineinger. 2017. *Representation Matters: Women in the U.S. Congress*. New Brunswick, NJ: Center for American Women and Politics, Eagleton Institute of Politics, Rutgers, The State University of New Jersey. <https://www.cawp.rutgers.edu/sites/default/files/resources/representationmatters.pdf>.

Dittmar, Kelly, Kira Sanbonmatsu, and Susan J. Carroll. 2018. *A Seat at the Table: Congresswomen's Perspectives on Why Their Presence Matters*. New York: Oxford University Press.

Dodson, Debra L., and Susan J. Carroll. 1991. *Reshaping the Agenda: Women in State Legislatures*. New Brunswick, NJ: Center for American Women and Politics, Eagleton Institute of Politics, Rutgers University. <https://cawp.rutgers.edu/sites/default/files/resources/reshapingtheagenda.pdf>.

Dodson, Debra L., Susan J. Carroll, Ruth B. Mandel, Katherine E. Kleeman, Ronnee Schreiber, and Debra Liebowitz. 1995. *Voices, Views, Votes: The Impact of Women in the 103rd Congress*. New Brunswick: Center for the American Woman and Politics, Eagleton Institute of Politics, Rutgers University. <https://cawp.rutgers.edu/sites/default/files/resources/voices_views_votes.pdf>.

Dodson, Debra L. 2006. *The Impact of Women in Congress*. New York: Oxford University Press.

Dolan, Julie. 1998. "Support for Women's Interests in the 103rdCongress: The Distinct Impact of Congressional Women." *Women & Politics* 18 (4): 81–94.

Dolan, Kathleen. 2010. "The Impact of Gender Stereotyped Evaluations on Support for Women Candidates." *Political Behavior* 32 (1): 69–88.

Dovi, Suzanne. 2002. "Preferable Descriptive Representatives: Will Just Any Women, Black, or Latino Do?" *American Political Science Review* 96: 729–743.

Dovi, Suzanne. 2007. "Theorizing Women's Representation in the United States." *Politics & Gender* 3 (3): 297–320.

Downs, Anthony. 1957. "An Economic Theory of Political Action in a Democracy." *Journal of Political Economy* 65 (2): 135–150.

Duerst-Lahti, Georgia. 2002. "Governing Institutions, Ideologies and Gender: Toward the Possibility of Equal Political Representation." *Sex Roles: A Journal of Research* 47: 371–388.

Dumain, Emma. 2013. "Boehner Finds the Woman for the Job." *CQ Roll Call*, October 22.

Dunn, Jennifer. Center for American Women and Politics Interview, June 15, 1998.

Dworkin, Andrea. 1983. *Right-Wing Women*. New York: Perigee.

Elder, Laurel. 2012. "The Partisan Gap among Women State Legislators." *Journal of Women, Politics, and Public Policy* 33 (1): 65–85.

Elder, Laurel, and Steven Greene. 2012. *The Politics of Parenthood: Causes and Consequences of the Politicization and Polarization of the American Family*. Albany, NY: State University of New York Press.

Elder, Laurel. 2018. "Why So Few Republican Women in State Legislatures? The Causes and Consequences." In *The Right Women: Republican Party Activists, Candidates, and*

Legislators, edited by Malliga Och and Shauna Shames, 157–175. Colorado: Praeger/ABC-Clio Press.

Elder, Laurel. 2020. "The Growing Partisan Gap among Women in Congress." *Society* 57: 520–526.

Elder, Laurel. 2021. *The Partisan Gap: Why Democratic Women Get Elected, But Republican Women Don't*. New York: New York University Press.

Eligon, John, and Michael Schwirtz. 2012. "Senate Candidate Provokes Ire with 'Legitimate Rape' Comment." *The New York Times*, August 19.

Ellmers, Renee. 2015. Center for American Women and Politics Interview, December 2.

Erler, Abbie H. 2018. "Moving Up and Getting Out: The Career Patterns of Republican Women State Legislatures." In *The Right Women: Republican Party Activists, Candidates, and Legislators*, edited by Malliga Och and Shauna Shames, 176–196. Colorado: Praeger/ABC-Clio Press.

Erzeel, Silvia, and Karen Celis. 2016. "Political Parties, Ideology and the Substantive Representation of Women." *Party Politics* 22 (5): 576–586.

Evans, Jocelyn Jones. 2005. *Women, Partisanship, and the Congress*. New York: Palgrave MacMillan.

Fabj, Valeria. 1993. "Motherhood as Political Voice: The Rhetoric of the Mothers of Plaza de Mayo." *Communication Studies* 44 (1): 1–18.

Fauntroy, Michael K. 2007. *Republicans and the Black Vote*. Boulder, CO: Lynne Rienner Publishers, Inc.

Fenno, Richard F. 1977. "U.S. House Members in Their Constituencies: An Exploration." *The American Political Science Review* 71 (3): 883–917.

Fenno, Richard F. 1978. *Home Style: House Members in Their Districts*. Boston: Little-Brown.

Fenno, Richard. 1997. *Learning to Govern: An Institutional View of the 104th Congress*. Washington, D.C.: The Brookings Institution.

Finlay, Barbara. 2006. *George W. Bush and the War on Women*. Chicago: The University of Chicago Press.

Foster, Carly Hayden. 2008. "The Welfare Queen: Race, Gender, Class and Public Opinion." *Race, Gender & Class* 15 (3/4): 162–179.

Fowler, Tillie. 1995. Center for American Women and Politics Interview, August 3.

Fox, Lauren. 2018. "Republican Women Wonder When They'll Get a Female Speaker of the House." *CNN*, April 24.

Fox, Richard Logan. 1997. *Gender Dynamics in Congressional Elections*. Thousand Oaks, CA: Sage Publications.

Foxx, Virginia. 2015. Center for American Women and Politics Interview, March 18.

Fraga, Luis R., and David Leal. 2004. "Playing the 'Latino Card': Race, Ethnicity, and National Party Politics." *Du Bois Review* 1 (2): 297–317.

Frankel, Lois. 2015. Center for American Women and Politics Interview, December 2.

Frantzich, Stephen, and John Sullivan. 1996. *The C-SPAN Revolution*. Norman, OK: The University of Oklahoma Press.

Frederick, Brian. 2009. "Are Female House Members Still More Liberal in a Polarized Era? The Conditional Nature of the Relationship between Descriptive and Substantive Representation." *Congress and the Presidency* 36: 181–202.

Frederick, Brian P. 2013. "Gender and Roll Call Voting Behavior in Congress." *The American Review of Politics* 34: 1–20.

Freeman, Jo. 1986. "The Political Culture of the Democratic and Republican Parties." *Political Science Quarterly* 101 (3): 327–356.

Freeman, Jo. 1987. "Who You Know Versus Who You Represent: Feminist Influence in the Democratic and Republican Parties." In *The Women's Movements of the United States and Western Europe: Feminist Consciousness, Political Opportunity and Public Policy*, edited by Mary Katzenstein and Carol Mueller, 215–244. Philadelphia: Temple University Press.

Freeman, Jo. 2000. *A Room at a Time: How Women Entered Party Politics*. Lanham, MD: Rowman & Littlefield.

Freeman, Jo. 2008. *We Will Be Heard: Women's Struggles for Political Power in the United States*. Lanham, MD: Rowman & Littlefield.

Fridkin, Kim L., and Patrick J. Kenney. 2014. *The Changing Face of Representation: The Gender of U.S. Senators and Constituent Communication*. Ann Arbor: University of Michigan Press.

Frostenson, Sarah. 2017. "The Women's Marches May Have Been the Largest Demonstration in US History." *Vox*, January 31.

Gajanan, Mahita. 2019. "Alexandria Ocasio-Cortez's First House Speech Broke a C-SPAN Record: Here's What She Said." *Time Magazine*, January 18.

Gardner, Amy. 2010. "Sarah Palin Issues a Call to Action to 'Mama Grizzlies.'" *Washington Post*, May 14.

Gelb, J., and M. Palley. 1996. *Title IX: The Politics of Sex Discrimination. Women and Public Policies*. Charlottesville, VA: University of Virginia Press.

Gentzkow, Matthew, Jesse M. Shapiro, and Matt Taddy. 2019. "Measuring Group Differences in High-Dimensional Choices: Method and Application to Congressional Speech." *Econometrica* 87 (4): 1307–1340.

Gertzog, Irwin N. 2004. *Women and Power on Capitol Hill: Reconstructing the Congressional Women's Caucus*. Boulder, CO: Lynn Rienner Publishers.

Gilens, M. 1999. *Why Americans Hate Welfare: Race, Media, and the Politics of Anti-Poverty Policy*. Chicago: University of Chicago Press.

Granger, Kay. 2016. Center for American Women and Politics Interview, January 7.

Grimmer, Justin. 2013. *Representational Style in Congress: What Legislators Say and Why It Matters*. New York: Cambridge University Press.

Groppe, Maureen. 2018. "Brooks Says House GOP Women Looking for Answers as Their Ranks Shrink to Lowest Levels in 25 Years." *Indianapolis Star*, December 13.

Grossmann, Matt, and David A. Hopkins. 2015. "Ideological Republicans and Group Interest Democrats: The Asymmetry of American Party Politics." *Perspectives on Politics* 13 (1): 120–139.

Grossmann, Matt, and David A. Hopkins. 2016. *Asymmetric Politics: Ideological Republicans and Group Interest Democrats*. New York: Oxford University Press.

Gurin, P., and Townsend, A. 1986. "Properties of Gender Identity and Their Implication for Gender Consciousness." *British Journal of Social Psychology* 25: 139–148.

Hammond, Susan Webb. 1998. *Congressional Caucuses in National Policymaking*. Baltimore: Johns Hopkins University Press.

Hancock, Ange-Marie. 2004. *The Politics of Disgust: The Public Identity of the Welfare Queen*. New York: New York University Press.

Hansen, Eric R., and Sarah A. Treul. 2015. "The Symbolic and Substantive Representation of LGB Americans in the U.S. House of Representatives." *Journal of Politics* 77 (4): 955 967.

Hardy-Fanta, Carol, Pei-te Lien, Dianne M. Pinderhughes, and Christine M. Sierra. 2006. "Gender, Race, and Descriptive Representation in the United States: Findings from the Gender and Multicultural Leadership Project." *Journal of Women, Politics & Policy* 28 (3–4): 7–41.

Harris, Douglas. 2005. "Orchestrating Party Talk: A Party-Based View of One-Minute Speeches in the House of Representatives." *Legislative Studies Quarterly* 30 (1): 127–141.

Harris, Douglas B. 2013. "Let's Play Hardball: Congressional Partisanship in the Television Era." In *Politics to the Extreme: American Political Institutions in the Twenty-First Century*, edited by Scott A. Frisch and Sean Q. Kelly, 93–116. New York: Palgrave Macmillan.

Hartzler, Vicky. 2016. Center for American Women and Politics Interview, December 1.

Hawkesworth, Mary. 2003. "Congressional Enactments of Race-Gender: Toward a Theory of Raced-Gendered Institutions." *American Political Science Review* 97 (4): 529–550.

Hawkesworth, Mary, Kathleen J. Casey, Krista Jenkins, and Katherine E. Kleeman. 2001. *Legislating by and for Women: A Comparison of the 103rd and 104th Congresses*. New Brunswick, NJ: Center for American Women and Politics, Rutgers University. https://cawp.rutgers.edu/sites/default/files/resources/congreport103-104.pdf.

Heberlig, Eric S., and Bruce A. Larson. 2021. *Congressional Parties, Institutional Ambition, and the Financing of Majority Control*. Ann Arbor: University of Michigan Press.

Heffernan, Trova. 2012. *A Woman First: The Impact of Jennifer Dunn*. Washington State Legacy Project, Office of the Secretary of State. Centralia, WA: Gorham Printing.

Hero, R., and Tolbert, C. 1995. "Latinos and Substantive Representation in the U.S. House of Representatives: Direct, Indirect, or Nonexistent?" *American Journal of Political Science* 39 (3): 640–652.

Hinojosa, Magda, Jill Carle & Gina Serignese Woodall. 2018. "Speaking as a Woman: Descriptive Presentation and Representation in Costa Rica's Legislative Assembly." *Journal of Women, Politics & Policy* 39 (4): 407–429.

Holman, Mirya R., and Anna Mahoney. 2018. "Stop, Collaborate, and Listen: Women's Collaboration in US State Legislatures." *Legislative Studies Quarterly* 43 (2): 179–206.

Horowitz, Juliana Menasce, Ruth Igielnik, and Kim Parker. 2018. "Women and Leadership 2018: Wide Gender and Party Gaps in Views about the State of Female Leadership and the Obstacles Women Face." *Pew Research Center*, July 20.

Huddy, Leonie, and Nadya Terkildsen. 1993. "Gender Stereotypes and the Perception of Male and Female Candidates." *American Journal of Political Science* 37 (February): 119–147.

Ingraham, Laura. 1996. "Convention Preview: How the Gender Gap Is Driving the Dole Girl Crazy." *The Washington Post*, August 4.

Israel, Josh. 2012. "Former GOP Congresswoman Blasts New GOP Women's Caucus: 'They're Not Voting in Best Interest of All Women.'" *Think Progress*, May 25.

Jaffe, Sarah. 2018. "Why Did a Majority of White Women Vote for Trump?" *New Labor Forum* 27 (1): 18–26.

Jardina, Ashley. 2019. *White Identity Politics*. New York: Cambridge University Press.

Jeydel, Alana, and Andrew Taylor. 2003. "Are Women Legislators Less Effective? Evidence from the U.S. House in the 103rd–105th Congress." *Political Research Quarterly* 56 (1): 19–27.

Johnson, Nancy. 1995. Center for American Women and Politics Interview, August 7.

Jones, James R. 2017. "Racing through the Halls of Congress: The Black 'Nod' as an Adaptive Strategy for Surviving in a Raced Institution." *Du Bois Review* 14 (1): 165–187.

Kabaservice, Geoffrey. 2012. *Rule and Ruin: The Downfall of Moderation and the Destruction of the Republican Party, From Eisenhower to the Tea Party.* New York: Oxford University Press.

Khan, Mariam. 2021. "Marjorie Taylor Greene Declares She Is 'Freed' after Being Booted from House Committees." *ABC News*, February 5.

Kane, Paul. 2019. "North Carolina runoff a test of women's standing in the Republican Party." *The Washington Post*, July 8.

Kanter, Rosabeth Moss. 1977a. *Men and Women of the Corporation.* New York: Basic Books.

Kanter, Rosabeth Moss. 1977b. "Some Effects of Proportions on Group Life: Skewed Sex Ratios and Responses to Token Women." *American Journal of Sociology* 82 (5): 965–990.

Kanthak, Kristin, and George A. Krause. 2012. *The Diversity Paradox: Political Parties, Legislatures, and the Organizational Foundations of Representation in America.* New York: Oxford University Press.

Karol, David. 2009. *Party Position Change in American Politics: Coalition Management.* New York: Cambridge University Press.

Kathlene, Lyn. 1994. "Power and Influence in State Legislative Policymaking: The Interaction of Gender and Position in Committee Hearing Debates." *American Political Science Review* 88 (3): 560–576.

King, David C., and Richard E. Matland. 2003. "Sex and the Grand Old Party: An Experimental Investigation of the Effect of Candidate Sex on Support for a Republican Candidate." *American Politics Research* 31 (November): 595–612.

Kitchener, Caroline. 2020. "More Women Are Running for House Seats than Ever. Even 2018." *The Lily*, May 13.

Kitchens, Karen E., and Michele L. Swers. 2016. "Why Aren't There More Republican Women in Congress? Gender, Partisanship, and Fundraising Support in the 2010 and 2012 Elections". *Politics & Gender* 12 (4): 648–676.

Klatch, Rebecca E. 1987. *Women of the New Right.* Philadelphia: Temple University Press.

Koger, Gregory, and Matthew J. Lebo. 2017. *Strategic Party Government: Why Winning Trumps Ideology.* Chicago: University of Chicago Press.

Kurtzleben, Danielle. 2018. "More than Twice as Many Women Are Running for Congress in 2018 Compared with 2016." *NPR*, February 20.

Lawless, Jennifer L., and Kathryn Pearson. 2008. "The Primary Reason for Women's Underrepresentation? Reevaluating the Conventional Wisdom." *Journal of Politics* 70 (1): 67–82.

Lawless, Jennifer L., Sean M. Theriault, and Samantha Guthrie. 2018. "Nice Girls? Sex, Collegiality, and Bipartisan Cooperation in the US Congress," *Journal of Politics* 80 (4): 1268–1282.

Lazarus, Jeffrey, and Amy Steigerwalt. 2018. *Gendered Vulnerability: How Women Work Harder to Stay in Office.* Ann Arbor, MI: University of Michigan Press.

Lee, Frances. 2009. *Beyond Ideology: Politics, Principles, and Partisanship in the U.S. Senate.* Chicago: University of Chicago Press.

Lee, Frances. 2016. *Insecure Majorities: Congress and the Perpetual Campaign.* Chicago: University of Chicago Press.

Lipinski, Daniel. 2004. *Congressional Communication: Content and Consequences.* Ann Arbor: University of Michigan Press.

Lopez, Ian Haney. 2015. *Dog Whistle Politics: How Coded Racial Appeals Have Reinvented Racism and Wrecked the Middle Class.* New York: Oxford University Press.

Lucas, Jennifer C. 2017. "Gender and Race in Congressional National News Media Appearances in 2008." *Politics & Gender* 13 (4): 569–596.

Lummis, Cynthia. 2016. Center for American Women and Politics Interview, February 29.

Madison, Lucy. 2012. "Republicans Push 'New Perspective' on Women." *CBS News*, May 22.

Mahoney, Anna Mitchell. 2018. *Women Take Their Place in State Legislatures: The Creation of Women's Caucuses*. Philadelphia, PA: Temple University Press.

Malecha, Gary Lee, and Daniel J. Reagan. 2012. *The Public Congress: Congressional Deliberation in a New Media Age*. New York: Taylor & Francis.

Maltzman, Forrest, and Lee Sigelman. 1996. The Politics of Talk: Unconstrained Floor Time in the U.S. House of Representatives. *Journal of Politics* 58 (3): 819–830.

Mann, Thomas E. 1988. "The Permanent Minority in American Politics." *Brookings Review* 6 (1): 33–38.

Mann, T. E., and Ornstein N. J. 2012. *It's Even Worse than It Looks: How the American Constitutional System Collided with the New Politics of Extremism*. New York: Basic Books.

Mansbridge, Jane. 1999. "Should Blacks Represent Blacks and Women Represent Women? A Contingent 'Yes.'" *Journal of Politics* 61: 628–657.

Mansbridge, Jane. 2003. "Rethinking Representation." *The American Political Science Review* 97 (4): 515–528.

Masket, Seth. 2020. *Learning from Loss: The Democrats 2016–2020*. New York: Cambridge University Press.

Mason, Lilliana. 2018. *Uncivil Agreement: How Politics Became Our Identity*. Chicago: University of Chicago Press.

Mason, Lilliana, and Julie Wronski. 2018. "One Tribe to Bind Them All: How Our Social Group Attachments Strengthen Partisanship." Political Psychology 39 (1): 257–277.

Maxwell, Angie, and Todd Shields. 2019. *The Long Southern Strategy: How Chasing White Voters in the South Changed American Politics*. New York: Oxford University Press.

Mayhew, David. 1974. *Congress: The Electoral Connection*. Yale University Press.

McAdam, Doug, John D. McCarthy, and Mayer N. Zald. 1996. *Comparative Perspectives on Social Movements: Political Opportunities, Mobilizing Structures and Cultural Framing*. Cambridge: Cambridge University Press.

McCall, Leslie. 2005. "The Complexity of Intersectionality." *Signs* 30 (3): 1771–1800.

McCarty, Nolan, Keith T. Poole, and Howard Rosenthal. 2006. *Polarized America: The Dance of Ideology and Unequal Riches*. Cambridge, MA: MIT Press.

McDermott, Monika L. 1997. "Voting Cues in Low-Information Elections: Candidate Gender as a Social Information Variable in Contemporary US Elections." American Journal of Political Science 41: 270–283.

McMorris Rodgers, Cathy. 2015. Center for American Women and Politics Interview, December 4.

McRae, Elizabeth Gillespie. 2018. *Mothers of Massive Resistance: White Women and the Politics of White Supremacy*. New York: Oxford University Press.

McSally, Martha. 2016. Center for American Women and Politics Interview, March 16.

Meinke, Scott R. 2016. *Leadership Organizations in the House of Representatives: Party Participation and Partisan Politics*. Ann Arbor, MI: University of Michigan Press.

Melich, Tanya. 1996. *The Republican War Against Women: An Insider's Report from Behind the Lines*. New York: Bantam Books.

Meng, Grace. 2015. Center for American Women and Politics Interview, October 21.

Meyers, Jan. 1997. Center for American Women and Politics Interview, November 18.

Mimms, Sarah. 2011. "Is Cathy McMorris Rodgers More than a Token?" *The Atlantic*, September 19.

Molinari, Susan. 1995. Center for American Women and Politics Interview, June 27.

Molinari, Susan. 1998. *Representative Mom: Balancing Budgets, Bill, and Baby in the U.S. Congress*. Doubleday.

Montanaro, Domenico. 2018. "It Was a Big, Blue Wave: Democrats Pick up Most House Seats in a Generation." *NPR*, November 14.

Morella, Connie. 1995. Center for American Women and Politics Interview, June 22.

Morris, Jonathan S. 2001. "Reexamining the Politics of Talk: Partisan Rhetoric in the 104th House." *Legislative Studies Quarterly* 26: 101–121.

Murphy, Jane C. 2005. "Legal Images of Fatherhood: Welfare Reform, Child Support Enforcement, and Fatherless Children." *Notre Dame Law Review* 81 (1): 325–386.

Myrick, Sue. 1998. Center for American Women and Politics Interview, February 25.

Newhauser, Daniel, Sarah Mimms, and National Journal. 2014. "In a Republican Congress, Few Gavels for Women," *The Atlantic*, October 6.

Nickerson, Michelle M. 2012. *Mothers of Conservatism: Women and the Postwar Right*. Princeton, NJ: Princeton University Press.

Noel, Hans. 2013. *Political Ideologies and Political Parties in America*. New York: Cambridge University Press.

Noem, Kristi. 2015. Center for American Women and Politics Interview, November 17.

Norton, Noelle H. 1999. "Committee Influence over Controversial Policy: The Reproductive Policy Case." *Policy Studies Journal* 27 (2): 203–216.

Och, Malliga, and Shauna Shames, eds. 2018. *The Right Women: Republican Party Activists, Candidates, and Legislators*. Colorado: Praeger/ABC-Clio Press.

Och, Malliga. 2018. "The Grand Old Party of 2016: No Longer a Party of Old White Men?" In *The Right Women: Republican Party Activists, Candidates, and Legislators*, edited by Malliga Och and Shauna Shames, 3–24. Colorado: Praeger/ABC-Clio Press.

Olson, Mancur. 1965. *The Logic of Collective Action: Public Goods and the Theory of Groups*. Cambridge, MA: Harvard University Press.

Osborn, Tracy L. 2012. *How Women Represent Women*. New York: Oxford University Press.

Osborn, Tracy, and Jeanette Morehouse Mendez. 2010. "Speaking as Women: Women and Floor Speeches in the Senate." *Journal of Women, Politics, and Policy* 31 (1): 1–21.

Pathe, Simone. 2018. "Elise Stefanik Wants to Play in Primaries to Help Republican Women." *Roll Call*, December 4.

Pearson, Kathryn, and Logan Dancey. 2011a. "Elevating Women's Voices in Congress: Speech Participation in the House of Representatives." *Political Research Quarterly* 64 (4): 910–923.

Pearson, Kathryn, and Logan Dancey. 2011b. "Speaking for the Underrepresented in the House of Representatives: Voicing Women's Interests in a Partisan Era." *Politics and Gender* 7: 493–519.

Pearson, Kathryn. 2015. *Party Discipline in the U.S. House of Representatives*. Ann Arbor: The University of Michigan Press.

Pearson, Kathryn. 2015b. "Gendered Partisanship in the US House of Representatives." Working Paper presented at the University of Utah. <https://poli sci.utah.edu/_documents/gendered-partisanship.pdf>.

Petrocik, John R. 1996. "Issue Ownership in Presidential Elections, with a 1980 Case Study." *American Journal of Political Science* 40 (3): 825–850.

Petrocik, John R., William L. Benoit, and Glenn J. Hansen. 2003. "Issue Ownership and Presidential Campaigning, 1952–2000." *Political Science Quarterly* 118 (4): 599–626.

Phillips, Anne. 1995. *The Politics of Presence.* New York: Oxford University Press.

Philpot, Tasha S. 2007. *Race, Republicans, and the Return of the Party of Lincoln.* Ann Arbor: The University of Michigan Press.

Pitkin, Hanna. 1967. *The Concept of Representation.* Berkeley: University of California Press.

Poole, Keith T. 2007. "Changing Minds? Not in Congress!" *Public Choice* 131: 435–451.

Poole, Keith T., and Howard Rosenthal. 1997. *Congress: A Political-Economic History of Roll Call Voting.* New York: Oxford University Press.

Pryce, Deborah. 1995. Center for American Women and Politics Interview, September 28.

Reingold, Beth, and Michele Swers. 2011. "An Endogenous Approach to Women's Interests: When Interests are Interesting in and of Themselves." *Politics and Gender* 7 (3): 429–435.

Reingold, Beth, and Adrienne R. Smith. 2012. "Welfare Policymaking and Intersections of Race, Ethnicity, and Gender in U.S. Legislatures." *American Journal of Political Science* 56 (1): 131–147.

Reingold Beth, Rebecca J. Kreitzer, Tracy Osborn, and Michele L. Swers. 2021. "Anti-abortion Policymaking and Women's Representation." *Political Research Quarterly* 74 (2): 403–420.

Rinehart, Sue Tolleson. 1991. "Do Women Leaders Make a Difference? Substance, Style and Perceptions." In *Gender and Policymaking: Studies of Women in Office,* edited by D. L. Dodson, 93–102. New Brunswick, NJ: Center for the American Woman and Politics, Rutgers University.

Roberti, Amanda. 2017. *"Women Deserve Better"*: Pro-Woman Issue Framing of Regulatory Abortion Policy in the States. Dissertation submitted to the Graduate School. New Brunswick: Rutgers, the State University of New Jersey.

Roberts, Steven V. 1984. "Congress Stages a Preemptive Strike on the Gender Gap." *New York Times,* May 6.

Roby, Martha. 2016. Center for American Women and Politics Interview, February 2.

Rocca, Michael S. 2007. "Nonlegislative Debate in the U.S. House of Representatives." *American Politics Research* 35 (4): 489–505.

Rocco, Philip, and Simon F. Haeder. 2018. "How Intense Policy Demanders Shape Postreform Politics: Evidence from the Affordable Care Act." *Journal of Health Politics, Policy, and Law* 43 (2): 271–304.

Rolfes-Haase, Kelly L., and Michele L. Swers. 2021. "Understanding the Gender and Partisan Dynamics of Abortion Voting in the House of Representatives." In *Politics & Gender, First View,* 1–35. New York: Cambridge University Press. DOI: https://doi.org/10.1017/S1743923X20000719

Ros-Lehtinen, Ileana. 1997. Center for American Women and Politics Interview, October 9.

Ros-Lehtinen, Ileana. 2016. Center for American Women and Politics Interview, March 1.

Rosenthal, Cindy Simon, ed. 2002. *Women Transforming Congress.* Norman, OK: University of Oklahoma Press.

Rosin, Hanna. 1997. "Pretty on the Outside." *New York Magazine,* April 28: 20–23.

Ross, Michael. 1994. "GOP Plans to Cut Funds for Black Caucus, Others." *The Los Angeles Times,* December 7.

Roukema, Marge. 1997. Center for American Women and Politics Interview, September 22.

Russell, Annelise. 2018. "U.S. Senators on Twitter: Asymmetric Party Rhetoric in 140 Characters." *American Politics Research* 46 (4): 695–723.

Rymph, Catherine E. 2006. *Republican Women: Feminism and Conservatism from Suffrage through the Rise of the New Right.* Chapel Hill, NC: University of North Carolina Press.

Sanbonmatsu, Kira. 2002. "Gender Stereotypes and Vote Choice." *American Journal of Political Science* 46 (1): 20–34.

Sanbonmatsu, Kira. 2004. *Democrats, Republicans, and the Politics of Women's Place.* Ann Arbor, MI: University of Michigan Press.

Sanbonmatsu, Kira. 2021. "Public Support for 'More' Women in Congress." *Politics, Groups, and Identities* 9 (3): 646–656.

Sanbonmatsu, Kira, and Kathleen Dolan. 2009. "Do Gender Stereotypes Transcend Party?" *Political Research Quarterly* 62: 485–494.

Saward, Michael. 2006. "The Representative Claim." *Contemporary Political Theory* 5 (3): 297–318.

Saward, Michael. 2010. *The Representative Claim.* New York: Oxford University Press.

Schickler, Eric. 2016. *Racial Realignment: The Transformation of American Liberalism, 1932 1965.* Princeton, NJ: Princeton University Press.

Schneider, Monica, and Angela Bos. 2016. "The Interplay of Candidate Party and Gender in Evaluations of Political Candidates." *Journal of Women, Politics & Policy* 37 (3): 274–294.

Schreiber, Ronnee. 2002. "Injecting a Woman's Voice: Conservative Women's Organizations, Gender Consciousness, and the Expression of Women's Policy Preferences." *Sex Roles* 47 (7–8): 331–342.

Schreiber, Ronnee. 2012. *Righting Feminism: Conservative Women and American Politics with New Epilogue.* New York: Oxford University Press.

Schreiber, Ronnee. 2016. "Gender Roles, Motherhood, and Politics." *Journal of Women, Politics, and Policy* 37 (1): 1–23.

Schuller, Rebecca. 2019. "Yes, the GOP Has a Woman Problem—Yes, It Can Be Solved." *The Hill,* July 26.

Sellers, Patrick. 2010. *Cycles of Spin: Strategic Communication in the U.S. Congress.* New York: Cambridge University Press.

Shapiro, Ari. 2020. "Minnesota Rep. Tom Emmer on How the GOP Whittled Away at Democrats' House Majority." *NPR,* November 10.

Shames, Shauna. 2018. "Higher Hurdles for Republican Women: Ideology, Inattention, and Infrastructure." In *The Right Women: Republican Party Activists, Candidates, and Legislators,* edited by Malliga Och and Shauna Shames, 95–106. Colorado: Praeger/ABC-Clio Press.

Shogan, Colleen. 2001. "*Speaking Out: An Analysis of Democratic and Republican Woman Invoked Rhetoric in the 105th Congress.*" In *Women and Congress: Running, Winning, Ruling,* edited by Karen O'Connor, 129–146. New York: Haworth Press, Inc.

Sinclair, Barbara. 2006. *Party Wars: Polarization and the Politics of National Policymaking.* Norman, OK: University of Oklahoma Press.

Sinclair, Barbara. 2016. *Unorthodox Lawmaking: New Legislative Process in the U.S. Congress.* Washington, D.C.: Sage CQ Press.

Skocpol, Theda. 1996. *Boomerang: Clinton's Health Security Effort and the Turn against Government in U.S. Politics,* 1st ed. New York: W. W. Norton.

Skocpol T., Williamson V. 2012. The Tea Party and the remaking of Republican conservatism. New York: Oxford University Press.

Smith, Jada F. 2012. "Forming a Caucus, Republican Women Send a Message." *The New York Times*, May 22.

Smooth, Wendy. 2006. "Intersectionality in Electoral Politics: A Mess Worth Making." *Politics & Gender* 2 (2006): 400–414.

Sparks, Holloway. 2003. "Queens, Teens, and Model Mothers." In *Race and the Politics of Welfare Reform*, edited by Sanford F. Schram, Joe Soss, and Richard C. Fording. Ann Arbor: University of Michigan Press, 171–195.

Stearney, Lynn M. 1994. "Feminism, Ecofeminism, and the Maternal Archetype: Motherhood as a Feminine Universal." *Communication Quarterly* 42 (2): 145–159.

Stefanik, Elise. 2015. Center for American Women and Politics Interview, October 20.

Swers, Michele. 1998. "Are Women More Likely to Vote for Women's Issue Bills than Their Male Colleagues?" *Legislative Studies Quarterly* 23 (3): 435–448.

Swers, Michele L. 2002. *The Difference Women Make: The Policy Impact of Women in Congress*. Chicago: University of Chicago Press.

Swers, Michele L. 2005. "Connecting Descriptive and Substantive Representation: An Analysis of Sex Differences in Co-Sponsorship Activity." *Legislative Studies Quarterly* 30 (3): 407–433.

Swers, Michele, and Carin Larson. 2005. "Women and Congress: Do They Act as Advocates for Women's Issues?" In *Women and Elective Office: Past, Present, and Future*, 2nd ed., edited by Sue Thomas and Clyde Wilcox. New York: Oxford University Press, 110—128.

Swers, Michele L. 2013. *Women in the Club: Gender and Policymaking in the Senate*. Chicago: The University of Chicago Press.

Swers, Michele. 2016. "Pursuing Women's Interests in Partisan Times: Explaining Gender Differences in Legislative Activity on Health, Education, and Women's Health Issues." *Journal of Women, Politics & Policy* 37 (3): 249–273.

Tarrow, Sidney. 1994. *Power in Movement: Social Movements, Collective Action and Mass Politics*. New York: Cambridge University Press.

Tate, K. 2003. *Black Faces in the Mirror: African Americans and Their Representatives in the U.S. Congress*. Princeton, NJ: Princeton University Press.

Teele, Dawn Langan, Joshua Kalla, and Frances Rosenbluth. 2018. "The Ties That Double Bind: Social Roles and Women's Underrepresentation in Politics." *American Political Science Review* 112 (3): 525—541.

Theriault, Sean M. 2008. *Party Polarization in Congress*. New York: Cambridge University Press.

Thomas, David R. 2006. "A General Inductive Approach for Analyzing Qualitative Evaluation of Data." *American Journal of Evaluation* 27 (2): 237–46.

Thomas, Ralph. 2007. "Jennifer Dunn, Who Inspired Face of Today's State GOP, Dies at 66." *The Seattle Times*, September 6.

Thomas, Sue. 1994. *How Women Legislate*. New York: Oxford University Press.

Thomas, Sue, and Catherine Wineinger. 2020. "Ambition for Office: Women and Policymaking." In *Good Reasons to Run: Women as Political Candidates*, edited by Shauna Shames, Rachel Bernhard, Mirya R. Holman, and Dawn Teele, 75–92. Philadelphia, PA: Temple University Press.

Thomsen, Danielle M. 2015. "Why So Few (Republican) Women? Explaining the Partisan Imbalance of Women in the U.S. Congress." *Legislative Studies Quarterly* 40 (2): 295–323.

Thomsen, Danielle M. 2017. Opting Out of Congress: Partisan Polarization and the Decline of Moderate Candidates. New York: Cambridge University Press.

Thomsen, Danielle. 2020. "Ideology and Gender in U.S. House Elections." *Political Behavior* 42: 415–442.

Thurman, Karen. 1995. Center for American Women and Politics Interview, June 30.

Tolchin, Martin. 1977. "House Bars Medicaid Abortions and Funds for Enforcing Quotas." *The New York Times*, June 18.

Valdini, Melody E. 2019. *The Inclusion Calculation: Why Men Appropriate Women's Representation*. New York: Oxford University Press.

Vega, Arturo, and Juanita Firestone. 1995. "The Effects of Gender on Congressional Behavior and the Substantive Representation of Women." *Legislative Studies Quarterly* 20 (2): 213–222.

Volden, C., A. E. Wiseman, and D. E. Wittmer. 2013. "When Are Women More Effective Lawmakers Than Men?" *American Journal of Political Science* 57 (2): 326–341.

Volden, C., A. E. Wiseman, and D. E. Wittmer. 2018. "Women's Issues and Their Fates in the US Congress." *Political Science Research and Methods* 6 (4): 679–696.

Vucanovich, Barbara. 1995. Center for American Women and Politics Interview, July 20.

Vucanovich, Barbara, and Patricia D. Cafferata. 2005. *Barbara F. Vucanovich: From Nevada to Congress, and Back Again*. Reno, NV: University of Nevada Press.

Wagner, Ann. 2016. Center for American Women and Politics Interview, April 28.

Wallace, Sophia J. 2014. "Representing Latinos: Examining Descriptive and Substantive Representation in Congress." *Political Research Quarterly* 67 (4): 917–929.

Wang, Amy B. 2021. "GOP Rep. Liz Cheney Says Trump 'Does Not Have a Role as a Leader of Our Party Going Forward.'" *The Washington Post*, February 7.

Weisman, Jonathan. 2012. "Indiana Senate Candidate Draws Fire for Rape Comments." *The New York Times*, October 23.

Weldon, Laurel. 2002. "Beyond Bodies: Institutional Sources of Representation for Women in Democratic Policymaking." *Journal of Politics* 64 (4): 1153–1174.

Williams, R. Seth. 2011. "In the Court of Common Pleas First Judicial District of Pennsylvania Criminal Trial Division in Re: Misc. No. 0009901-2008 County Investigating: Grand Jury XXIII." Pennsylvania Grand Jury Report, January 14.

Wineinger, Catherine. 2018. "War against Women." In *Women in the American Political System: An Encyclopedia of Women as Voters, Candidates, and Office Holders,* edited by Dianne Bystrom and Barbara Burrell, Vol. 2: ABC-Clio.

Wineinger, Catherine. 2021. "How Can a Black Woman Be a Republican? An Intersectional Analysis of Identity Claims in the 2014 Mia Love Campaign." *Politics, Groups, and Identities* 9 (3): 566–588. https://doi.org/10.1080/21565503.2019.1629316

Wineinger, Catherine, and Mary Nugent. 2020. "Framing Identity Politics: Right-Wing Women as Strategic Party Actors in the UK and US." *Journal of Women, Politics, & Policy* 41 (1): 91–118.

Winter, Nicholas J. G. 2005. "Framing Gender: Political Rhetoric, Gender Schemas, and Public Opinion on U.S. Health Care Reform." *Politics & Gender* 1 (3): 453–480.

Winter, Nicholas J. G. 2006. "Beyond Welfare: Framing and the Racialization of White Opinion on Social Security." *American Journal of Political Science* 50: 400–420.

Winter, Nicholas J. G. 2010. "Masculine Republicans and Feminine Democrats: Gender and Americans' Explicit and Implicit Images of the Political Parties." *Political Behavior* 32: 587–618.

Wolbrecht, Christina. 2000. *The Politics of Women's Rights: Parties, Positions, and Change.* Princeton, NJ: Princeton University Press.

Wolbrecht, Christina. 2002. "Explaining Women's Rights Realignment: Convention Delegates 1972–1992." *Political Behavior* 24 (3): 237–282.

Wong, Scott. 2017. "Female Lawmakers Flee for Higher Office, Retirement." *The Hill,* May 17.

Xydias, Christina. 2018. "Republican Female Lawmakers' Contributions to Legislative Debates in the 113th U.S. Congress." In *The Right Women: Republican Party Activists, Candidates, and Legislators,* edited by Malliga Och and Shauna Shames, 247–258. Colorado: Praeger/ABC-Clio Press.

Zanona, Melanie, and Ally Mutnick. 2020. "Recruitment Push Fuels Record Number of Women in the House GOP." *Politico,* November 4.

Index

For the benefit of digital users, indexed terms that span two pages (e.g., 52–53) may, on occasion, appear on only one of those pages.

Note: Tables and figures are indicated by *t* and *f* following the page number